GUIDE TO

FRENCH BED & BREAKFAST

2ND EDITION

Notes for reprint of 2nd Edition
July 1995

★ PLEASE READ THIS LIST ★

Please remember you are received as house guests and as such it is normal for you to arrive neither too early nor too late – between 4pm and 7pm – and to telephone if you are going to be late.

Entry No.	Alteration
45	Fax: 31 22 75 99
57	Michel is now on his own.
59	To get there: LEFT at church. From October 1995, Mme Simand will be under entry 366B in Limousin-Dordogne.
95	Rooms: 4 double rooms, 2 with handbasin; sharing shower & w.c.
99	Children's dinner 5 Frs per year of age. Open all year except 1-20 Sept, 1996. No wheelchair access.
125	Price: 250 Frs for two, including breakfast.
192	Monsieur speaks a little English. Fax No: 85 33 02 79.
228	Ren Rijpstra has moved: see entry 366A in Limousin-Dordogne.
235	Map Ref No: 10
237	New owner: Muriel CABIN-SAINT-MARCEL.
238	Meals: Mme. Choquet cooks dinner every night except Sundays. To get there: At Noyers-sur-Cher, before intersection of D675 & N76, turn right into rue de la Mardelle, just before railway.
277	Owners: Alain DAVID & Nicole DUBOIS.
288	To get there: RIGHT onto D151.
300	Les Essards is south-west of Saintes, not east.
305	Tel: 49 46 30 81 or 49 41 41 76 Fax: 49 47 64 12 "French-dilapidated" is unfair; sorry!
348	The Tricketts are nearly always there; our apologies!
379	Owners: Annie CASTEX et ses enfants.

With many thanks to all our readers and house-owners who have pointed out errors and inaccuracies.

Alastair Sawday's

GUIDE TO

FRENCH BED
& BREAKFAST

2ND EDITION

ASP

Alastair Sawday Publishing

ACKNOWLEDGEMENTS

So many people have helped with this edition that I can't name them all, let alone the many readers who have written with their advice. I had no idea that people would be so inspired to write, and with such praise. What has given particular pleasure has been the regular flow of thanks for new friendships in France. There has also been a flood of recommendations for new entries. We will get round to inspecting them soon. I should also thank the many French house-owners who have been fullsome in their praise and encouragement.

Most of the inspections for this edition were done by Guy Hunter-Watts, who set out rather grandly in a smart camper-van. It was destroyed in an accident but he loyally continued in an old Renault 4 van. Reactions to the Renault were useful guides to the type of welcome travellers would receive!

The huge bulk of the work this year has been done by the indefatigable, loyal and talented Ann Cooke-Yarborough. With 26 years in France as training she has coped brilliantly both with the eccentricities of house-owners and the oddities of a very small publishing company. When she started she couldn't even use a computer. I owe her book-fulls of thanks.

Alastair Sawday: *Editor*

Managing Editor : Ann Cooke-Yarborough
Assistant Editor : Guy Hunter-Watts
Design : Springboard Design, Bristol
Computer programming : Jerome Ungoed-Thomas
Data-processing : Ann Cooke-Yarborough
Administration : Ann Cooke-Yarborough
Promotion : Sheila MacDonald
Inspiration : Richard Binns and Michel Smith for their wonderful books
            on France
Moral support : Trevor Hockey of the Clifton Bookshop, Bristol.
Typesetting/Data Conversion : Avonset, Midsomer Norton, nr Bath.
Printers : BPC, Paulton, Avon
UK Distributors : Alastair Sawday Publishing and Portfolio
US Distributors : New Amsterdam Books, New York State
US Promotion : Marlene Doley
Inspections : Guy Hunter-Watts and Patricia Herrera Cornejo, Diana Harris,
            Philippa Ryder, Clive and Patricia Brooks, Eric and Audrey
            Anstead, Colin and Alyson Browne, Flora Olney.
Back-up in France : Mark and Fiona Berridge of Château Mont Epinguet
Extra photographs : Trudi Bine, Pippa and Tim Gore, Michael Hodson,
            Penny Cook, Mrs J. Avery, Dave Clifton
Maps : Bartholomews
Everything else : Ann Cooke-Yarborough

(A special thank-you to Ted Kersker who sent money from the USA for tea and biscuits!)

INTRODUCTION

Welcome to the second edition of this Guide, bigger and better and even more indispensable ... and still the only one of its kind.

A good novel will take you on somebody's journey. A good biography gives you access to someone else's life. This Guide opens the door to the private homes of hundreds of people in France. They are, for the most part, warm, interesting people who – through their personalities, their homes, their children and friends – have much to give you, not least their friendship.

The 1994 edition was a bold beginning, a slightly mad adventure embarked upon in a fit of enthusiasm and conviction. We were innocents in the publishing jungle. Inevitably things went wrong: our distribution system collapsed, leaving us to tackle it on our own; the book-sellers' computer was reluctant to absorb any information we offered it; newspaper articles omitted our address. But the saving grace was the book itself. Somehow lots of people found it and used it, told their friends about it and lent it to their neighbours. For many it has become a constant companion when in France, a source of amusing encounters, beautiful houses, friendships and, simply, a lot of fun. It has also, by the way, saved many people a great deal of money.

To my astonishment and delight we have received a steady stream of letters from users of the Guide. Forgive me for quoting from a few of them:

"I want to thank you for the most entertaining holiday I have spent for years. Although I have travelled the length and breadth of France for 25 years I had never even heard of the French B&B's. We now have a whole new set of French friends".

"Ordinary hotels pale by comparison with most of the Chambres d'Hôtes we visited; they offered tender and surprising insights into French family life".

... and from one of the French owners: "...votre guide a été pour nous une "bouffée d'oxygène" par la qualité de gentillesse, la sensibilité de nos hôtes anglais. Aujourd'hui nous avons deux dames Anglaises qui sont exquises; venues pour une nuit ça fait 5 jours que nous avons la joie de partager avec elles notre vie de famille".

... and another: "Si votre seconde édition doit surpasser la première il ne pourra s'agir que d'une 'tête de cuvée' comme on dit pour le vin".

My cockles are still warm. If you don't believe those quotes (I never do) we'll copy the letters and send them to you. But you must be wondering about negative comments, of which there have been blessedly few. My favourite described one of the few uninspected houses and features in the Prize section. It is far and away the most critical letter we have had, yet its author remains keen to use the next edition.

INTRODUCTION

Of course we made mistakes and I hope that this edition has ironed most of them out. I take comfort from J.M. Keynes: 'It is a good thing to make mistakes so long as you are found out quickly'.

In adding another 100 homes we have taken care to include a mixture and not to veer instinctively to the safe and the comfortable. Some of the most nourishing experiences are to be had with, say, farmers who may not have the most elegant rooms. What does that matter if the house is an architectural treat and the hosts a social one? Let me share a typical conundrum for an inspector.

My family and I stayed in a handsome stone farmhouse whose owners bent in every direction to make us all welcome, even letting the children camp on the lawn and clearing out their log-shed to let us create a camp-kitchen. The rooms were adequate, but the decor was endearingly awful: thick purple furry curtains and matching bed-spreads. To include or not to include? It is included, because the memorable decor is a small price to pay for the fine house and hosts.

English Owners. What to do with the many English house-owners who want to be in the Guide? Some have lovingly restored old houses (and even rescued them from certain ruin) and have a keen eye for the authentic. We have used our judgement, resolving to keep English owners to a small maximum percentage in any one area. Our aim is still to introduce you to the Frenchness of the France we love.

Hotels v Chambres d'Hôtes. A controversy rages about the damage done to the traditional hotels by the growth in the B&B system. I suspect, however, that the real damage is being done by those modern hotels ... usually built and franchised out by multinational hotel-chains at the bottom end of their market ... that are sprouting like malevolent toadstools on the fringes of many French towns.

I love those wonderful French family-run hotels and have no wish to undermine them. But I DO want to undermine those unspeakable modern ones! There is little to recommend them and they compete unfairly with the traditional hotels. Many of the Chambres d'Hôtes, on the other hand, bring people to the dying villages and small towns of France, adding life and money to the community. That must, surely, be a Good Thing.

ABOUT THIS BOOK

This is the only book of its kind. There are other Guides to French B&B, but none so personal, so well-documented, and with such a rich variety of houses. Some books heap praise on only the grandest houses, while others provide brief notes on thousands of them. Most are written in French. Above all we think that the photographs make this book.

The Chambres d'Hôtes do not have to be officially recognised to be included in this Guide but we have included a symbol for those that belong to the Gîtes de France system. Generally we agree that if there are more than 6 rooms in a house it shouldn't be a Chambre d'Hôte; I hope that you approve of the exceptions.

Eco-Tourism. This much-abused buzz-word does not perhaps fit well with a book that is bought largely by car-drivers; but by promoting the local economy, home stays, home-grown and even organic food, and bicycling we are doing our little bit. Let us have your ideas for doing it better.

Inspections. Nearly all the houses have now been inspected by us. We circle the number of the house if we have not seen it ourselves, although it is only included after recommendation of some sort, perhaps from a reader. Our inspectors are unreformable Francophiles and make allowances for inconveniences when the overall atmosphere is right. We hope you do too.

Each B&B owner pays a small sum per room to be included, small enough not to be a bribe! This scheme works in favour of the smaller Chambres d'Hôtes.

Who was left out. We have abandoned places which we got wrong last year, such as the goat-farm where the goats were so thinly separated from guests that the latter awoke thinking the goats were in the room.

There must be hundreds of lovely places that we have not yet heard of. Please tell us about them. Otherwise we have tried to be consistent in leaving out the ugly (usually modern), the noisy, the tasteless and ... most eagerly ... the unwelcoming. (The latter choice was made easier by our use of an old Renault 4 van in the recent inspections. Some owners were distinctly sniffy..!)

Remember, however, that one man's meat is another man's fish. Some of our favourite places have not gone down well with everybody, and vice versa. But I will continue to resist the temptation to play 100% safe. A Guide that appealed to all travellers would be anodyne indeed.

Comfort. Most of these Chambres d'Hôtes are as comfortable as your own home, and perhaps more so. A few are very simple but no less worthy of inclusion. Modern comfort is NOT a critical factor for us; indeed a B&B that lays primary store by its modern 'amenities' – such as TV and mini-bar – may well be excluded unless otherwise remarkable.

HOW TO USE CHAMBRES d'HÔTES

... always with sensitivity and kindness, as you would the homes of your own friends. Bear in mind that most owners genuinely enjoy having guests and appreciate a good chat. But remember, too, that they may be leading their own lives while you are there: milking the cows, tending the children, going off to work in town etc. So don't stay all day unless it seems OK to do so, and don't expect to eat late breakfasts. If you're staying a second night please tidy your room!

Getting There. Always carry a telephone card (available from the ubiquitous 'tabac') and some spare coins, and practise a few stock phrases such as 'nous aurons une heure de retard'. Or you can, if desperate, ring French-speaking friends at home to ask them to make a call on your behalf.

The British Telecom Charge card, by the way, works in France and is cheaper than using a pay-phone. The operator voice is English.

Asking directions can be fun, with or without the language. But a good map is essential; don't try to make it through the hinterland of rural France without the relevant Michelin map, or even better, their road Atlas of France (you may have to buy it in France).

Payment. Please pay in cash; most of the Chambres d'Hôtes cannot accept credit cards and have not heard of Eurocheques. The prices are low enough so try to make payment uncomplicated. Francs are the answer, and a well-tried one. Almost every town has a cash-dispenser which will disgorge francs against your Visa/Master Card.

Bookings. Telephone ahead for a booking if possible. It is frustrating to navigate your way up narrow lanes to a full house, although most owners will help you find somewhere else. PLEASE telephone your hosts if you decide to cancel a booking, even if at the last minute (they may be waiting up for you with a hot drink). If you are asked for a deposit, please be prepared to forfeit it if you cancel. That is only fair.

Meals. Breakfast usually includes the usual hot drinks and lots of bread and jam. If you are lucky there will be juice and perhaps some other delight. But don't expect platefuls of eggs, porridge, waffles, and cheeses ... or whatever you are used to.

Many of the Chambres d'Hôtes serve dinner and I urge you to join in. If you speak a little French you will gain more than just a meal. If your French is of the faltering variety you will still enjoy it hugely. In private homes you can eat some of the best of regional cooking, often with fresh home-grown ingredients. Readers have waxed eloquent about the sumptuous meals they have had, to their surprise and delight and often around a family table.

If you are vegetarian please tell us where you found good vegetarian cooking in France. It is still often a matter of omelettes and veg.

HOW TO USE THIS BOOK

Maps If you know where you are going (lucky you) turn to the first (general) map to check the number of the relevant area map. Then turn to that map page and hunt for the B&B you want. Each house has its own number, easy to find by leafing through the book.

Our directions take you to the house from one side only. If you approach another way, make adjustments with your road map. We use the French road categories as follows:

A = Autoroute = motorways with junctions that have the same name on both sides, so no need to indicate which way you come from.
N = Route Nationale. The old main roads, fast but through towns.
D = Départementale. Smaller country roads with relatively little traffic.

If our directions are not perfect then PLEASE tell us how to improve them.
Prices are for the room, in which the French quite reasonably expect two to sleep. If on your own you will probably have a double bed and pay for two people. Unfair, so some hosts may relent a little.

Please be forgiving if you find that the price we have given has changed a little when you get there. We don't ask owners to guarantee to hold the price and we don't know how long this edition of the Guide will last. If prices do change it is unlikely to be by much.

Bathrooms vary from the luxurious to those endearing old arrangements where the hip-bath and loo are behind a screen at the end of the room. I rather enjoy the latter kind but there are more of the former. Some have a shower and no bath; some have no loo. Be prepared to accept unpredictability as part of the adventure. Having said that, most bathrooms are excellent by any standards.

Children It is always worth asking if the children can sleep on the floor of your room for a small sum; but don't be offended if the answer is 'no'. One hint: farms are ideal for children; chickens and rabbits make excellent babysitters.

SYMBOLS

 Working farm

 Organic produce available

 English spoken

 Access for wheelchairs

 Children welcome

 Pets welcome

 Member of Gîtes de France

 No Smoking

 Bike hire or loan

 Swimming

 Uninspected properties

 Inspected properties

Explanation of Symbols Treat each one as a guide rather than a concrete indicator. A few notes:

 Your hosts may speak any form of English, from pidgin to perfect.

 Children are positively welcomed. The text gives restrictions where relevant.

 You can either borrow or hire bikes here.

 Some, but not necessarily all, ingredients are organically grown.

 indicates access on the ground floor but not full facilities for handicapped users. Ring ahead to discuss your precise needs.

 are welcome if well behaved. Check when booking if there are restrictions (such as 'not in bedrooms) or a small supplement to pay.

 Applies only to totally non-smoking houses. Some that accept smoking in the main rooms may not want it in the bedrooms.

 Swimming may be in a pool, a lake or a river.

INTRODUCTION

PRIZE WRITING

In the first edition I promised a prize for the best inspection report written by a reader. The winner's offering has earned 2 free nights in a Chambre d'Hôte in Normandy, the Château de Mont Epinguet. There is an unofficial runner-up, whose criticism of one of the few uninspected properties is irresistible. A bottle of bubbly will find its way to the writer ... with my thanks.

The prize offer applies to the second edition too, so take your writing kit to France with you ... along with your sense of humour.

Readers' Prize-Winning Piece: Michael and Jean Wilson from Sunderland:
   ** "There were two phrases in your Tips for Travellers section that I did not expect to need: "Où pourrais-je accrocher ce linge humide?" – we were hoping for sun! and "Est-ce que les poules dorment toujours dans cette chambre?" – was this a joke? But both were needed.

On our arrival at Fougeolles – we were greeted by 2-year-old Mathias, who, with 3 ducks in tow, came to investigate our car. As our 3-day stay progressed Mathias introduced us to Monsieur Lapin (his rabbit), Le Cheval and Le Chien. He would climb the stone stairs into our bedroom hand-in-hand with our daughter Helen for a forage in our biscuit box.

Mama served us with tea on arrival and shared her son's charming disposition. Breakfast in the courtyard, with, of course, the famous three ducks and a pet chicken, were very much a family affair. On our one morning of drizzle (hence the 'linge humide') we squeezed into the family dining-room around the big old wooden table. The wall was draped with old photographs, forgotten ornaments adorned the mantelshelf over the enormous fireplace. Breakfast was always an unhurried affair and it was usually a struggle to leave for a day out. Then it was always a pleasure to come 'home', often to hear Grandpère playing the piano ... Mathias never far away ... and that ever glorious French sunshine filtering the whole scene."

and the Runner-Up, Jonathan Austin quoting Penelope Hasler's diary:
   ** "This was the worst place I have ever stayed in. We made our way to our room which can be summed up in one word: disgusting! It has bunk beds covered with synthetic fur fabric – brown – and a double bed – orange. Around the walls are pinned posters of pop stars, men and horses. Beside the bed is a china dog that lights up. The whole room has an aroma of old clothes. The loo and shower are small, dark and have an even less pleasant aroma, not that that will reach here as they are downstairs and through the sitting-room! Feeling overcome by the seediness we went for a walk ... The 'garden' has rabbits in cages, a chicken run, old caravan and dead car. There are cages of budgerigars and even a chipmunk. We returned to our accommodation at 10.00pm to find the place in pitch darkness. We struggled back to our room where numerous flies had gathered. First task was to kill the flies which we did with the help of my sandals. After the massacre J. found the bed so shaky, creaky and uncomfortable that he slept on the floor ..."
(Ed. note: this was one of the few uninspected houses in the first edition and has been dropped!).

YOUR ADVICE TO US

 We need this, and enjoy letters, however critical. Please use, and copy with abandon, the special page at the end of this book.

Alastair Sawday

Famille Pinier ... what more can I say?

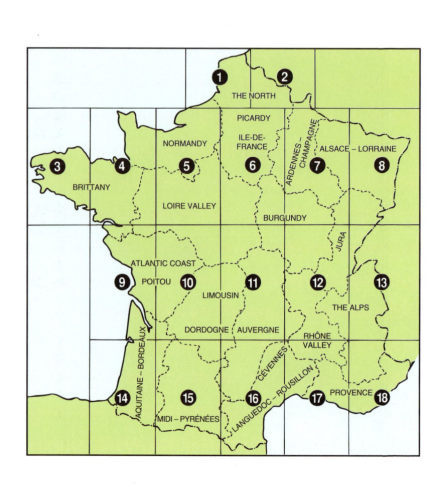

THE NORTH

PICARDY

NORMANDY

ILE-DE-
FRANCE

ARDENNES –
CHAMPAGNE

ALSACE – LORRAINE

BRITTANY

LOIRE VALLEY

BURGUNDY

JURA

ATLANTIC COAST

POITOU

LIMOUSIN

DORDOGNE   AUVERGNE

THE ALPS

RHÔNE
VALLEY

AQUITAINE – BORDEAUX

CÉVENNES

LANGUEDOC – ROUSILLON

PROVENCE

MIDI – PYRÉNÉES

CONTENTS

	ENTRIES	MAP
The North – Picardy – Ile-de-France		
• Aisne	1-5	❻
• Nord	6	❷
• Oise	7-12	❻
• Pas-de-Calais	13-25	❶
• Somme	26-39	❶ ❷ ❻
• Val d'Oise	40	❻
Normandy		
• Calvados	41-59	❹ ❺
• Eure	60-72	❺ ❻
• Manche	73-96	❹
• Orne	97-105	❺
• Seine-Maritime	106-111	❶ ❺
Brittany		
• Côtes-d'Armor	112-119	❸ ❹
• Finistère	120-139	❸
• Ille-et-Vilaine	140-145	❹
• Loire-Atlantique	146-148	❹ ❾
• Morbihan	149-155	❸
The Ardennes – Champagne		
• Ardennes	156	❼
• Marne	157-159	❼
• Somme	160-161	❼
Alsace – Lorraine		
• Meuse	162-164	❻ ❼
• Moselle	165-167	❽
• Bas-Rhin	168-170	❽
Burgundy		
• Côte d'Or	171-176	❼ ⓬

CONTENTS

	ENTRIES	MAP
• Nièvre	177-187	❻ ⓫ ⓬
• Saône-et-Loire	188-198	⓬
• Yonne	199-207	❻ ❼

The Loire Valley

• Cher	208-217	⓫
• Eure-et-Loir	218-222	❺ ❻
• Indre	223-228	❿ ⓫
• Indre-et-Loire	229-236	❺ ❿
• Loir-et-Cher	237-241	❺
• Loiret	242-248	❻
• Maine-et-Loire	249-271	❹ ❺ ❿
• Mayenne	272-275	❹ ❺
• Sarthe	276-284	❺
• Vienne (North)	286	❿

The Atlantic Coast

• Charente	287-289	❿
• Charente-Maritime	290-302	❾ ❿
• Vienne (Centre/South)	303-313	❿
• Baie de Gascogne	314	❾

Aquitaine – Bordeaux

| • Gironde | 315-319 | ❾ ❿ ⓯ |
| • Landes | 320-322 | ⓮ |

Limousin – Dordogne

• Corrèze	323-329	❿
• Creuse	330-331	⓫
• Dordogne	332-348	❿ ⓯
• Lot	349-353	⓫ ⓯
• Lot-et-Garonne	354-361	⓯
• Haute-Vienne	362-366	❿ ⓫

The Midi-Pyrénées

• Ariège	367-378	⓯ ⓰
• Haute-Garonne	379-385	⓯
• Gers	386-389	⓯
• Hautes-Pyrénées	390-391	⓯
• Tarn-et-Garonne	392-397	⓯

CONTENTS

	ENTRIES	MAP

Languedoc-Rousillon – Cévennes
- Aude ——————————— 398-400 ❶❻
- Gard———————————— 401-411 ❶❼
- Hérault ——————————— 412-422 ❶❻ ❶❼
- Lozère———————————— 423 ❶❻
- Pyrénées-Orientales ————— 424-427 ❶❻
- Tarn ——————————— 428-441 ❶❻

The Auvergne
- Allier ——————————— 442 ❶❶
- Aveyron ——————————— 443-450 ❶❶ ❶❻
- Cantal ——————————— 451-453 ❶❶
- Haute-Loire ————————— 454-455 ❶❶
- Puy-de-Dôme ————————— 456-457 ❶❶

Provence – The Mediterranean
- Alpes-Maritimes ——————— 458-462 ❶❽
- Bouches-du-Rhône —————— 463-472 ❶❼
- Var ———————————— 473-481 ❶❽
- Vaucluse —————————— 482-498 ❶❼

The Alps – Jura
- Haute-Alpes ————————— 499 ❶❽
- Isère———————————— 500-501 ❶❷
- Jura ———————————— 502-504 ❶❷
- Savoie ——————————— 505-509 ❶❸
- Haute-Savoie ————————— 510-515 ❶❸

The Rhône Valley
- Ardèche —————————— 516-517 ❶❷ ❶❼
- Drôme———————————— 518-525 ❶❷ ❶❼
- Rhône ——————————— 526 ❶❷
- Gaule ——————————— 527 ➖

Tips for travellers in France
ETA
Eurodrive
Journeys
Green Initiatives
Order Form
Report Form
Index

Amiens	Bâle	Bayonne	Besancon	Bordeaux	Brest	Caen	Calais	Clermont-Ferrand	Dijon	Genève	Grenoble	Le Harve	Lille	Limoges	Lyon	Le Mans	Marseille
568																	
918	1028																
560	151	888															
726	836	184	696														
614	1097	814	956	622													
239	783	770	643	578	373												
155	683	1062	595	870	718	343											
546	478	555	337	372	751	544	690										
459	244	833	104	641	856	542	603	282									
684	259	932	177	695	1081	767	828	323	199								
711	403	815	287	658	1108	794	855	286	296	144							
179	746	842	606	650	482	107	283	571	505	730	757						
115	610	989	522	797	814	344	112	617	530	755	782	284					
542	612	412	472	220	599	437	686	178	417	486	464	548	613				
607	389	813	249	550	1004	690	751	178	192	156	104	653	678	356			
349	703	619	563	427	402	151	415	382	462	687	714	223	420	286	610		
923	694	683	564	649	1319	1005	1067	459	507	435	282	969	994	637	316	926	
345	253	1095	257	903	920	568	471	546	264	424	559	531	387	680	455	526	771
906	677	519	547	484	1092	989	1050	364	490	418	300	952	977	432	299	718	169
527	35	1016	139	824	1085	771	653	466	232	294	438	734	569	600	377	691	693
362	209	1031	199	839	884	541	488	495	213	366	508	504	404	629	404	491	720
530	847	518	707	326	296	284	674	452	606	725	738	380	601	303	628	183	961
1078	737	838	719	804	1474	1161	1222	614	662	478	334	1124	1149	792	471	1081	188
277	538	649	398	457	545	255	421	295	297	522	549	283	348	272	445	138	761
148	554	771	413	579	596	240	292	400	313	538	565	203	219	396	461	203	776
1054	825	483	695	448	1056	972	1198	465	638	566	448	1100	1125	514	447	821	317
157	412	906	324	714	731	379	271	502	284	470	580	342	198	531	476	338	791
417	849	629	708	437	245	177	522	536	608	833	860	286	566	374	756	154	1071
115	682	814	542	622	499	124	219	507	441	666	693	87	220	484	589	196	905
659	441	701	301	519	909	742	803	147	244	214	139	705	730	325	59	507	309
503	145	1122	244	930	1077	725	617	571	338	404	548	688	544	706	483	684	798
984	755	744	625	710	1380	1067	1128	520	568	496	335	1030	1055	698	377	987	64
852	913	299	783	244	852	768	996	397	726	654	536	858	923	310	535	617	405
381	656	537	516	345	484	233	525	300	415	527	534	305	452	204	430	82	745

Distances between major towns

Example: Montpellier – Toulon 230km

Metz
Montpellier
Mulhouse
Nancy
Nantes
Nice
Orléans
Paris
Perpignan
Reims
Rennes
Rouen
Saint-Étienne
Strasbourg
Toulon
Toulouse
Tours

754																
228	676															
56	703	184														
707	796	835	671													
926	324	848	875	1116												
402	744	526	382	303	916											
331	759	542	304	383	931	130										
902	152	824	851	760	472	786	907									
189	774	371	206	518	946	265	143	922								
672	907	837	636	107	1226	297	348	871	483							
419	888	670	440	379	1060	219	139	1036	231	303						
507	292	429	456	599	464	392	513	440	528	661	641					
163	781	114	148	864	953	560	489	929	346	829	577	535				
831	230	754	781	1022	153	822	837	378	852	1132	966	370	859			
990	240	912	939	556	560	582	706	204	841	667	794	528	1017	466		
558	636	644	494	198	900	112	234	739	369	236	277	425	715	806	535	

© Bartholomew

2

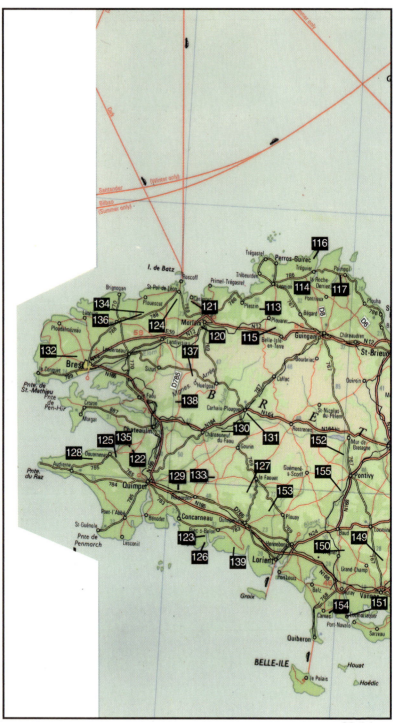

© Bartholomew

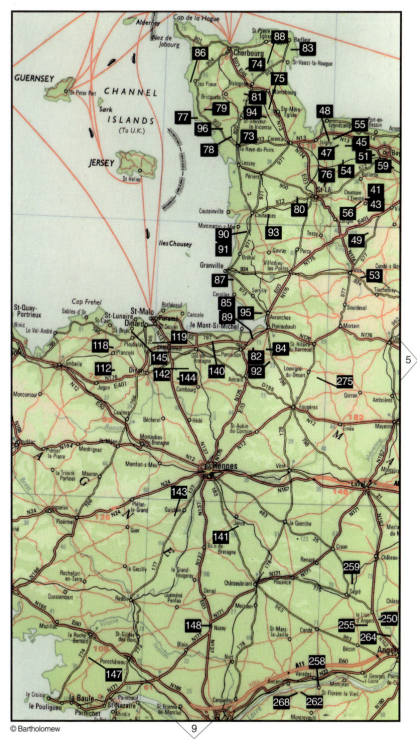

© Bartholomew

4

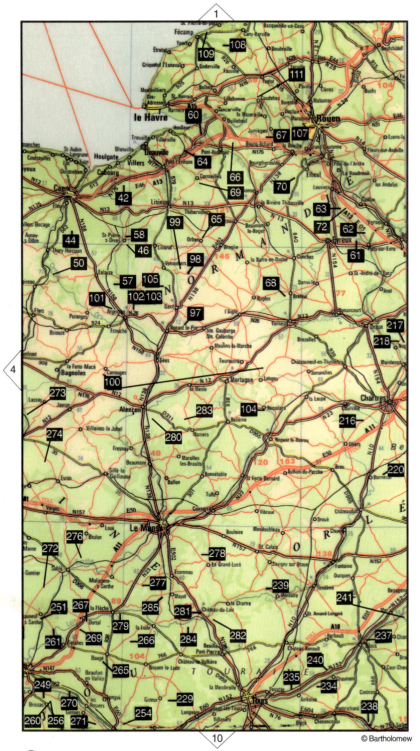

© Bartholomew

© Bartholomew

6

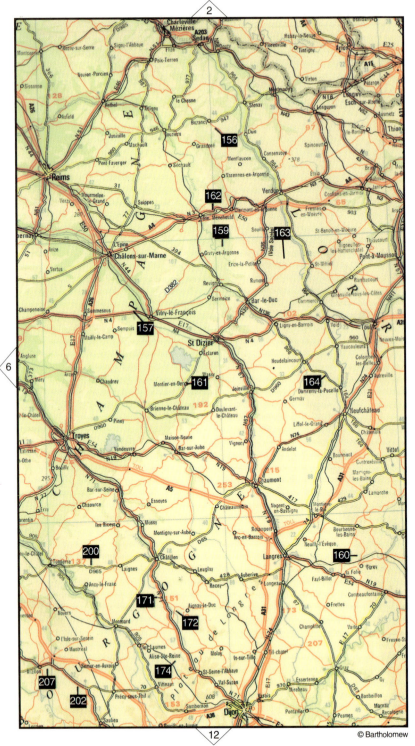

© Bartholomew

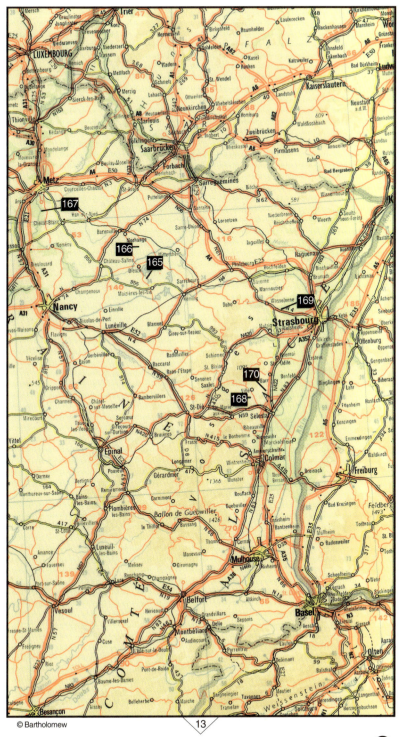

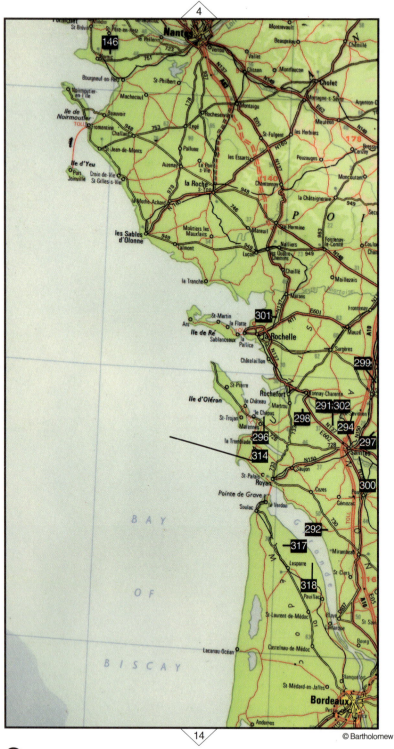

© Bartholomew

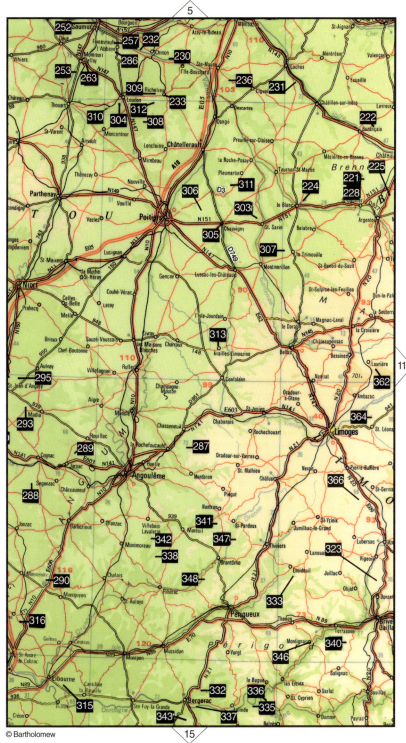

© Bartholomew

10

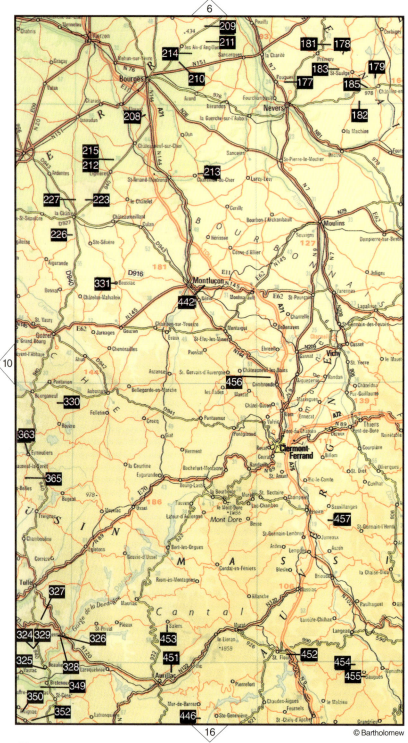

© Bartholomew

11

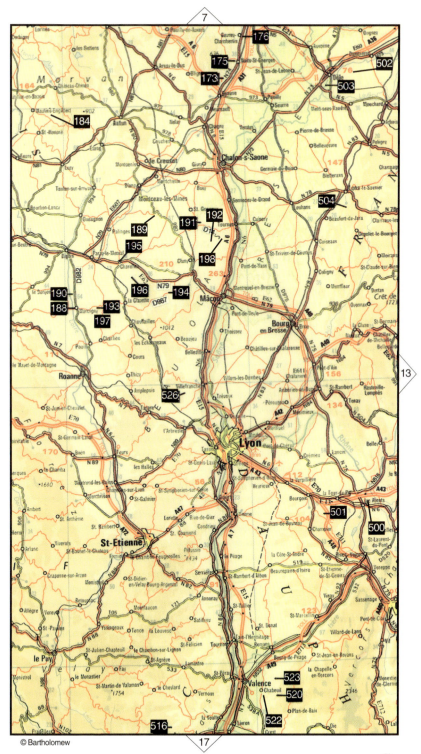

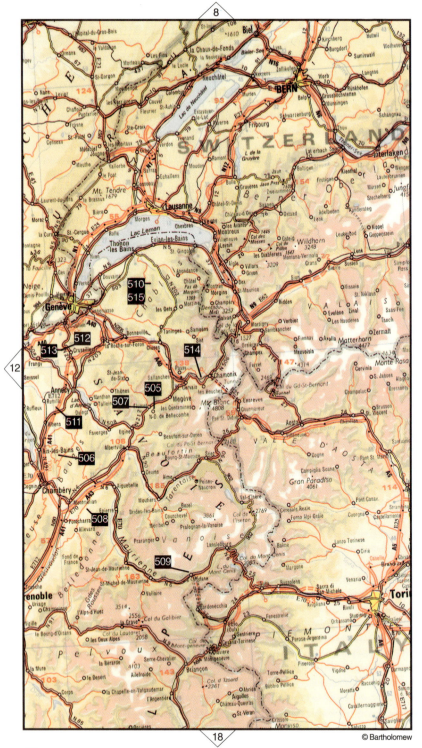

© Bartholomew

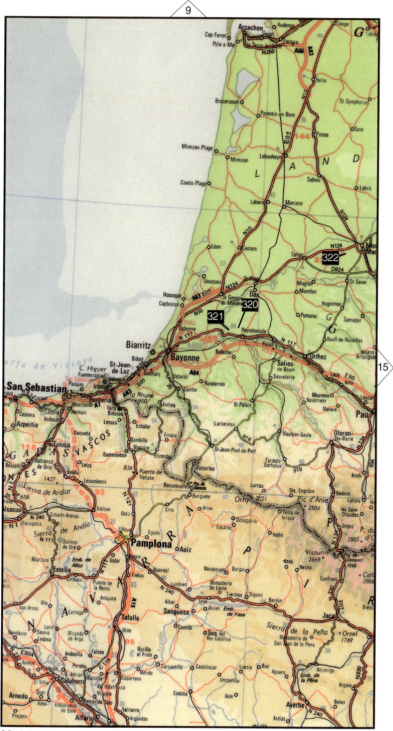

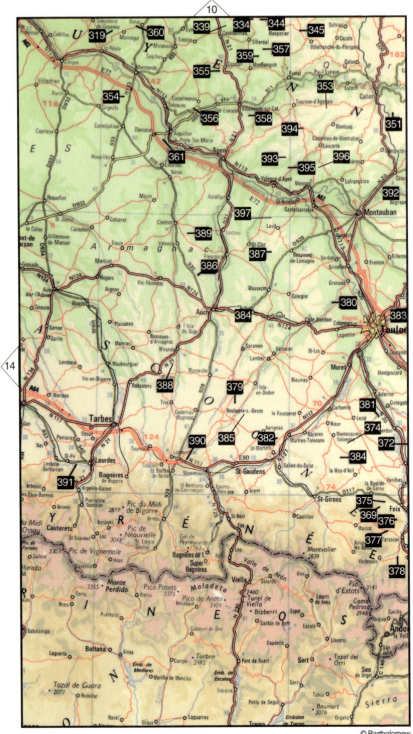

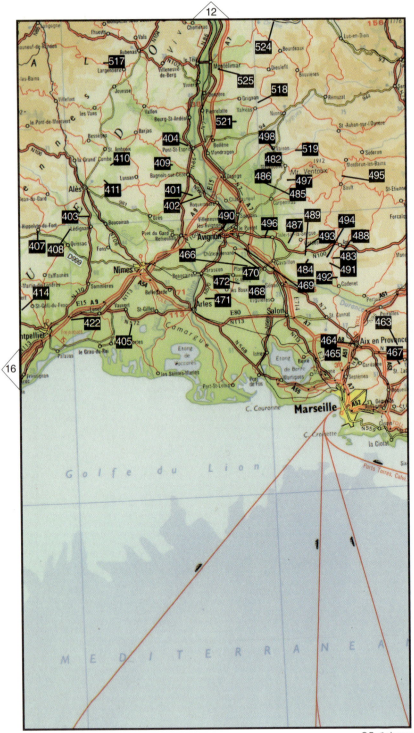

Light traffic on the D128

Set amid parkland and lakes (fishing is encouraged), this working farm has been in the Duffié family for over 200 years, though the house itself was rebuilt after the 1914-18 war. Guests stay in a more recently renovated barn; the bedrooms are modern and comfortable. Breakfast and evening meals are served in a separate dining-room.

Rooms: 1 double room and 1 twin room, each with own bathroom

Price: 250 Frs for two, including breakfast.

Meals: Dinner 100 Frs, including wine (book ahead).

Open: All year.

The North – Picardy – Ile-de-France

To get there: *From Soissons, N2 towards Laon. At Bucy-le-Long, D925 towards Vailly. House on right, just before entering Missy.*

Map Ref No: 6

M & Mme Georges DUFFIE
La Biza
02880 Missy-sur-Aisne
Aisne
Tel: 23 72 83 54
Fax: 23 72 91 43

1

A fine, solid (French) Empire 'maison bourgeoise' in dressed stone standing in a large mature garden offers a big welcome to travellers struggling to reach (or to escape) the Champagne wells. The house is well set back from the road and guestrooms look out over the fields; you will wake to the dawn chorus of sheep and birds. A relaxed and friendly home, furnished with family antiques, where you are received like long-lost cousins.

Rooms: 1 twin room with own bathroom, 2 triple rooms sharing a bathroom.

Price: 250 Frs for two, including breakfast.

Meals: None (5 minutes walk to restaurants).

Open: All year.

The house is dated 1611, the furnishings are elegant 19th century and the estate was once the property of Napoleon's Finance Minister. Extensive grounds running down to the river Aisne create an almost rural impression though you are 3 minutes walk from the town centre. Fish in the river, swim in the pool, play tennis or, less energetically, draughts on the giant 10ft x 10ft board. A tranquil place, clean air and most agreeable hosts.

Rooms: 2 double rooms, 3 triple rooms, all with own shower & wc.

Price: 310-350 Frs for two, including breakfast.

Meals: Dinner 90Frs, excluding wine (book ahead).

Open: All year.

To get there: *From Soissons, N31 towards Reims. In Braine, house is set back on this road next to Peugeot/BP garage.*

Map Ref No: 6

To get there: *From Compiègne, N31 towards Soissons; after 22km, left to Vic-sur-Aisne; opposite Mairie, right and first right again.*

Map Ref No: 6

Mme Jacqueline MARTIN
14 rue St Rémy
02220 Braine
Aisne
Tel: 23 74 12 74

(2)

Jean & Anne MARTNER
Domaine des Jeanne
Rue Dubarle
02290 Vic-sur-Aisne, Aisne
Tel: 23 55 57 33
Fax: 23 55 57 33

3

Rather a special place. Troughs with flowers, doves cooing, a garden with play-house ... a friendly home where Madame rushes about after her teenage family and will babysit for guests. A piano, old photos and vases of flowers add to the atmosphere. Cottage-style bedrooms with pretty bed-linen and marble-topped wash-stands. Ample breakfasts include eggs and yoghurt; robust farmhouse dinners, 'en famille' if you wish. Pool for children.

Rooms: 1 double room, 1 twin room and 1 single room, all with own bathrooms; 1 double room and 1 twin room sharing a bathroom.

Price: 230 Frs for two, including breakfast.

Meals: Dinner 80 Frs, excluding wine.

Open: All year.

To get there: *From Soissons, N2 towards Paris. At 4th main crossroads, D172 left towards Hartennes. About 3km on, D177 left to Léchelle.*

Map Ref No: 6

Jacques & Nicole MAURICE
Ferme Léchelle
02200 Berzy-le-Sec
Aisne
Tel: 23 74 83 29

4

This imposing 17th-century house is set in a wooded valley. Fine old furniture fills the house and comfortable guestrooms. The Simonnots, easy-going and lighthearted, love having guests. Madame's 5-course dinners, eaten 'en famille' by the big open fireplace, are the star attraction; there are invariably 12 or 13 people present – quite a house-party! Children's playroom and swings.

Rooms: 1 double room and 1 twin room, each with own bathroom; 2 double rooms and 1 twin room with hand-basins and shared bathrooms.

Price: 180-250 Frs for two, including breakfast.

Meals: Dinner 80 Frs, including wine.

Open: 15 April to 15 October.

To get there: *From A26-E17, Laon/Chambry exit south on N2. D516 to Bruyères-et-Montbérault; left opposite church; D903 to Chérêt; signposted.*

Map Ref No: 6

Mme Monique SIMONNOT
Le Clos
02860 Chérêt
Aisne
Tel: 23 24 80 64

5

THE NORTH – PICARDY – ILE-DE-FRANCE

The rather bleak setting only serves to enhance the warmth inside, the fruit of loving restoration. The whole house was destroyed in 1916, rebuilt in 1920; the staircase warmed the German occupier in the 2nd world war, so this one is modern. An endearing, personal cocktail of furnishings – parquet floors and marble fireplaces, great wardrobes and dressers, cheap prints and a gorgeous pair of Art Deco vases – plus good bathrooms and friendly hosts make this a perfect stopover near Calais.

Rooms: 2 double rooms and 1 suite for 5, all with own shower & wc.

Price: 220-300 Frs for two, including breakfast.

Meals: None (100m).

Open: All year.

This 18th-century auberge, run by the easy-going Mme Gitterman whose late husband's paintings and sculpture decorate the rooms (in a separate building), has a special charm. Wood-panelled bedrooms and a sunken bath surrounded by hand-painted tiles. Parakeets and toucans (plus their distinctive flavour), loose and caged, among houseplants and sleeping cats. The small garden feels tropical too – but a busy road passes nearby.

Rooms: 1 double room and 2 twin rooms. 3 bathrooms. One extra twin room available.

Price: 200 Frs for two, including breakfast.

Meals: None.

Open: All year.

To get there: *From Cambrai, N44 towards St Quentin. Farm is at Bonavis junction where D917 and N44 meet.*

Map Ref No: 2

To get there: *From Beauvais, N1 towards Paris; right on D927 towards Pontoise. Village 4km after Méru – house on left, after church; signposted.*

Map Ref No: 6

Michel & Thérèse DELCAMBRE
Ferme de Bonavis
Route Nationale
59266 Banteux
Nord
Tel: 27 78 55 08

6

Mme Odette GITTERMAN
25 rue Nationale
60110 Amblainville
Oise
Tel: 44 52 03 22

7

Two labradors greet visitors in the huge cobbled courtyard of this cereal farm surrounded by woods. Charmingly renovated farm cottages provide clean, modern bedrooms with good bedding. Within a converted barn is a playroom and a stone-walled dining-room with an old dresser and painted jugs. The Hamelins are smiling, light-hearted and keen to please.

Rooms: 3 twin rooms, all with bathrooms; 1 extra room for children.

Price: 300 Frs for two, including breakfast.

Meals: Dinner 80 Frs, including wine (advance booking).

Open: All year except January.

One of our very favourites. The trees in the huge garden were part of an ancient forest. The house, dated early 1900s, is full of flowers and plants, Monsieur's sculpture, Madame's painting and objects collected when they were teaching and nursing in Africa. Share their fascinating company at dinner on the veranda – fish is popular, served with wine or cider. There are no rules, the house exudes peace and tenderness and everything, it seems, is possible.

Rooms: 1 double & 1 twin, each with own bathroom.

Price: 290 Frs for two, including breakfast.

Meals: Dinner 100 Frs, including aperitif, wine, digestif (book ahead).

Open: All year.

To get there: *From A1, Senlis exit onto N324 to Crépy-en-Valois, then D332 towards Lévignen and Betz. 3km after Lévignen, Macquelines is on right.*

Map Ref No: 6

To get there: *From Beauvais, N31 towards Gournay-en-Bray. At Orsimont, left onto D129, through St Germer-de-Fly, to Le Coudray; in village.*

Map Ref No: 6

M Philippe HAMELIN
Ferme de Macquelines
60620 Betz
Oise
Tel: 44 87 20 21

8

Marc & Eugénie Le MARCHAND
de SAINT PRIEST
58 rue Paul Dubois
60850 Le Coudray-St Germer
Oise
Tel: 44 81 56 74

9

Next to the church in Bonvillers, this brick and beam presbytery, dated 1787, has guestrooms in an annexe. There is a pretty garden and an 18th-century 'cave' (temperance is seldom considered a virtue in the wine-producing regions!). Rooms are comfortable and traditionally furnished; some have 'salons' or mini-kitchens. We'd be grateful for readers' reports as we have had mixed reactions to the food and wine. The welcome, however, has been much appreciated by all.

Rooms: 4 double rooms and 1 twin room, all with own shower-rooms. Also a gîte for 4-5.

Price: 195-255 Frs for two, including breakfast.

Meals: Dinner 72-85 Frs, excluding wine.

Open: All year.

To get there: *From Beauvais, N1 to Breteuil. There, D916 towards St Just and Clermont. After 5km, left to Bonvillers (D112).*

Map Ref No: 6

M Christian LOUREIRO
17 rue de l'Eglise
60120 Bonvillers
Oise
Tel: 44 51 91 54

10

A sweeping drive leads up to this well-proportioned manor with its characteristic stone tower (housing a marble staircase), thick walls and barn-flanked courtyard. The guestroom is modern and has its own living area. Breakfast (and dinner, if requested) is served in a magnificent dining-room, reminiscent of a hunting-lodge, with stags' heads above a grand fireplace. Elegance, luxury and charm.

Rooms: 1 twin room with own bathroom.

Price: 300 Frs for two, including breakfast.

Meals: Dinner 65-100 Frs, including wine (book ahead).

Open: All year.

To get there: *From Crépy-en-Valois, D332 towards Betz. 3km after Lévignen, left to Bargny. Farm is first group of houses on left when you arrive in Bargny.*

Map Ref No: 6

Lucie & Jacques TRIBOULET
211 rue de la Gruerie
60620 Bargny
Oise
Tel: 44 87 23 52

11

An idyllic village setting surrounded by rolling farmland. Guests sleep in a modern extension (though on beds that are a bit less modern?) to the farmhouse, a fine old building of uncertain age. Mme Verhoeven is a charming hostess. She will, if requested, cook a traditional evening meal with organic produce from her delightful kitchen garden, and the jams at breakfast are, of course, home-grown and homemade.

Rooms: 2 double rooms, each with shower.

Price: 220 Frs for two, including breakfast.

Meals: Dinner 85 Frs (book ahead).

Open: All year.

To get there: *From Beauvais, D901 towards St Omer-en Chaussée. At Troissereux, D133 towards Songeons. There, D143 towards Gournay-en-Bray. On leaving forest, right to Buicourt; house near church.*

Map Ref No: 6

Mme VERHOEVEN
3 rue de la Mare
60380 Buicourt
Oise
Tel: 44 82 31 15

Hold your head high, drive up the long poplar-lined avenue, through two sets of wrought-iron gates and sweep magnificently onto the semi-circular court. Your hosts will greet you affably. Their 1850s house is elegant with huge pieces of period furniture and a delicious whiff of decadence. There are big, comfortable guestrooms, a gorgeous black-and-white tiled floor, a huge fireplace and a sense of light even in winter. Home-made brioche for breakfast.

Rooms: 1 large double room, 2 smaller rooms above, all in one dwelling with one bathroom.

Price: 200 Frs for two, including breakfast.

Meals: Not available.

Open: All year.

To get there: *From Abbeville, N25 towards Amiens; left on D925 towards Arras; after St Riquier, left on D941; through Auxi-le-Château; right on D938 to Beauvoir Wavens: château is first building on right as you enter village.*

Map Ref No: 1

René AUGUSTIN
Château de Drucas
Beauvoir Wavens
62390 Auxi-le-Château
Pas-de-Calais
Tel: 21 04 01 11

This small stud farm, the drive flanked by old stables, has been recently restored to offer self-contained guest accommodation. Rooms, which look out onto the courtyard and surrounding wooded hills, have simple, modern decor and lovely window-boxes. The orchard-garden leads down to a river. Children welcomed; an amiable, family-orientated set-up.

Rooms: 2 double rooms and 2 twin rooms, all with own bathrooms.

Price: 250 Frs for two, including breakfast.

Meals: None.

Open: All year, except Christmas & New Year

A quiet, 200-year-old farmhouse, surrounded by fields but no longer 'working'. An appealing homely atmosphere; the house is full of family photographs and old furniture. The guestrooms are traditionally decorated and furnished. Madame is an enthusiastic cook and serves good-value country suppers in the evenings. Peaceful and friendly.

Rooms: 2 double rooms with own bathrooms.

Price: 190 Frs for two, including breakfast.

Meals: Dinner 80 Frs, excluding wine.

Open: 1 April to 1 November.

To get there: *From Boulogne-sur-Mer, D940 towards St Léonard. There, at 2nd lights, D234 to Echinghen; in village centre.*

Map Ref No: 1

To get there: *From Calais, N43 towards St Omer. At Nordausques, D218, then D217 towards Ruminghem. Signposted in Muncq-Nieurlet hamlet.*

Map Ref No: 1

Jacqueline & Jean-Pierre
BOUSSEMAERE
Rue de l'Eglise
62360 Echinghen
Pas-de-Calais
Tel: 21 91 14 34

Mme Françoise BRETON
Rue du Bourg
62890 Muncq Nieurlet
Pas-de-Calais
Tel: 21 82 79 63

The imposing neo-classical façade of this magnificent château, set in parkland with 15 hectares of orchard and beautifully-tended flower gardens, belies its relaxed atmosphere. Understated modern decor; an individual colour scheme in each of the bedrooms. A large, light dining-room with still-life paintings of apples and pears – and delicious homemade apple juice and raisin-bread for breakfast. A warm welcome for children.

Rooms: 4 double rooms, all with own bathrooms (extra beds available).

Price: 210 Frs for two, including breakfast.

Meals: None.

Open: All year.

To get there: *From Doullens, N25 towards Arras. In L'Arbret, first left to Saulty and follow signposts.*

Map Ref No: 1

Pierre DALLE
82 rue de la Gare
62158 Saulty
Pas-de-Calais
Tel: 21 48 24 76
Fax: 21 48 18 32

16

At the end of a long drive through farmland, beyond gateposts crowned with old bomb shells, this secluded 19th-century manor, a working dairy farm, exudes a quiet air of traditional country hospitality. The rooms, which have a separate entrance and living-room, are comfortable and furnished with antiques, though the loos are down a long corridor. There is a tranquil wooded garden. Madame, friendly and aproned, offers a home-grown, home-cooked dinner.

Rooms: 2 twin rooms and 2 double rooms, all with own bathrooms, sharing 2 wcs .

Price: 160-180 Frs for two, including breakfast. (25 Frs for extra bed).

Meals: Dinner 65 Frs, including wine.

Open: All year.

To get there: *From Calais, A16 for Boulogne. At Marquise, D238 to Wierre Effroy. Follow D234 southwards; left onto D233 and left to Le Breucq.*

Map Ref No: 1

Jacques & Isabelle de MONTIGNY
Le Breucq
62142 Belle-et-Houllefort
Pas-de-Calais
Tel: 21 83 31 99

17

Set in lovely parkland, at the end of a sweeping gravel drive, this imposing château, built in 1745, is being sympathetically restored by the down-to-earth hosts, though a little damp may still be felt. Bedrooms are furnished with period pieces, bright colours and four-poster beds. There is a walled flower garden. Salons and dining-room are on a grand scale, with chandeliers and a huge oak table. But don't be deterred; the atmosphere is relaxed and casual.

Rooms: 2 double rooms with own bathrooms.

Price: 300 Frs for two, including breakfast.

Meals: Dinner 100 Frs, including wine.

Open: All year.

This small farmhouse has been simply and sensitively renovated. The guestrooms, which have their own entrance and day area, with fridge and small library, enjoy views onto thick forests. They are light and airy with open beams. The hosts are kind and helpful and will give you a substantial breakfast with regional produce. There is a barbecue, and bicycles to explore the surrounding countryside.

Rooms: 2 double rooms with own bathrooms.

Price: 220 Frs for two, including breakfast.

Meals: None (barbecue available).

Open: All year.

To get there: *From Arras, N25 towards Doullens. At L'Arbret, right on D8 to Avesnes-le-Comte. D75 to Grand-Rullecourt (4km); château in village centre.*

Map Ref No: 1

To get there: *From Boulogne-sur-Mer, D341 to Desvres, then D215 towards Menneville; just outside Desvres, left at sign "Le Mont Eventé".*

Map Ref No: 1

M Patrice de SAULIEU
Château de Grand-Rullecourt
Avesnes-le-Comte
62810 Grand-Rullecourt
Pas-de-Calais
Tel: 21 58 06 37

M & Mme DESALASE
Le Mont Eventé
Menneville
62240 Desvres
Pas-de-Calais
Tel: 21 91 77 65

A working farm – anyone in search of rural France will find it here. The parents run the auberge; the children run the farm. No pretensions: traditional-style rooms, simple yet tasteful, soft colours and comfortable. A gourmet's paradise with everything home-grown or home-made: pain de campagne, cheeses, foie gras, cassoulet de canard, terrine, rillettes. Produce can be bought. Children are welcome and will adore running around the farmyard and garden.

Rooms: 4 double rooms, all with own bathrooms.

Price: 210 Frs for two, including breakfast.

Meals: Dinner 70 Frs, excluding wine.

Open: All year. Closed Mondays.

To get there: *From Boulogne, N42 towards St Omer. At Escoeuilles, D216 to Bas-Loquin.*

Map Ref No: 1

M & Mme DUSAUTOIR
Ferme-Auberge des Peupliers
Bas-Loquin
62850 Haut-Locquin
Pas-de-Calais
Tel: 21 39 63 70

20

A grand, tranquil place to stay near the ferry; gentle views over the valley – and the battlefields of Agincourt ringing with history just 3 km away, though neither Henry V nor Laurence Olivier (nor Kenneth Branagh) actually stayed here. House and owner are definitely English, with a smart, chintzy feel enlivened by Mrs James's art gallery and a series of regular painting courses run in the house.

Rooms: 2 twin rooms, each with own bathroom.

Price: 290 Frs for two, including breakfast. (Family room 350 Frs.)

Meals: Dinner on request.

Open: All year.

To get there: *From Hesdin, D928 towards St Omer, then D155 left to Fressin. On entering village cross bridge, take 2nd left; house is 200m on left.*

Map Ref No: 1

Mrs Lesley JAMES
La Maison des Violettes
Rue de l'Avocat
62140 Fressin, Hesdin
Pas-de-Calais
Tel: 21 81 80 94

21

The pretty bedrooms of the 'Manoir Francis' have white stone walls, tiled floors and large beds. Most have fireplaces and overlook the lovely garden. Many 'extras', from board games to, possibly, a glass of wine upon arrival. Cooked breakfasts on request, but don't miss the 'pain aux noix'. Dinner is available in winter and can be eaten with the young owners or in private. Elegant, unobtrusive hospitality.

Rooms: 2 twin rooms with own bathrooms; 2 twin rooms sharing a bathroom.

Price: 250 Frs for two, including breakfast.

Meals: Dinner 70 Frs, including wine (Oct – Mar).

Open: All year.

To get there: *From Montreuil, D901 to Neuville. In Neuville, on sharp bend, D113 towards Marles-sur-Canche. Shortly after la Chartreuse follow signposts for 3km.*

Map Ref No: 1

Dominique LEROY
1 rue de l'Eglise
62170 Marles-sur-Canche
Pas-de-Calais
Tel: 21 81 38 80
Fax: 21 81 38 56

22

The large bedrooms of this fine house, a recent conversion of the centuries-old stables of the Château de Bois-en-Ardres, overlook wooded gardens. Decorated in pastels, with large country-style beds, they have everything – from razors to chocolates. There's a children's room and a billiard table in the breakfast room; after 6 children of his own, Monsieur is keen on games! The retired hosts enjoy good and cheerful conversation and their welcome is genuine.

Rooms: 2 double rooms and 1 triple, all with own bathrooms and extra beds available.

Price: 200 Frs for two, including breakfast.

Meals: Not available.

Open: All year (except 23-26 December).

To get there: *From Calais, N43 towards St Omer. At Bois-en-Ardres, house is second property on right; signposted.*

Map Ref No: 1

Bernard & Geneviève LETURGIE
La Chesnaie
N43 Bois-en-Ardres
62610 Ardres
Pas-de-Calais
Tel: 21 35 43 98

23

A typical U-shaped 19th-century château with heavy symmetry, solid masonry and marble fireplaces in every room. It stands in its own park where guests will find a tennis court, pool and fishing and, at a distance, a camping site with restaurant (let us know if it disturbs). Big, comfortable rooms and very convenient on the way to or from the ferry. Nearby is the biggest underground bunker in the world where Hitler stored the V2s with which he planned to crush England.

Rooms: 1 double, 2 twin rooms, all with own shower and wc.

Price: 280 Frs for two, including breakfast.

Meals: Restaurant on the spot in season.

Open: All year.

Laurels flank the drive leading to this imposing stone manor-house, built and added to between the 17th and 19th centuries. It originally belonged to the château next door. Rooms are high-ceilinged, bright and comfortable, with antique furniture and collections of shells and theatre masks. Madame is very much the pivot of her family and has photographs of them everywhere. There is a lovely, mature, sheltered garden.

Rooms: 1 family suite and 1 double room, both with bathrooms.

Price: 200 Frs for two, including breakfast.

Meals: None.

Open: All year.

To get there: *From Calais, N43 towards St Omer. 2km after Nordausques, left onto D221 to Ganspette; signposted.*

Map Ref No: 1

To get there: *From Arras, N39 towards Le Touquet. After 5km, left along D56 towards Duisans. House on left.*

Map Ref No: 1

Gérard PAUWELS
Château du Ganspette
62910 Eperlecques
Pas-de-Calais
Tel: 21 93 43 93
Fax: 21 95 74 98

(24)

Mme Annie SENLIS
Le Clos Grincourt
18 rue du Château
62161 Duisans
Pas-de-Calais
Tel: 21 48 68 33

25

Madame takes pride in welcoming guests to this attractive 200-year-old farmhouse at the end of the drive flanked by old stables with red doors. The one guestroom has traditional floral decoration. The garden is Monsieur's pride and is full of flowers; indeed, the village is a 'ville fleurie' so there's lots of competition. You are near a large forest with lovely walks. Two very kind hosts who enjoy sharing their home and interests.

Rooms: 1 double room with own shower-room.

Price: 280 Frs for two, including breakfast.

Meals: None.

Open: All year.

Joanna has had seven children and is a sculptress. Breakfast is served, with jam made from her own organic fruit, in a conservatory full of her works nestling amongst the hothouse plants. The air of ecccentricity extends to the guestrooms which are furnished in an ancient-and-modern mix with bright colours and adequate bathrooms. Plumb in the centre of an attractive village with a fine mature garden looking out over fields, this is an unusual and interesting stopover.

Rooms: 2 double rooms, each with own shower or bath & wc.

Price: 250 Frs for two, including breakfast.

Meals: Not available.

Open: All year.

To get there: *From Abbeville, N1 towards Nouvion. At Hautvillers, D105 to Forest l'Abbaye; signposted.*

Map Ref No: 1

To get there: *From Abbeville, D925 towards St Riquier. After 2.5km, Vauchelles signposted on right. House on main square next to church.*

Map Ref No: 1

M & Mme Michel BECQUET-CHATEL
161 place des Templiers
80150 Forest l'Abbaye
Somme
Tel: 22 23 24 03

Mme Joanna CREPELLE
121 place de l'Eglise
80132 Vauchelles-les-Quesnoy
Somme
Tel: 22 24 18 17

These are real farmers who know how to treat their guests; 15 pairs of wellies are kept for those who want to discover the secrets of flax, sugar beet, peas and cattle au naturel. Hélène is a treat, bubbling with enthusiasm for her rooms, England (she used to teach English), the heron she saw this morning or her shop where she sells linen produced with the farm's flax. A converted timber-frame stable block houses the guestrooms. It is clean, very comfortable and totally French.

Rooms: 4 double rooms, one studio, each with own shower or bath & wc.

Price: 300 Frs for two, including breakfast.

Meals: None (2 restaurants in village).

Open: All year.

To get there: *From Abbeville, D82 to Caours. House on far side of village; signposted.*

Map Ref No: 1

Marc & Hélène de LAMARLIERE
La Rivièrette
2 rue de la Ferme
80132 Caours, Somme
Tel: 22 24 77 49
Fax: 22 24 76 97

A fine, solid 16th-17th-century manor with turrets, a wide sweeping driveway and large lounging lawn dogs. It is now a sporty, outdoors home where the children can ride bicycles and horses. If the house seems overfilled with furniture, there is space enough in the park and a rambling kitchen garden. Madame radiates energy and serves wonderful meals, using her home-grown vegetables, in a pale green châteauesque dining-room.

Rooms: 1 double room and 1 suite for four, with bathrooms; 2 double rooms sharing a bathroom.

Price: 350-400 Frs for two, including breakfast.

Meals: Dinner 110 Frs, excluding wine.

Open: All year.

To get there: *From Abbeville, N28 towards Rouen. At St Maxent, D29 to Oisemont, then D25 towards Sénarpont. Signposted on outskirts of Foucaucourt.*

Map Ref No: 1

Mme Elisabeth de ROCQUIGNY
Oisemont
80140 Foucaucourt
Somme
Tel: 22 25 12 58

A modest house with a pretty garden that would suit a family looking for easy access to the surrounding towns and forested countryside. The four rooms are generally let as two family suites and are decorated in modern provincial style with lots of cut flowers. Madame particularly welcomes children and likes to include guests in her household.

Rooms: 2 family suites for four, each with own bathroom.

Price: 240 Frs for two, including breakfast.

Meals: Not available.

Open: All year.

The Goisques are green-fingered, with a beautiful garden and large nursery. Their oh-so-French house has a charming glass-and-ironwork veranda. The entrance hall is tiled with a mosaic and an impressive oak staircase leads up to the rooms. These have beautiful wooden floors and Louis XVI furniture. An attractive and relaxing house where you may be welcomed with, for example, fresh raspberries in season.

Rooms: 1 double room and 1 twin room, each with own wash-basin. Shared bathroom.

Price: 220 Frs for two, including breakfast.

Meals: None.

Open: All year.

To get there: *From Abbeville, D925 to St Riquier. In village, left at first junction; fourth house on right.*

Map Ref No: 1

Mme GENCE
12 rue Drugy
80135 Saint-Riquier
Somme
Tel: 22 28 83 19

To get there: *From Amiens, N29 towards Neufchâtel-en-Bray. 13km after Poix-de-Picardie, at Coq Gaulois junction, right to Digeon.*

Map Ref No: 6

M Bruno GOISQUE
Château de Digeon
80590 Digeon
Somme
Tel: 22 38 07 12

A 200-year-old stable-block beside Madame's Tudor-style cottage has been converted for guests. There is a charming air of vague disorder about this deliciously ramshackle place, with chickens scratching in a huge, rambling garden. Madame is warm and friendly; she keeps the rooms spotless and serves breakfast 'en famille' with the help of her teenage children.

Rooms: 3 double rooms and 1 twin room, all with bathrooms.

Price: 240-320 Frs for two, including breakfast.

Meals: Not available.

Open: All year.

The guest bedrooms, filled with flowers and Louis XVI furniture, overlook the fine English-style garden; Madame is a fanatical gardener. She likes to chat over breakfast, which is served on porcelain that matches the pale green of the curtains in the elegant dining-room.

Rooms: 3 double rooms, all with own bathrooms. (Additional rooms available at son's nearby farm.)

Price: 380 Frs for two, including breakfast. Reservation only.

Meals: None.

Open: All year, except between Christmas and New Year.

To get there: *From Amiens, N29 towards Poix, then left on D162 to Creuse; signposted.*

Map Ref No: 6

To get there: *From Abbeville, D40 towards St Valéry-le-Crotoy. Right in Port-le-Grand and follow small road for 2km; path for Bois Bonance is on right, 300m after a railing.*

Map Ref No: 1

Mme Monique LEMAITRE
26 rue Principale
80480 Creuse
Somme
Tel: 22 38 91 50

Jacques & Myriam MAILLARD
Le Bois Bonance
Port-le-Grand
80132 Abbeville
Somme
Tel: 22 24 11 97

Rommel stayed here and we know he had good taste (but his soldiers broke the fireplace tiles chopping wood on them). Nestling in rolling, wooded country, this very attractive house was the first to offer B&B hospitality in the Somme and the tradition holds. Irreproachably comfortable rooms with great views and a magnificent panelled dining-room where Madame lays a fine breakfast. Don't leave without tasting the home-produced cider and honey or meeting Monsieur's "trotteur" horse.

Rooms: 3 double rooms, one with own bathroom & wc, 2 with own shower and sharing wc.

Price: 220-230 Frs for two, including breakfast.

Meals: Not available.

Open: All year.

To get there: *From Abbeville, N28 towards Rouen. After 28km, left at Bouttencourt on D1015 to Sénarpont then D211 towards Amiens. After 4.5km, left into Le Mazis; follow Chambres d'Hôtes signs.*

Map Ref No: 6

Dorette & Aart ONDER DER LINDEN
80430 Le Mazis
Somme
Tel: 22 25 90 88
Fax: 22 25 76 04

34

In the very beautiful valley of the Somme, this working farm with 15 hectares of lakes along the river is an obvious attraction for those who enjoy fishing or boating. There are views of a bridge and lock from the bedrooms. The friendly Madame Randjia offers regional specialities using organic ingredients. Meals, served in the flower-filled dining-room/lounge are easy, family gatherings.

Rooms: 2 double rooms and 1 twin room, all with own bathrooms.

Price: 260 Frs for two, including breakfast.

Meals: Dinner 85 Frs, excluding wine.

Open: All year.

To get there: *From A1, Péronne exit onto N29 westwards and immediately right on D146 towards Feuillères. Before village, D146E to Frise. First farm after bridge.*

Map Ref No: 2

M Michel RANDJIA
La Ferme de l'Ecluse
1 rue Mony
80340 Frise
Somme
Tel: 22 84 59 70

35

This converted chapel is all that remains of an old abbey. The smallish guestrooms are set right under the brown-painted rafters. The ground floor, also used by the 'gîte d'étape' (B&B bookings are not taken when groups are expected), has a corner kitchen and massive table which converts into ... a snooker table. Guests may use the garden and the area offers water sports, fishing and one of the greatest Gothic cathedrals in France. A pleasant and unusual stopover.

Rooms: 1 double room and 1 triple room, each with own bathroom

Price: 200 Frs for two, including breakfast.

Meals: None (in village).

Open: All year.

To get there: *From Amiens, N1 towards Beauvais. Between St Sauflieu and Essertaux, right on D153 to Loeuilly; signposted.*

Map Ref No: 6

Mme RICHOUX
36 route de Conty
80160 Loeuilly
Somme
Tel: 22 38 15 19

The spire of Amiens cathedral soars up into the sky nearby. 4 guestrooms and sitting-room, in an excellently-converted out-building, are furnished with a pleasing mix of old and new, adorned with fresh flowers and sweets and double-glazed against any road noise. If you arrive at a sensible time you will be offered a glass of home-made cider. Indeed, kind attentions are the hallmark here and breakfast in the dining-room is a feast. Pony-and-trap rides in summer.

Rooms: 3 double rooms and 1 twin, each own bathroom.

Price: 310 Frs for two, including breakfast.

Meals: None (within walking distance).

Open: All year.

To get there: *From Amiens, N1 towards Breteuil and Paris. Just before Dury, left towards St Fuscien; signposted 'Chambres d'Hôtes'.*

Map Ref No: 6

M Alain SAGUEZ
2 rue Grimaux
80480 Dury
Somme
Tel: 22 95 29 52

This exotic example of 19th-century architecture sits proudly on its hill offering views way out across the Somme Bay to the Channel, all flat and wet and appropriately melancholy. Madame has taken infinite care with the interior and gives monthly candlelit musical dinners. Her style is inimitable, her utterly quiet home an experience in itself. An ideal spot for walking, riding, fishing and birdwatching; or take Hélène's tour of antique dealers.

Rooms: 3 double & 2 twin, all with own bathrooms.

Price: 350-500 Frs for two, including breakfast (min. 2 nights).

Meals: Dinner: 'gastronomique" 250 Frs, 'familial' 150 Frs, both including wine & coffee.

Open: All year.

To get there: *From Abbeville, D901 towards Beauvais. In Liercourt, right on D3 (Chambres d'Hôtes sign) towards Mareuil then left on D13 towards Huppy. House on left ('Welcome' sign) up 900m drive.*

Map Ref No: 1

Hélène THAON D'ARNOLDI
Manoir de la Renardière
80580 Erondelle
Somme
Tel: 22 27 13 00
Fax: 22 27 13 12

A rambling garden with pond, stone love-seats, swings and a large play-house give this old manor house the feel of a child's adventure story. Behind the wrought-iron front door, the emphasis is on family hospitality. Madame, often clad in a white linen apron, gives guests a big welcome. Bedrooms have marble fireplaces, square French pillows on the beds and floral 1950s country-style decor.

Rooms: 3 double rooms (one on the ground floor), each with own bathroom; 2 small rooms (a twin and a single) suitable for children.

Price: 200 Frs for two, including breakfast.

Meals: Not available.

Open: All year.

To get there: *From Amiens, D929 towards Albert. At Pont-Noyelles, left onto D115 towards Contay; signposted in Bavelincourt.*

Map Ref No: 1

M Noël VALENGIN
Bavelincourt
80260 Villers Bocage
Somme
Tel: 22 40 51 51

Hazeville is an exceptional experience; from your artist host to his highly aristocratic and refined home (built in 1560); from your rather exotic rooms in the pigeon-tower (even older) to the private pool for a pre-breakfast swim (8-9 am only). You will be flooded with history and art, given a generous breakfast on hand-painted china (to match the wall covering) and carefully directed to all the secret treasures of the Vexin. Well-behaved children over 7 welcome.

Rooms: 1 double & 1 twin room, both with bathrooms.

Price: 600 Frs for two, including breakfast.

Meals: None (wide choice within 5-10km).

Open: Weekends and school holidays.

To get there: *From Rouen, N14 towards Paris. 20km before Pontoise, at Magny-en-Vexin, right onto N183 to Arthies. Left onto D81, through Enfer; château on left.*

Map Ref No: 6

Guy & Monique DENECK
Château d'Hazeville
95420 Wy-Dit-Joli-Village
Val d'Oise
Tel: 34 67 06 17
Fax: 34 67 17 82

(40)

Three generations of the family have worked this peaceful dairy farm, in its extensive grounds on the outskirts of Caumont l'Eventé. Locals from the town will even tell you that it is too quiet. There are horses, chickens, ducks, and ... cows. Madame is most kind, and her food, much of it home-produced, is a treat. Bikes and horses – no charge!

Rooms: 2 double rooms and 1 twin room, each with bathroom.

Price: 170 Frs for two, including breakfast.

Meals: Dinner 70 Frs, excluding wine.

Open: All year.

To get there: *From Caen, D9 towards Torigni-sur-Vire. At Caumont l'Eventé, D53 through Sept Vents. After village, take chestnut-lined drive on right and follow "La Rivière" signs.*

Map Ref No: 4

Normandy

Geneviève & Raoul ACHARD de LELUARDIERE
Ferme de la Rivière, Sept Vents
14240 Caumont l'Eventé
Calvados
Tel: 31 68 70 44

A beautiful old cider farm set in blissful rural peace with sweeping views over the gardens and beyond. Madame's admirable restoration job pays homage to the farm's past (no timbers cut, windows slotted in behind original frame) and it figures in French interior design mags. She also provides sumptuous breakfasts in her tranquil, almost church-like dining-room. Of the three rooms, splurge and go for the vast "Bleue" (though all are excellent). Careful children welcome.

Rooms: 1 double room and 1 twin, each with own bathroom.

Price: 260-280 Frs for two, including breakfast (minimum 2 nights).

Meals: None (many eating places nearby).

Open: All year, except for Christmas.

Guests at the charming, ivy-covered 19th-century staging inn awake to the sound of church bells, in rooms with fine furnishings. A typical dinner may feature a chicken, spit-roasted over a copper pan. Then a wonderful farmhouse breakfast in a traditional Norman kitchen. The hosts, who rear horses, are energetic and sociable. There is a rambling garden, kitchen facilities and a pleasant living-room. Ideal for children (as long as they are over three).

Rooms: 3 double rooms, all with bathrooms.

Price: 270 Frs for two, including breakfast.

Meals: Dinner 130 Frs, including wine/cider.

Open: All year.

To get there: *From Caen, N175 to Dozulé and D85 to Cambremer. 5.4km after Cambremer, left to St Aubin Lebizay; signposted.*

Map Ref No: 5

To get there: *From Bayeux , D6 to Juvigny then D9 to Caumont-l'Eventé. Opposite Caumont church, D28 towards Balleroy. After 200m, look for Gîtes de France sign on right.*

Map Ref No: 4

Bernard BATAILLE
La Cour l'Epée
14340 St Aubin-Lebizay
Calvados
Tel: 31 65 09 45

Claude BOULLOT
Le Relais
19 rue Thiers
14240 Caumont-l'Eventé
Calvados
Tel: 31 77 47 85

This handsome château, recently renovated, has some fine period ceilings and furnishings. The huge guestrooms fill with morning light. Bathrooms have luxury 'toiletries' and efficient showers. Dinner (5 courses) can be taken 'en famille' if wished. Madame is a superb cook, worthy of French tradition (vegetarian dishes on request), and has a charming husband and a delightful daughter. A thoroughly restful environment, though the road is near. Riding possible.

Rooms: 2 double rooms and 2 suites, all with own bathrooms.

Price: 460 Frs for two, including breakfast.

Meals: Dinner 200 Frs, including aperitif, wine & calvados.

Open: All year.

Standing in rolling countryside, this beautiful manor-house is a delight and extremely comfortable. Madame Corpet has been welcoming guests for years and does it with huge charm and professionalism. Meals, 'en famille', are delicious; Madame serves lots of fish, 'fruits de mer' and, in the morning, a very satisfying breakfast. Children welcome. Golf and horse-riding nearby.

Rooms: 2 double rooms, 1 twin room, all with bathrooms.

Price: 600 Frs for two, including breakfast.

Meals: Dinner 250 Frs, including wine.

Open: 1 March to 31 December.

To get there: *From Caen, N158 towards Falaise. At la Jalousie, right on D23; right on D235 just before Bretteville-sur-Laize; signposted.*

Map Ref No: 5

To get there: *From Bayeux, N13 west then D30 exit south to Aignerville.*

Map Ref No: 4

Anne-Marie & Alain CANTEL
Château des Riffets
14680 Bretteville-sur-Laize
Calvados
Tel: 31 23 53 21

Yves & Francine CORPET
Manoir de l'Hormette
Aignerville
14710 Trévières, Calvados
Tel: 31 22 51 79
Fax: 31 22 75 90

Parts of this old farmhouse are over 500 years old and its position, in 3 acres of orchards overlooking the Auge valley, does true justice to this area of Normandy. Relax in the quiet garden or try fishing for multicoloured carp in the pond. Visit some lovely old Norman country towns, the peace memorial at Caen or the Cheese Museum. Then dine in one of the 'good little restaurants' Madame will point out before returning to old beams and rural silence for the night.

Rooms: 2 double rooms, 2 triple rooms, all with own bath or shower, 2 sharing a wc.

Price: 250 Frs for two, including breakfast.

Meals: Not available.

Open: All year.

Another gorgeous Norman farmhouse, this time dating as far back as the 15th century when it was the building used by the monks of the Abbey as their dormitory. Much of the original church remains. Madame runs the farm – horses, cows and sheep – and still has time for her guests. The house is unpretentiously lovely, with a fine stone staircase, a big fireplace, exposed beams and some stone columns in the oldest part.

Rooms: 1 twin room, 2 suites for three; own bathrooms.

Price: 200 Frs for two, including breakfast.

Meals: Dinner 80 Frs, including cider.

Open: All year.

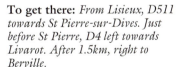

To get there: *From Lisieux, D511 towards St Pierre-sur-Dives. Just before St Pierre, D4 left towards Livarot. After 1.5km, right to Berville.*

Map Ref No: 5

To get there: *From Bayeux, N13 west. After 14km, D30 to Ecrammeville and follow signposts (farm is near church).*

Map Ref No: 4

Annick DUHAMEL
Le Pressoir
Berville
14170 St Pierre-sur-Dives
Calvados
Tel: 31 20 51 26

Louis & Annick FAUVEL
Ferme de l'Abbaye
14710 Ecrammeville
Calvados
Tel: 31 22 52 32

The whole house is exceptionally light and airy, although Grandmère rules over it like a dragon; her bust adorns the fireplace and her portrait hangs on the wall. But she planted a marvellous garden; there is a pond, a moat, huge swings, and magnificent plants. More like a manor, the house has an imposing frontage, a palatial dining-room and splendid bedrooms. "Wonderful", said our inspector.

Rooms: 3 double rooms and 1 suite for four, all with bathrooms.

Price: 290 Frs for two, including breakfast.

Meals: None.

Open: 1 March to 31 December.

This restored farm raises poultry, including geese which are spit-roasted in winter! Guests are warmly greeted by the well-educated, youngish hosts and there's a relaxed atmosphere. Bedrooms are big, clean and bright, with their own entrance, kitchen and sitting-room. Good puddings round off appetising dinners, eaten with the family if wished. Vegetarian dishes upon request. Children welcome (cots, games and bikes).

Rooms: 2 twin rooms (one on ground floor), with bathrooms.

Price: 180 Frs for two, including breakfast.

Meals: Dinner 75 Frs, including wine.

Open: All year.

To get there: *From Cherbourg, N13 to Isigny. There, right on D5 towards Le Molay. Left near Vouilly church. Château on right after 500m.*

Map Ref No: 4

To get there: *From Caen, N175 towards Avranches. At St Martin-des-Besaces, left onto D165; house is on right 4km along.*

Map Ref No: 4

Marie-José & James HAMEL
Château de Vouilly
Vouilly
14230 Isigny-sur-Mer
Calvados
Tel: 31 22 08 59

Jacqueline & Gilbert LALLEMAN
Carrefour des Fosses
14260 Brémoy
Calvados
Tel: 31 77 83 22

In the green pasturelands and hills of 'La Suisse Normande', this friendly couple have built a traditional-style house where they offer comfortable B&B rooms with brand new, spacious bathrooms, perfectly delicious regional dinners and rides with pony and trap through the secret byways of the area. The house may lack character but your hosts make up for it in personal warmth and "savoir-vivre" and you wake to stunning views over the hushed hills in your first-floor room. Excellent value.

Rooms: 1 double room, 1 suite, each with own shower & wc.

Price: 180 Frs for two, including breakfast.

Meals: Dinner 75 Frs, including cider.

Open: All year.

A lovely 18th-century family-run farmhouse with a very homely atmosphere. The bedroom is comfortable and traditional in style; the en-suite shower-room is new. Breakfast is served in the guest dining-room. A useful base from which to visit the Bayeux Tapestry and the Normandy Landing beaches and the impressive Peace Monument in Caen.

Rooms: 1 double room with shower-room.

Price: 220 Frs for two, including breakfast.

Meals: Not available.

Open: All year.

To get there: *From Caen, D562 towards Flers. About 25km on at Le Fresne, D1 towards Falaise. After 4km, house on right: signposted.*

Map Ref No: 5

Roland & Claudine LEBATARD
Arclais
14690 Pont d'Ouilly
Calvados
Tel: 31 69 81 65

To get there: *From Bayeux, N13 west towards Carentan. Vaucelles is first village on that road.*

Map Ref No: 4

M & Mme Michel LEGRAND
Vaucelles
14400 Bayeux
Calvados
Tel: 31 92 84 03

The stones of the old farmhouse are utterly authentic, the floorboards, beams and stone fireplaces warmly genuine and the farmyard fowls sound as real in the morning as they taste at dinner. The farm produces its own cider and vegetables. Lovingly-decorated rooms with hand-sewn curtains; intimate spaces outside with flowers and shrubs. When you come back from your day, your hard-working hosts have plenty of time for you despite their herd of dairy cows.

Rooms: 1 family room for 3-4, 2 double rooms, 1 twin room and 1 suite for 4, all with own shower & wc.

Price: 190 Frs for two, including breakfast.

Meals: Dinner 70 Frs, including wine.

Open: All year.

To get there: *From Bayeux, D12 towards Courseulles-sur-Mer and Banville. In village centre, right down rue du Camp Romain to No24.*

Map Ref No: 5

Arlette & Gérard LESAGE
24 rue du Camp Romain
14480 Banville
Calvados
Tel: 31 37 92 18

This typical old farmhouse, in its own woodland and surrounded by farmland, is an ideal stop for those wishing to explore the Normandy countryside. Rooms, some with their own balconies, are comfortable and well decorated. There is a large garden where you are welcome to have your own picnic. Children (and adults...) will appreciate the table tennis and miniature golf at La Gage. Tennis, swimming and riding close by.

Rooms: 2 double rooms with own bathrooms; 2 twin rooms & 1 room for 3-4 people, with own showers but sharing wc.

Price: 170-220 Frs for two, including breakfast.

Meals: None (restaurant 500m).

Open: All year.

To get there: *From Vire centre, D524 towards Tinchebray & Flers; house signposted after 2km on RIGHT.*

Map Ref No: 4

Camille MARIE
La Gage
14500 Roullours
Calvados
Tel: 31 68 17 40

This working dairy farm, built in the 1760s, has been in the family for two generations and has the warm atmosphere of an authentic Norman home. Comfortable, traditionally-furnished rooms, with beautiful, low wooden ceilings, have been converted from a wine-store (above ground!). Given some advance warning, Madame will provide a mouthwatering selection of 'plats régionaux' served in the charming family dining-room.

A blissful place to stay after arriving in Normandy or before returning home. It is stunningly handsome, a great Norman farmhouse – more of a manor-house in style – that doubles as a ferme-auberge and serves honest and delicious meals. The rooms are simple and comfortable, the atmosphere serene, and the views across the 'marais' would cure any attack of the blues. Utterly genuine and totally quiet...if you don't count the ducks.

Rooms: 2 twin rooms and 1 triple, all with bathrooms. (Extra beds available.)

Rooms: 2 double rooms with own bathrooms; 2 twin rooms with shared bathroom.

Price: 220 Frs for two, including breakfast.

Price: 200 Frs for two, including breakfast.

Meals: Dinner 75 Frs (book ahead).

Meals: Dinner 80 Frs, including cider.

Open: All year.

Open: Easter to 31 October.

To get there: *From Bayeux, D5 west, through Le Molay Littry, towards Bernesq and Briqueville. Right about 0.75km before Bernesq; Le Ruppaley on this road.*

To get there: *From Bayeux, N13 to La Cambe, then D113 south. After 1km, D124 towards St Germain-du-Pert (1.5km).*

Map Ref No: 4

Map Ref No: 4

Marcelle & Jean-Claude MARIE
Le Ruppaley
14710 Bernesq
Calvados
Tel: 31 22 54 44

Paulette & Hervé MARIE
Ferme Auberge de la Rivière
St Germain-du-Pert
14230 Isigny-sur-Mer
Calvados
Tel: 31 22 72 92

Secluded, down its own drive, this old stone house, built in 1714, is now a dairy farm. The salon is very French and just the place for a quiet read. Big rooms with country furniture (one has a four-poster); the slightly worn bathrooms are more than made up for by these light sunny bedrooms. The family is charming and helpful but not intrusive. Special extras are comfortable garden chairs, a pond for fishing and homemade yoghurt. Some stay a week.

Rooms: 2 doubles & 1 suite, all with own shower & wc.

Price: 210 Frs for two, including breakfast.

Meals: Dinner 110 Frs, including wine or cider.

Open: All year.

To get there: *From Caen, A13 towards Cherbourg then exit for Carpiquet and Caumont-l'Eventé. 500m before Caumont-l'Eventé, left at Chambres d'Hôtes sign into private drive.*

Map Ref No: 4

Mme Alain PETITON
La Suhardière
14240 Livry
Calvados
Tel: 31 77 51 02

The seat of a seigneurial tax-collector, the 15th-century fortified farm, still working, offers the perfect rural refuge. Warm and attentive, M & Mme Plassais, self-confessed paysans, ensure privacy and calm. Of the three bedrooms, 'Mathilde' and 'Guillaume' are good value, spacious with simple decoration and large open fireplaces. Breakfast, with the hosts, must be eaten before 9 a.m. Fishing and horse-riding nearby.

Rooms: 1 double room, 1 twin room and 1 room for 2-4 people, all with own bathrooms.

Price: 190 Frs for two, including breakfast.

Meals: Not available.

Open: All year.

To get there: *From Falaise, D63 towards Trun. After Fresné-La-Mère, right towards Pertheville-Ners and follow signs.*

Map Ref No: 5

Michel & Rolande PLASSAIS
Le Chêne Sec
14700 Pertheville-Ners
Calvados
Tel: 31 90 17 55

Yet another 17th-century farmhouse deep in the countryside; one could spend an enchanted holiday staying all over France in them. To cap it all, this one produces cider! There are no pretensions here, just good solid farm fare, old-fashioned furnishings and fittings, a homely atmosphere, and lots of good walks. The guestrooms are independent, marvellous for those wanting to stay a few days and do their own cooking.

Rooms: 1 double room and 1 triple, each with own bathroom and self-catering facilities.

Price: 200-220 Frs for two, including breakfast.

Meals: None (self-catering).

Open: 1 Feb – 31 October.

On a small hill, surrounded by farmland, this charming old farmhouse has a very hospitable anglophile owner with fluent English. Guestrooms are immaculate, each with a distinctive, clear style and colour scheme and traditional furniture. There is a welcoming, open fireplace and the house looks out onto a full-flowered, herb-scented English-plan garden. 'Plats régionaux' are served in the evening with a warming shot of calvados!

Rooms: 1 double, 2 twin & 1 family room for 5, all with bathrooms.

Price: 220 Frs for two, including breakfast.

Meals: Dinner 100 Frs, including wine.

Open: All year.

To get there: *From Caen, N13 towards Lisieux. At Vimont, D47 to St Pierre-sur-Dives. Left onto D16 to Bretteville-sur-Dives; signposted.*

Map Ref No: 5

To get there: *From Bayeux, N13 towards Caen. After 6km, right to Nonant; right at church. House is 300m down this road.*

Map Ref No: 4

Michèle RENAULDON
Ferme de Glatigny
14170 Bretteville-sur-Dives
Calvados
Tel: 31 20 78 34

58

Xavière SIMAND
La Poulinière
14400 Nonant
Calvados
Tel: 31 92 51 03

59

Le Vieux Pressoir is a haven of flowers, peace and femininity. From the dried flowers to the antique lace laid across each bed or the cushion stuck with antique hatpins, everything is done to bring the pleasure of the surrounding countryside into the house. The antique lights and large fireplace add to the experience of the table d'hôte in the evening, in the company of a quiet gentle couple who will rise at dawn if you need to catch an early ferry.

Rooms: 5 rooms: 2 with own bathrooms, 3 with hand-basin only and a shared bathroom.

Price: 230 Frs for two, including breakfast.

Meals: Dinner 120 Frs, including cider.

Open: All year.

To get there: *From Le Havre cross Pont de Tancarville onto N178 towards Caen. At Foulbec, D312 towards Honfleur. In Conteville, left after church, following signpost "Hameau Potier Pressoir".*

Map Ref No: 5

Pierre & Odile ANFREY
Le Vieux Pressoir
Le Clos Potier
27210 Conteville
Eure
Tel: 32 57 60 79

60

These are purpose-built rooms in a typical Norman setting: comfortable, spotless, long on mod cons, short on soul. But you are only 20km from Monet's Giverny, where you'll find all the soul you need. Alongside, in a converted 18th-century barn, is the guest living-room (with coin-operated telephone) opening onto a terrace and the garden; Madame plans to set up a rural Norman scene on the mezzanine when she can find the mannequins ... really!

Rooms: 3 double & 2 twin rooms, all with shower or bath & wc.

Price: 270 Frs for two, including breakfast.

Meals: None (picnic here or restaurant nearby).

Open: All year.

To get there: *From A13, exit 15 at Chauffour, then N13 towards Evreux. After Caillouet, D534 towards Boncourt and follow signs.*

Map Ref No: 5

Brigitte BEGHINI
Les Ormes
5 rue Divette
27120 Boncourt, Eure
Tel: 32 36 92 44 or 32 36 73 01
Fax: 32 26 39 11

61

This farm – a monks' lodging house in the 11th century – has enchanting modern rooms. Very French details, such as embroidered white linen and toiletries in the bathrooms, all point to the tremendous care and pride Sandrine takes in having guests to stay, though the towels are French size (i.e. rather small) too! She has even provided a 'Cabane d'Ali Baba' for children to play in.

Rooms: 2 double rooms and 1 twin room, each with own bathroom.

Price: 270 Frs for two, including breakfast.

Meals: None.

Open: All year.

This is a lovingly-maintained home full of country furniture and huge beams. Janine is a hostess who takes great care over presentation and welcoming details. She grows fruit and vegetables and will very occasionally prepare dinner for guests. Enthusiastic about her region, she can provide armchair guiding through Giverny, Rouen and the great abbeys of Normandy. She is also taking English lessons so as to be able to chat with her guests; rare dedication!

Rooms: 1 double room and 1 family room for five, each with own bathroom.

Price: 230-260 Frs for two, including breakfast.

Meals: None (in village or 6km away).

Open: All year.

To get there: *From A13, exit 16 towards Vernon. Left on D57 towards Cocherel. After 4km, D65 left towards Menilles and 1st right; farm is on this road.*

Map Ref No: 5

To get there: *From Evreux, D155 north. 300m after Les Faulx hamlet, right for Heudreville. House in cul-de-sac opposite church.*

Map Ref No: 5

Sandrine BESNARD
Ferme de la Moinerie
27120 Houlbec Cocherel
Eure
Tel: 32 26 00 44

Mme Janine BOURGEOIS
La Ferme
4 rue de l'Ancienne Poste
27400 Heudreville-sur-Eure
Eure
Tel: 32 50 20 69

Here is a family home in the truest sense. The Bulteys are totally unpretentious and welcome adults and children equally to their farm. The house is particularly well-provided for disabled guests. The rooms are spacious, with old brass beds and large wardrobes. You can borrow bicycles to explore and, in the evening, enjoy Madame's traditional Norman cookery.

Rooms: 2 double rooms with own bathrooms; 1 double room with shower only.

Price: 200 Frs for two, including breakfast.

Meals: Dinner 80 Frs, excluding wine.

Open: All year.

No great château this but a family house (the Préaumonts have 17 grandchildren) that also serves as farm offices. Perhaps rather run-down but supremely friendly with an air of faded grandeur. Guests will warm to Madame's relaxed manner and children love it here: there are billiards, ping-pong and 'babyfoot' for rainy days, the farm to explore and old family photos to interrogate on the grand staircase. Little finery inside but architectural interest outside in its two distinct periods.

Rooms: 2 double rooms, one with own bath & wc, one with own shower & wc.

Price: 260 Frs for two, including breakfast.

Meals: Not available.

Open: All year.

To get there: *From A13 exit 28, go into Beuzeville. Opposite Credit Agricole Bank, take road for St Pierre-du-Val then left into Rue des Coutances; house is 1km along.*

Map Ref No: 5

To get there: *From Lisieux, D519 towards Orbec. At Orbiquet, left onto D145. Go through St Germain-la-Campagne; château on left as you leave village.*

Map Ref No: 5

Mme Régine BULTEY
Les Coutances
27210 Beuzeville
Eure
Tel: 32 57 75 54

Bruno & Laurence de PREAUMONT,
Château du Grand Bus
St Germain-la-Campagne
27230 Thiberville, Eure
Tel: 32 44 71 14
Fax: 32 46 45 81

Your Franco-British hosts have totally renovated their 200-year-old Norman farmhouse, exposing plastered beams, fireplaces and old tiled floors and creating 5 guestrooms, all differently decorated with Nicky's spoils from travels to exotic places. She is also a Cordon Bleu cook – and Régis makes the cheese and cider and grows the vegetables for her delicious meals. They are young, charming, hospitable and love having guests.

Rooms: 2 double & 3 twin rooms, all with own bathrooms.

Price: 230 Frs for two, including breakfast.

Meals: Dinner 100 Frs, including wine.

Open: All year.

The authentic 18th and 19th-century rooms have sweeping views across the Seine without, and fine antiques within. (The bathrooms are gratifyingly modern.) The sitting-room's painted ceiling adds further elegance, as do the porcelain and silver used for meals on the terrace or in the hunting room. Your host is an antiques dealer and he has hung oil paintings and trophies in most rooms.

Rooms: 4 double rooms and 3 twin rooms, all with own bathrooms.

Price: 530 Frs for two, including breakfast.

Meals: Dinner 180 Frs, including wine.

Open: March to January.

To get there: *From A13, Le Havre exit, onto D139 towards Pont Audemer. In Fourmetot, left towards Corneville. Farm is 1km from turning on left.*

Map Ref No: 5

To get there: *From A13, exit 25 (Bourg-Achard) on D313 towards Yvetot. After 4km, right for the Château.*

Map Ref No: 5

Régis & Nicky DUSSARTRE
L'Aufragère
La Croisée
27500 Fourmetot, Eure
Tel: 32 56 91 92
Fax: 32 57 75 34

M Patrice FAVREAU
Château du Landin
Le Landin
27350 Routot
Eure
Tel: 32 42 15 09

An impressive house, not just a château but also an important site in the Hundred Years War. You enter across a rickety wooden bridge over the moat and there are underground passages beneath the whole building. Maryvonne is anything but imposing, however, and takes great care over her guests' comfort. The service is luxurious: silver tableware, fruit juice in crystal glasses in the mornings, a beautifully-served tea in the afternoon.

Rooms: 2 double rooms and 1 twin room, all with bathrooms; shared loo.

Price: 350 Frs for two, including breakfast.

Meals: None.

Open: 1 March – 31 December.

A gorgeous place, surrounded by hills, woods and Norman farm buildings. Superb reception rooms with country-house decor, fires in winter, a real 2-pocket billiard table and a terrace. Large, stylishly-decorated guestrooms have polished floors, lovely old beds and very good bathrooms. You will be welcomed by the keen-to-please owners (choose your own room if they aren't all taken) who want you to enjoy your stay. A great place for large family reunions.

Rooms: 5 double, 1 twin & 2 single rooms, all with bathrooms.

Price: 330-530 Frs for two, including breakfast.

Meals: None (restaurants 4-5km).

Open: All year.

To get there: *From Breteuil, D141 towards Rugles; through forest. At Bémécourt, take left turn (300m after the traffic lights).*

Map Ref No: 5

To get there: *From Lisieux, D510 towards Cormeilles. Almost at Cormeilles, right onto D22 towards Thiberville. After 4km, château on right: signposted.*

Map Ref No: 5

Mme Maryvonne LALLEMAND-LEGRAS
Le Vieux Château
27160 Bémécourt
Eure
Tel: 32 29 90 47

M & Mme NOIROT-NERIN
Château de Saint Gervais
27260 Asnières
Eure
Tel: 32 45 37 87
Fax: 32 46 49 76

Madame Paris has created an easy-going mood in this Norman townhouse. There is a neat garden with an apple orchard and a well, and inside the house pot-plants are literally everywhere. In the rooms some of the furnishings don't quite 'work', but the bedroom with the old carved bed and wardrobe is a must. A good place in the summer and cosy in the winter.

Rooms: 2 double rooms and 1 twin room, all with bathrooms. Cot available.

Price: 200 Frs for two, including breakfast.

Meals: Not available.

Open: All year, except 15 days in January.

A brook runs by the lush garden filled with birdsong. In an old converted barn, the guestrooms are furnished with beautiful pieces. One has a brass Art-Déco bed made by the grandfather, the other a romantic curtained bed. Madame, cultured and highly knowledgeable about the area, is a skilled cook of both Norman and exotic dishes. Not suitable for children.

Rooms: 2 double rooms with own bathrooms; 1 twin room for young people, with shared bathroom.

Price: 280 Frs for two, including breakfast.

Meals: Dinner 130 Frs, including wine.

Open: 15 March to 15 December.

To get there: *From Elbeuf, D840 to St Pierre-des-Fleurs. There, right onto D26; house is signposted on left after 4.5km.*

Map Ref No: 5

To get there: *From Dieppe, D915 to Gisors. Cross Gisors then D181 towards Vernon. In Dangu, rue du Gué is beside the river Epte. Look for house with green shutters.*

Map Ref No: 6

Mme Micheline PARIS
La Michaumière
72 rue des Canadiens
27370 Tourville-la-Campagne
Eure
Tel: 32 35 31 28

70

Nicole POULAIN de SAINT PERE
Les Ombelles
4 rue du Gué
27720 Dangu, Eure
Tel: 32 55 04 95
Fax: 32 55 59 87

71

This place has got it all! The house (listed 15th-century farmhouse), the pond with black and white swans, the position (total country peace near Monet's house at Giverny), the furniture (each piece so carefully chosen, some tenderly hand-painted) and, 'enfin', an exceptional hostess who is calm and generous with her time and attention. She cooks an excellent Norman meal with home-grown organic ingredients and house cider. Your delight is complete.

Rooms: 2 double rooms, 2 twin rooms, each with own shower & wc.

Price: 240 Frs for two, including breakfast.

Meals: Dinner 85 Frs, including homemade cider.

Open: All year.

To get there: *From Rouen, N15 towards Paris. At Gaillon (about 40km), right on D10 towards La-Croix-St Leufroy. After about 7km, enter La Boissaye and follow signs for Chambres d'Hôtes.*

Map Ref No: 5

Clotilde & Gérard SENECAL
Manoir de la Boissière
Hameau la Boissaye
27490 La-Croix-St Leufroy Eure
Tel: 32 67 70 85
Fax: 32 67 03 18

Geneviève and Joseph, an elderly Norman couple of great warmth and charm, are palpably happy to have you in their recently built and centrally-heated house a kilometre outside town. It is traditionally furnished, with a lovely garden that conveys a sense of peace. You are not far from the coast and there is excellent shopping in the market town.

Rooms: 2 double rooms, each with own bathroom.

Price: 160 Frs for two, including breakfast.

Meals: Not available.

Open: All year.

To get there: *From Barneville-Carteret, D903 towards Coutances. Approximately 400m before La Haye-du-Puits, turn left; signposted.*

Map Ref No: 4

Jospeh & Geneviève BELLEE
Route de Barneville
St Symphorien-le-Valois
50250 La-Haye-du-Puits
Manche
Tel: 33 46 11 13

NORMANDY

Built in 1751, and with two of the nicest hosts imaginable, the château is delectably ramshackle and unspoiled. The cavernous Mussolini Room has French windows onto a massive balcony with views across the lawn, and bath and loo behind a screen. The Colonial Room has pith-helmets and colonial mementoes, while the Hat Room. ..... Big garden for children, a hugely relaxed atmosphere, ideal for family holidays. A very special place.

Rooms: 2 double rooms with bathrooms; 1 double and 1 twin sharing a bathroom.

Price: 200-240 Frs for two, including breakfast (50 Frs extra for child in room).

Meals: None.

Open: All year, except January.

To get there: *From Cherbourg, N13 towards Valognes. After 8 miles, right on D119 towards Ruffosses. Cross motorway bridge; signposted.*

Map Ref No: 4

Mark & Fiona BERRIDGE
Château Mont Epinguet
50700 Brix
Manche
Tel: 33 41 96 31
Fax: 33 41 98 77

74

There is great charm to this rather shabby working farm in a fine setting, an old manor with its private chapel in vast grounds. The rooms overlook the park. The decor is slightly haphazard and your hosts are suitably unpretentious, Monsieur's dry wit as surprising and pleasing as the pieces of art nouveau furniture for those who know the language and appreciate the natural, unsophisticated approach. Excellent value for a stopover, and you may want to stay.

Rooms: 3 double rooms, 2 sharing shower & wc, 1 with own bath & wc.

Price: 165-190 Frs for two, including breakfast.

Meals: Not available.

Open: All year.

To get there: *From Cherbourg, N13 south; leave at Ste Mère-l'Eglise exit. At top of sliproad, Cauquigny is signposted on right. Follow this road for 4km, then signs for Chambres d'Hôtes.*

Map Ref No: 4

Albert & Michèle BLANCHET
La Fière
Route de Pont l'Abbé
50480 Ste Mère-l'Eglise
Manche
Tel: 33 41 32 66

75

An impressive, creeper-covered 18th-century farmhouse set around a lovely dark-gravel courtyard flanked by old stables and outbuildings. Rooms are rather dark but very comfortable, with homely family furniture. The elderly hosts are friendly (Anglophile!) and very accommodating; one has a real sense of being invited into their home. There is a pretty flower garden with tables and chairs and a sandpit.

Rooms: 2 double rooms with shared bathroom.

Price: 180 Frs for two, including breakfast.

Meals: Not available.

Open: All year.

This part of the coast has a micro-climate and thus attracts a lot of holiday-makers. There are 25 miles of fine white sandy beaches stretching away from town. They are just 600m from this unusual 1930's Tunisian-style house which looks out across the sea so it matters not that the rooms are on the small side. The town is a very traditional Norman resort and there is stacks to do, particularly for families. Don't miss the memorable 'moules marinières' in Carteret.

Rooms: 2 double rooms with bathrooms; extra beds available.

Price: 200 Frs for two, including breakfast.

Meals: None (good places in walking distance).

Open: All year.

To get there: *From Cherbourg, N13 and N174 to St Lô. At St Georges-Montcocq, D191 to Villiers Fossard. In village, right on C7; house is 800m on right.*

Map Ref No: 4

To get there: *From Cherbourg, D904 to Barneville-Carteret. There, take road to lighthouse; signposted.*

Map Ref No: 4

Jacques & Denise BUISSON
Le Suppey
50680 Villiers Fossard
Manche
Tel: 33 57 30 23

M et Mme CESNE
Ti Gwenn
74-76 route du Cap Barneville
50270 Carteret-Le Cap
Manche
Tel: 33 04 62 84

Perfect if you want solitude; you will hear little but church bells and the occasional tractor. Shops are 5km away; the beach is 6km. This long Norman farmhouse was bought in 1988 and restored by your English hosts with a mixture of modern and traditional styles. They make their own cider, keep goats, rabbits and chickens and are happily integrated. Breakfasts are delicious with homemade jams, fresh orange juice, fresh croissants, etc.

Rooms: 2 double rooms, each with own bathroom.

Price: 160 Frs for two, including breakfast.

Meals: None (5km).

Open: All year.

Fiercely independent and proud of their farm, the family are also unusually passionate about conserving their fine buildings and local wildlife. They are hard-working, easy-going and enthusiastic about meeting foreign travellers. The garden and house are as attractive as the rooms are simple (the decor is a novel assault upon the senses but authentically French – of a kind). It is a treat to stay here, especially for families; total quiet and superb beaches.

Rooms: 2 double rooms, sharing a bathroom.

Price: 200 Frs for two, including breakfast.

Meals: Not available.

Open: All year.

To get there: *From La Haye-du-Puits, D903 towards Barneville-Carteret. At Bolleville, right on D127 to St Nicolas-de-Pierrepont; left before church; house on right after cemetery.*

Map Ref No: 4

Richard & Jay CLAY
La Ferme de l'Eglise
50250 St Nicolas-de-Pierrepont
Manche
Tel: 33 45 53 40

To get there: *From Barneville-Carteret, D904 towards Cherbourg. Right on D513 towards Bricquebec. At Sénoville, signposted 'Chambres d'Hôtes – Le Manoir'.*

Map Ref No: 4

Joseph DELAROCQUE
Le Manoir
50270 Sénoville
Manche
Tel: 33 04 33 24

Set in manicured grounds graced by peacocks, the house is luxurious and hotel-like but there's a warm welcome. Immaculate rooms have delicate antique furnishings and everything a guest may need. Buffet breakfasts include Madame's excellent breads. Good food, cooked on a wood-fired stove, is served by a maid. Sitting-room with marble fireplace and piano. Bikes are Monsieur's passion. Good value.

Rooms: 8 double rooms and 7 twin rooms, all with bathrooms. (2 rooms specially adapted for physically disabled guests.) Extra beds available.

Price: 310 Frs for two, including breakfast.

Meals: Dinner 95 Frs, including wine.

Open: All year.

To get there: *From St Lô, D972 towards Coutances. In St Gilles, D77 towards Pont-Hébert for 3km; signposted.*

Map Ref No: 4

This secluded village house, set in attractive farmland and well placed for visitors to enjoy the cultural and social attractions of Valognes, is run by a hospitable elderly couple, very informative on local history and sights, who still keep some sheep. The rooms are comfortable, with family furnishings and new bathrooms. A kitchen is available for guests' use.

Rooms: 2 double rooms, sharing a bathroom.

Price: 150 Frs for two, including breakfast.

Meals: None (self-catering).

Open: All year.

To get there: *From Cherbourg, N13 to Valognes, then D902 towards Bricquebec. After 2km, left on D87 to Yvetot-Bocage. At the church go towards Morville and take first left.*

Map Ref No: 4

Raymond & Mireille DELISLE
Château de la Rocque
50180 Hébécrevon
Manche
Tel: 33 57 33 20
Fax: 33 57 51 20

Léon & Lucienne DUBOST
Le Haut Billy
Route de Morville
50700 Yvetot-Bocage
Manche
Tel: 33 40 06 74

Racehorses are bred here – the other beasts pale into insignificance beside the "trotteurs"; it is fascinating to watch them training. Your hosts are simple, no-fuss folk, as is their house. It has one plain, perfectly adequate guestroom, a homely dining-room adorned with pictures of prizewinners, be they horses, cows or geese. Breakfast on local "craquelin" biscuits. A good stopping place on the way to Brittany; get up to see Mont St Michel magical in the early morning light.

Rooms: 1 double room with shared bathroom (extra bed available).

Price: 190 Frs for two, including breakfast.

Meals: None (many eating places nearby).

Open: All year.

To get there: *From Avranches, N175 towards Pontorson. After Precey, left on D200 towards Macey. You will find the house after a few minutes.*

Map Ref No: 4

Adolphe DUGUEPEROUX
Les Chaliers
50170 Macey-Pontorson
Manche
Tel: 33 60 01 27

With its flower-lined drive and lush lawn, this old wind-beaten manor-house is a welcome refuge from the wild coastline below. One of the bedrooms, the 'Chambre de la Comtesse', is in a tower at the top of the house and has a sumptuously-carved bed. Everywhere the atmosphere is of light and gentleness.

Rooms: 2 double rooms, each with own bathroom.

Price: 250 Frs for two, including breakfast.

Meals: None (auberge within walking distance).

Open: All year.

To get there: *From Cherbourg, D901 to Barfleur. There, D1 towards St Vaast. After signpost marking the end of Barfleur, 2nd right and 1st left.*

Map Ref No: 4

Mme Claudette GABROY
Le Manoir
50760 Monfarville
Manche
Tel: 33 23 14 21

A beautiful house in a romantic setting next to a large lake and a château. The Gavard's farm has a domestic atmosphere with its large collection of children and dogs; the family dog will even accompany you on walks. Wonderful old varnished staircase and bannister-rail and excellent meals served next to a huge fireplace in the lovely dining-room.

Rooms: 2 twin rooms and 2 double rooms, all with bathrooms. (Extra beds and cot available.)

Price: 190 Frs for two, including breakfast.

Meals: Dinner 75 Frs, including wine.

Open: All year.

Le Petit Manoir has a superb view of Mont St Michel. In the enclosed courtyard there are passion fruit and fig trees. Annick and Jean are livestock farmers; they also produce their own honey, jams and cider. Jean is mayor and the council meets in his kitchen. The rooms are clean and adequate, if short on storage space, but the welcome easily makes up for that. This is a fascinating area; don't miss historic Dinan.

Rooms: 2 double rooms with own bathrooms.

Price: 200 Frs for two, including breakfast.

Meals: Not available.

Open: All year.

To get there: *From Avranches, N175 towards Mt St Michel. After 12km, 1st right (exit Mt St Michel). After 500m, left on D43 towards Rennes. At roundabout, D40 towards Rennes for 5.5km, then D308 left; signposted.*

Map Ref No: 4

To get there: *From Mt St Michel, D275 towards Pontaubault. At Montitier, D107 to Servon. There, take D113 left. House on left; signposted.*

Map Ref No: 4

Jean-Paul & Brigitte GAVARD
La Ferme de L'Etang
'Boucéel'
Vergoncey
50240 St James, Manche
Tel: 33 48 34 68

Annick & Jean GEDOUIN
Le Petit Manoir
50170 Servon
Manche
Tel: 33 60 03 44
Fax: 33 60 17 79

Once inside the high walls of the château you will feel sheltered from the flood tide, although you can hear it coming. Some say it's like living a century ago...or more. Le Rozel, the first owner, was one of William the Conqueror's companions. It has both mediaeval austerity and, on the safer inner part, 18th-century French charm. The furnishings are irreprochably French (salon a little fragile, to be protected from lively children) and so are your hosts. Are you still tempted to go to an hotel?

Rooms: 1 suite for 3 or 4 with shower & wc.

Price: 450 Frs for two, including breakfast.

Meals: None (good choice 2-15km).

Open: All year.

A small dairy farm where they have also made their own cider for two centuries; make sure you try it. The large, blissfully quiet guestroom looks out over the old cider press and the fields. Breakfast will be tempting, with milk fresh from the cows, homemade jams and the smells of baking. The sea is within walking distance and the pretty town of Granville with its fish restaurants just 5km away. And such likeable hosts.

Rooms: 1 room for up to four people, with bathroom.

Price: 160 Frs for two, including breakfast.

Meals: None (5 km).

Open: All year.

To get there: *From Cherbourg, D904 towards Coutances. After Les Pieux, right onto D23 then left onto D117 to Le Rozel; signposted.*

Map Ref No: 4

To get there: *From Granville, D973 towards Avranches. After about 3km, left at Gîtes de France sign, left after 200m; house on left.*

Map Ref No: 4

Josiane GRANDCHAMP
Le Château
50340 Le Rozel
Manche
Tel: 33 52 95 08

Jean-Claude LAISNE
"Mallouet"
50400 Granville
Manche
Tel: 33 50 26 41

A lively and talkative person, Wendy has two small rooms in her old presbytery and a more spacious suite in a converted outhouse. There is a 25-metre-deep holy well in the courtyard. Her flair for interior design is most evident in the kitchen's stencilled motifs and there are unusual flourishes throughout. She cycles off at dawn for freshly-baked croissants from the village. In a wild and beautiful part of Normandy, this is the sort of place you would miss without this book.

Rooms: 2 twin rooms sharing shower room & wc; 1 suite with own bathroom.

Price: 200-275 Frs for two, including breakfast.

Meals: Not available.

Open: All year.

To get there: *From Cherbourg, N13 to Valognes then D902 towards Quettehou. After 9km, left on D119 at bottom of long hill; after 300m take left fork. House is on right after about 2km.*

Map Ref No: 4

Wendy LENDRUM
L'Ancien Presbytère
Sainte Croix
Teurtheville Bocage
50630 Quettehou, Manche
Tel: 33 23 90 32

A typical, 19th-century village house with pleasant rooms and warm, friendly, welcome. The hosts, retired farmers, serve breakfast in their own dining-room. There are tennis courts, a swimming pool and restaurants close at hand, and the proximity to Mont St Michel is a natural advantage. (When calling to book, better to have a French speaker to hand...)

Rooms: 1 double, 1 triple and 1 twin, sharing 2 bathrooms & 2 wcs.

Price: 180 Frs for two, including breakfast.

Meals: Not available.

Open: All year.

To get there: *From Avranches, N175 towards Pontorson. 3km after Precey, right to Servon.*

Map Ref No: 4

M & Mme LESENECHAL
Le Bourg
50170 Servon
Manche
Tel: 33 48 92 13

The English hosts keep an almost self-sufficient home; Ron and Marian came to France to seek 'The Good Life'. Theirs is an 18th-century village house, with traditional decor and large, centrally-heated bedrooms. A casual atmosphere for guests – breakfast is served in the hosts' own dining-room. Look out for their comprehensive collection of old irons!

Rooms: 2 double rooms, sharing a bathroom.

Price: 190 Frs for two, including breakfast.

Meals: None (restaurants in walking distance).

Open: All year.

A light, airy Normandy house set in secluded gardens and an orchard, with comfortable, traditional-style bedrooms but very near a main road. Dinner is prepared using produce from the garden; vegetarian cooking is a speciality. The hosts also run 3 and 5-day courses in photography, painting and crafts. Cycling, fishing, horse-riding and country walks nearby; beach 5km.

Rooms: 3 double rooms sharing 2 bathrooms.

Price: 200 Frs for two, including breakfast.

Meals: Dinner 90 Frs, excluding wine.

Open: All year.

To get there: *From Cherbourg, N13 to Carentan; then D971 to Quettreville-sur-Sienne.*

Map Ref No: 4

To get there: *From Cherbourg, N13 to Carentan; then D971 to Quettreville-sur-Sienne.*

Map Ref No: 4

Ron & Marian MURRELL
Le Bourg
50660 Quettreville-sur-Sienne
Manche
Tel: 33 45 62 30

Pat O'NEILL
Le Capelier
50660 Quettreville-sur-Sienne
Manche
Tel: 33 45 91 75

With an old stable-block converted for guest accommodation, there is a warm, authentic country feel to this 17th-century working farmhouse. Rooms, which have stripped wooden floors and comfortable furnishings, are ideal for families; cots in the attic rooms and a kitchenette. Madame is an excellent cook, offering mouthwatering 'plats régionaux', served 'en famille'.

Rooms: 2 double rooms, 1 twin room and 1 family room for four, all with own bathrooms.

Price: 180 Frs for two, including breakfast.

Meals: Dinner 80 Frs, including wine.

Open: All year.

A fine old village house, square and stone, recently converted by the young English owners, in a peaceful rural spot within easy reach of Coutances (the cathedral is a must), Bayeux (ditto...) and the Normandy beaches. Your hosts are shy but friendly and very willing to please. Lesley is a trained cook (meals are good value) and they both enjoy talking to their guests. The rooms are clean and functional with pine furniture and pastel colour schemes.

Rooms: 1 double room with own bathroom, 1 double & 1 single sharing a bathroom.

Price: 200 Frs for two, including breakfast.

Meals: Dinner 70 Frs, including wine.

Open: All year.

To get there: *From Avranches, N175 south then D998 to St James. There, D12 towards Antrain. House is on right.*

Map Ref No: 4

To get there: *From Coutances, D972 for 6km towards St Lô, then right onto D276 towards Belval Bourg for 3km: house on right, signposted.*

Map Ref No: 4

François & Catherine TIFFAINE
La Gautrais
50240 St James
Manche
Tel: 33 48 31 86

Paul & Lesley TROUT
La Guérandière
Belval, 50210 Cerisy-la-Salle
Manche
Tel: 33 45 21 03
or UK 0452 840541

Set in National Parkland with 8 acres of tranquil grounds, this 16th-century, fortified manor has been lovingly restored by its owner. Guestrooms are pleasant with muted, traditional decor and open fireplaces. Ben Trumble is an eccentric Englishman, very welcoming and sociable, who runs a fine Bugatti car. There are black-powder shooting and archery ranges on the estate and horse-riding nearby.

Rooms: 1 family room for 4 with bathroom; 1 triple and 1 twin with shared bathroom; extra beds available.

Price: 300 Frs for two, including breakfast.

Meals: Not available.

Open: April – November.

This 18th-century château has been fully restored and modernised. The comfortable rooms are centrally heated and overlook the courtyard. Breakfast is served in the dining-room and the hosts are welcoming and sociable. A lovely, convenient spot near Avranches; don't miss its Botanical Gardens whence the view across the bay to Mont St Michel is unforgettable.

Rooms: 2 double rooms with hand-basins; sharing a bathroom.

Price: 180 Frs for two, including breakfast.

Meals: Not available.

Open: All year.

To get there: *From Cherbourg, N13 to Ste Mère-Eglise and D67 via Chef-du-Pont. 1.5km after village turn right; signposted.*

Map Ref No: 4

Ben TRUMBLE
Manoir de Founecroup
50360 Picauville
Manche
Tel: 33 21 36 63

To get there: *From Avranches, D973 towards Granville, across Pont Gilbert; 300m after shopping precinct, take 1st left.*

Map Ref No: 4

Mme TURGOT
Le Château
Marcey-les-Grèves
50300 Avranches
Manche
Tel: 33 58 08 65

An 18th-century farmhouse, it is happily run by a kindly farmer's wife who shares her time between family, guests and dairy cows in a charming rural setting, surrounded by farmland and close to forest and coast. The simply-furnished bedrooms have old beams, traditional wardrobes and are centrally heated. Breakfast is served in the owner's dining-room. Beach 5km; horse-riding 6km.

Rooms: 2 doubles, each with own bathroom.

Price: 170 Frs for two, including breakfast.

Meals: None (3km).

Open: All year.

To get there: *From Cherbourg, D904 towards Lessay then D903 towards La Haye. Left very soon on D15 towards St Sauveur; farm is second on left.*

Map Ref No: 4

Bernadette VASSELIN
La Rocque de Bas
Canville la Rocque
50580 Port-Bail
Manche
Tel: 33 04 80 27

A converted 18th-century farmhouse set in 3 hectares of meadows; a seductive marriage of peace and elegance. The independent family suite has two comfortable and cheerfully-decorated bedrooms, a sitting-room, dining-room and bathroom, overlooking a large garden. The hosts are welcoming and sociable, speak fluent English and have a good sense of humour. Homemade jam at breakfast; excellent farmhouse dinners. Riding, fishing, tennis and forest walks nearby.

Rooms: 1 suite for 3-4 people, with sitting-room, dining-room and bathroom.

Price: 230 Frs for two (320 Frs for four), including breakfast.

Meals: Dinner from 100 Frs (book ahead).

Open: All year.

To get there: *From Argentan, N26 towards l'Aigle. 5km after le Merlerault, turn left; signposted.*

Map Ref No: 5

Catherine & Michel BLIAUT
Le Champ du Haut
61240 Les-Authieux-du-Puits
Orne
Tel: 33 39 19 63

Madame bubbles with energy; she loves children and gives guests a genuine welcome to this simple, unaffected Norman farmhouse which she and her husband have completely rebuilt. The guestrooms are low-ceilinged and comfortable, with a surprising mix of old and new furnishings. Make sure you dine with the Bourgaults and share their home-made cider and calvados. Breakfast next morning will include 'confiture de lait' – milk marmalade made to an old Paraguayan recipe!

Rooms: 1 double, 1 triple, 1 quadruple room, all with bathrooms.

Price: 230 Frs for two, including breakfast.

Meals: Dinner 100 Frs, including wine & coffee (book ahead).

Open: All year.

To get there: *From Rouen, N138 towards Alençon, through Bernay to Monnai. There, right onto D12; after 2km, follow signs to Chambres d'Hôtes.*

Map Ref No: 5

Gérard & Emilienne BOURGAULT
Les Roches
61470 Le Sap
Orne
Tel: 33 39 47 39

98

Real gourmet vegetarian food here, most unusual in the depths of agricultural France. "We aren't vegetarians but might easily convert if offered this sort of fare", says one of our readers. A comfortable house (with an enormous garden) run by a friendly British couple who offer children dinner for 3Frs per year of their age! and advice on how to get the best out of Normandy. Walk across to mediaeval Ticheville, drive to Monet's Giverny, Mathilda's Bayeux or, even, cheese-producing Camembert.

Rooms: 4 double rooms sharing 2 showers & 4 wcs. Further conversion in progress.

Price: 260 Frs for two, including breakfast.

Meals: 100 Frs for an excellent vegetarian meal.

Open: All year.

To get there: *D579 from Lisieux to Vimoutiers then D979 towards Alençon. 5km on, left on D12 towards l'Aigle. In Ticheville: house signposted on left.*

Map Ref No: 5

Jill BUTLER & Colin KIRK
La Maison du Vert
Le Bourg,
61120 Ticheville
Orne
Tel: 33 36 95 84

99

A genuine aristocratic family château in a fine park. The owner's ancestor fled to Scotland at the Revolution then recovered his estate and introduced the Adam style, hence the rare false marble trompe l'oeil decor in the hall. There are ancient towers (with loos), magnificent 18th-century inlaid panelling and period furniture (all family). You enter a real and much-loved home to be welcomed in all simplicity; you sleep in the main house, up the great staircase; breakfast and dine with the family.

Rooms: 1 twin & 2 double rooms, each with own bathroom & wc.

Price: 450 (the smaller double room) - 600 Frs for two, including breakfast.

Meals: Dinner 220 Frs, including aperitif, wine, coffee, digestif … (book ahead).

Open: All year (but book ahead end Nov-end March)

To get there: *From Verneuil-sur-Avre, N12 south-west to Carrefour Ste Anne (24km). Left on D918 towards Longny-au-Perche for 4.5km then left on D289 towards Moulicent. House signposted 800m on right.*

Map Ref No: 5

Jacques & Pascale DE LONGCAMP
La Grande Noë
61290 Moulicent
Orne
Tel: 33 73 63 30
Fax: 33 83 62 92

A typically warm welcome awaits you at this farmhouse in a tranquil spot between historic Falaise and Argentan. The independent, traditionally-furnished bedrooms, with old 'armoires' and exposed beams, have new bathrooms and their own mini-kitchens. Home-produced honey features at the leisurely breakfasts in the hosts' own dining-room.

Rooms: 2 double rooms, each with bathroom and corner kitchen.

Price: 200 Frs for two, including breakfast.

Meals: Dinner 70 Frs, including cider (book ahead).

Open: All year.

To get there: *From Argentan, N158 towards Caen. After sign for Moulin-sur-Orne, take next left. House 800m on left; signposted.*

Map Ref No: 5

M & Mme Rémy LAIGNEL
Le Mesnil
61200 Occagnes
Orne
Tel: 33 67 11 12

This really superb small château is surrounded by farmland and has a garden for guests. You will experience 'exclusive' service from your hosts, for there is only one guestroom; traditionally furnished, centrally heated, and plenty large enough for a family of three. After a leisurely breakfast, explore the shops and restaurants at nearby Argentan.

Rooms: 1 double room with bathroom. (Extra bed for child available.)

Price: 260 Frs for two, including breakfast.

Meals: Not available.

Open: All year.

Pierre is a hard-working farmer who grows cereals and raises livestock. Guestrooms have cane or brass bedsteads and fresh flowers. Madame spoils you at breakfast and dinner, with honey and Camembert produced by friends and veg from parents' garden. Meals are normally taken with the family, unless you don't want to join in. The sitting-room, playroom and kitchen facilities are a bonus. Try not to arrive too early.

Rooms: 2 double rooms, 1 triple room, 1 room for four. 2 rooms have private bathrooms and 2 share a bathroom.

Price: 195 Frs for two, including breakfast.

Meals: Dinner 75 Frs, excluding wine.

Open: All year.

To get there: *From Argentan, N26 towards Paris; D113 left towards Fel, then second small road on left after sign for Crennes village.*

Map Ref No: 5

To get there: *From Argentan, N26 towards L'Aigle & Paris. Left at Silli-en-Gouffern. At Ste Eugénie, last farm on left.*

Map Ref No: 5

M & Mme LE BOUTEILLER
Château de Crennes
61200 Crennes
Orne
Tel: 33 36 22 11

102

Pierre et Ghislaine MAURICE
La Grande Ferme
Sainte-Eugénie
61160 Aubry-en-Exmes
Orne
Tel: 33 36 82 36

103

This is a genuine 17th-century 'longère'. A haven of rural calm, despite the small campsite, it offers a prize-winning flower garden, an avenue of fruit trees and a lake fronting the farm courtyard. The interior has been maintained in period style: beams, antique furnishings and open fireplaces. Madame makes great meals with organic produce from her garden; Monsieur is jovial, practical and helpful. Both are very good company.

Rooms: 1 quadruple room with own bathroom.

Price: 190 Frs (double bed), 260 Frs (two beds) for two, including breakfast.

Meals: Dinner 75 Frs, excluding wine.

Open: Easter – 1 November.

In lovely countryside, just ten minutes from Vimoutiers, this is an 18th-century manor-house complete with 'pigeonnier' and moat. Kit and Toto, its English owners, have converted the dairy, where Camembert cheese was once produced, into charming bedrooms that look out across the farm to the valley beyond.

Rooms: 3 double rooms with bathrooms. Extra beds available.

Price: 200 Frs for two, including breakfast.

Meals: Dinner 100 Frs, including wine.

Open: All year.

To get there: *From Chartres, N23 towards Le Mans. 5.5km after Montlandon, at La Hurie, right then follow signs to Camping le Paradis.*

Map Ref No: 5

To get there: *From Vimoutiers, D916 towards Argentan. Just outside Vimoutiers, D26 towards Exmes; signposted at Survie.*

Map Ref No:5

M Louis PERNET
Le Paradis
61110 Bretoncelle
Orne
Tel: 37 37 25 08

Kitt & Toto WORDSWORTH
Les Gains
Survie
61310 Exmes
Orne
Tel: 33 36 05 56

The Auclerts are a quiet, kind couple who patently enjoy their house, their guests and each other. They have turned their typical 19th-century manor into a proper 20th-century residence with coordinated decor in each room and modern plumbing. You may or may not love the the wedding-cake-style dining-room with its cast iron garden furniture but only birdsong can be heard and Madame is most endearing.

Rooms: 3 double rooms, 1 twin room, 1 triple room, 1 suite, all with private bathroom & wc.

Price: 320 Frs for two, including breakfast.

Meals: Not available.

Open: All year.

In an ancient narrow street among the stone buildings of lovely old Rouen stands the 17th-century listed family home of Phillipe Aunay. He clearly enjoys, in equal measure, sharing the history of Rouen and the comfort of his beautiful (and quiet!) half-timbered townhouse, a treasure-trove of curios, with huge beams, surprisingly large windows and genuine antique Norman furniture. The bathrooms are crisply modern. Breakfast is generous and your reception is cheerful.

Rooms: 2 double rooms & 1 twin with bathrooms (can be used as suite with kitchen facilities); 1 single sharing a bathroom.

Price: 270 Frs for two, including breakfast.

Meals: Not available.

Open: All year.

To get there: *From Dieppe, D75 towards Veules-les-Roses; through Quiberville Plage, on into Quiberville village, then follow Chambres d'Hôtes signs.*

Map Ref No: 1

To get there: *In the centre of Rouen, 100m from the cathedral and 100m from the Horloge.*

Map Ref No: 5

M & Mme AUCLERT
Les Vergers, rue des Vergers
76860 Quiberville
Seine-Maritime
Tel: 35 83 16 10
Fax: 35 83 36 46

106

Philippe AUNAY-STANGUENNEC
45 rue aux Ours
76000 Rouen
Seine-Maritime
Tel: 35 70 99 68

107

'Bénédictine' is made at the nearby abbey town of Fécamp. Bosc-aux-Moines (Monks' Wood), now part of a 60-hectare cattle/arable farm, once belonged to an abbey. The old, red-brick farmhouse is secluded amidst an abundance of trees and birdlife. It has one sparkling clean, spacious, no-frills-style guestroom with separate bathroom upstairs (take towels and dressing-gowns). Meals are 'en famille' at a huge table; your hosts clearly enjoy making you feel at home.

Rooms: 1 double room with separate bathroom (extra beds available).

Price: 160 Frs for two, including breakfast.

Meals: Dinner 55 Frs, including homemade cider (book ahead).

Open: Easter – 15th November.

To get there: *From Fécamp, D150 to Valmont and Riville. At Riville, signposted from the town square.*

Map Ref No: 5

M & Mme Jean-Pierre DEFRANCE
Ferme de la Bosc-aux-Moines
76540 Riville
Seine-Maritime
Tel: 35 27 60 56

Monsieur takes justifiable pride in having built this house out of old materials and in the old Norman farmhouse style so that no-one can tell it's new. The rooms are spotless, the beds comfortable, the bathrooms large, the whole house hushed and restful. A low (and old) beamed dining-room welcomes you for breakfast; then you can take the path hewn out of the cliff face down to the wild rugged beaches, in superb contrast to the domestic cosiness you have just left.

Rooms: 3 double rooms, each with own bath or shower & wc.

Price: 270 Frs for two, including breakfast.

Meals: Not available.

Open: All year except 3 weeks in August.

To get there: *Leave Fécamp by D925; left at signpost to Senneville. In village take bumpy road towards the sea; house is first on left.*

Map Ref No: 5

M et Mme LETHUILLIER
Val de la Mer
76400 Senneville-sur-Fécamp
Seine-Maritime
Tel: 35 28 41 93

The 17th-century farmhouse stands in a hamlet which used to have seven water mills ('Sept Meules') – two still remain. The simple, carpeted guestrooms are in a converted attic overlooking the courtyard. They share basic shower and wc on the landing. Furnishings are as lacking in pretension as their friendly, retired owners; Madame is genuinely warm without being gushing. The surroundings are most attractive. Good walks in the forest of Eu; the sea and Somme Valley are also close.

Rooms: 2 double rooms with shared bathroom. (Extra beds available.)

Price: 95-170 Frs for two, including breakfast.

Meals: None (10km).

Open: 1 March – 30 November.

Caudebec is on the Seine, one of the main arteries of France, so the region has abbeys, churches, museums, villages by the dozen, all worthy of attention. The Villamaux are a kindly French family (one son is a pastry-cook) who keep pets, make their own jam and like to test their English on guests – or vice versa if visitors want to practise their French. Madame loves her quiet garden in the village centre and you will certainly feel relaxed here.

Rooms: 3 triple rooms, each with shower & wc.

Price: 235-250 Frs for two, including breakfast.

Meals: None (self-catering; in village).

Open: All year.

To get there: *From Abbeville, D925 to Eu and D1314 towards Neufchâtel-en-Bray. At Sept-Meules follow signs.*

Map Ref No: 1

To get there: *From Rouen, D982 towards Le Havre. After passing Pont de Brotonne, in Caudebec, right onto rue de la République (D131) towards Yvetot; No 68 is 500m on the right.*

Map Ref No: 5

Michel & Arlette TAILLEUX
Ferme de la Motte
76260 Sept-Meules
Seine-Maritime
Tel: 35 50 81 31

Christiane VILLAMAUX
68 rue de la République
76490 Caudebec-en-Caux
Seine-Maritime
Tel: 35 96 10 15

This 15th-century working farmhouse, a grand old Breton 'longère', has been in the Beaupère family for four generations. Guests are welcome to eat 'en famille'; few will resist Petits Pigeons, Lardons et Raisins and local cheeses. As far as possible only produce from the farm is used. Rooms are anonymous but comfortable. There are carp ponds for those with an interest and a rod.

Rooms: 2 twin and 2 double (one with extra bed), all with bathrooms.

Price: 240 Frs for two, including breakfast.

Meals: Dinner 70 Frs, excluding wine.

Open: All year.

Brittany

To get there: *From Dinan, N176 towards St Brieuc. At Plélan-le-Petit, take D19 (right) to St Michel-de-Plélan. House signposted left, 1km after village.*

Map Ref No: 4

Odile & Henri BEAUPERE
La Corbinais
22980 St Michel-de-Plélan
Côtes-d'Armor
Tel: 96 27 64 81

Awarded the Vieilles Maisons Françaises first prize for its restoration from virtual ruin after the Revolution, this has become a working château (Madame remembers horses coming into the house for sugar-lumps!). Now a stately residence with gracious hosts, it has a sense of 'vieille noblesse'. Rooms are elegant and impeccably furnished, with fireplaces and views over the gardens.

A tree-lined avenue and grand wrought-iron gates lead to this imposing château, over 500 years in the de Kermel family and beautifully maintained. Glorious sweeping lawns and rich greenery. The guestrooms are full of character, from the grand to the homely, all lovingly restored and furnished with heirlooms. The hosts are friendly and charmingly down-to-earth, effusive in their welcome to this treasure-house of family history.

Rooms: 2 twin rooms with own bathrooms.

Rooms: 3 double rooms and 2 twin rooms, all with own bathrooms.

Price: 500 Frs for two, including breakfast.

Price: 460-500 Frs for two, including breakfast.

Meals: None.

Meals: Dinner 190 Frs.

Open: All year.

Open: All year (except Christmas).

To get there: *From N12 towards Brest, Beg ar Chra/Plouaret exit between Guingamp and Morlaix; at Plouaret, D11 towards Lannion. After Run, D30 left towards St Michel-en-Grève then fourth left: follow signposts.*

To get there: *From St Brieuc, N12 to Guingamp, then D8 towards Tréguier. At Pommerit-Jaudy (lights) turn left; signposted 'Château de Kermezen'.*

Map Ref No: 3

Map Ref No: 3

Mme Gérard de BELLEFON
Manoir de Kerguéréon
Ploubezre
22300 Lannion
Côtes-d'Armor
Tel: 96 38 91 46

113

Comte & Comtesse de KERMEL
Château de Kermezen
22450 Pommerit-Jaudy
Côtes-d'Armor
Tel: 96 91 35 75

114

Go through an arch into an enclosed courtyard with a well. This enchanting grey-stone 17th-century presbytery, with blue shutters and climbing roses, has been sensitively restored over the last decade. Walled gardens and an orchard for picnics complete the sense of harmony and privacy. Rooms are charmingly furnished and have luxurious bathrooms. Madame is an accomplished cook offering an enticing evening menu, including vegetarian dishes.

Rooms: 1 double and 2 twin rooms, all with bathrooms.

Price: 280-300 Frs for two, including breakfast.

Meals: Dinner 125 Frs, including wine.

Open: All year.

On the wildest stretch of the Breton coast, this imposing château, originally a fortified bishop's seat (sic), is in orderly and luxurious contrast to the harsh landscape and climate. Rooms vary from the grand to the cosy, all of very high quality. The hosts could not be more unpretentious and welcoming. Breakfast/brunch is a sociable, family affair. Good regional dinners are available.

Rooms: 2 double rooms, 1 twin room, 1 triple room and 2 suites for 3-4 people; all with private bathrooms.

Price: 420-490 Frs for two, including breakfast.

Meals: Dinner from 210 Frs (on reservation).

Open: All year.

To get there: *From Guingamp N12 towards Morlaix, then Louargat exit. From Louargat church, D33 to Tregrom (7km). House in village centre, opposite church (blue door in wall).*

Map Ref No: 3

To get there: *From Guingamp, D8 to Plougrescant. In Plougrescant, right after the church (leaning spire) and right again 200m along.*

Map Ref No: 3

Nicole de MORCHOVEN
Le Presbytère Tregrom
22420 Plouaret
Côtes-d'Armor
Tel: 96 47 94 15

Vicomte & Vicomtesse de
ROQUEFEUIL
Manoir de Kergrec'h
22820 Plougrescant, Côtes-d'Armor
Tel: 96 92 59 13
Fax: 96 92 51 27

Ideal for families, this renovated farm, with a gorgeous flower-filled porch, has guestrooms inside the house and others, gîte-style, in a converted stable-block next door. The large, lawned garden has a pond, a barbecue and a crêperie (at weekends, the hosts' daughter makes galettes – dark Breton pancakes). Breakfast is served 'en famille' in a pretty kitchen. Children are welcomed by this lively couple.

Rooms: 2 double rooms with own bathrooms; 1 double, 1 twin and 1 triple, sharing a bathroom.

Price: 200 Frs for two, including breakfast.

Meals: Not available.

Open: All year.

To get there: *From St Brieuc, D6, D7 and D786 towards Lézardrieux. 2km after exit to Paimpol, right through Plounez, Ecole de Trieux, towards Kerloury. After 1km, take 3rd left: signposted.*

Map Ref No: 3

Irénée LE GOASTER
Ferme de Kerloury
22500 Paimpol
Côtes-d'Armor
Tel: 96 20 85 23

This 200-year-old farmhouse is typically Breton and has been in the family for four generations. Guestrooms are comfortable and have lovely, old country furniture. Breakfasts, and evening meals which must be requested, are cooked on a wood-fired range and served on attractive rough pottery at separate tables (the feel of a restaurant rather than a home). Your relaxed and friendly hosts may offer homemade cider.

Rooms: 3 double rooms, 1 twin and 1 triple, all with bathrooms.

Price: 230 Frs for two, including breakfast.

Meals: Dinner (Easter-15 November only) 75 Frs, excluding wine.

Open: All year.

To get there: *From Dinard, D168 to Ploubalay and D768 to Plancoët. There, D19 to St Lormel. Take turning opposite school; signposted.*

Map Ref No: 4

Evelyne LEDE
La Pastourelle
St Lormel
22130 Plancoët
Côtes-d'Armor
Tel: 96 84 03 77

This is a lovely part of Brittany. The house, a typical old stone building, is 400m from the beautiful river Rance and Plouer is a 'living' French town of great character. The area provides for the nature lover and the 'sportif', the gourmand and the gourmet. The Robinsons have renovated their attractive house with loving care, preserving the best features and creating an informal, relaxed atmosphere as well as 5 lovely guestrooms.

This young professional couple turned market gardeners are thoughtful hosts. Guests arrive to spotless, prettily decorated bedrooms. There are board games, a piano and a pretty garden. The house, comfortable and homely (with a big sloppy dog!), but rather dark, stands next to a busy intersection. Double-glazing is effective. Best in cooler months, perhaps.

Rooms: 1 double, 2 twins with own bathrooms; 1 double, 1 twin sharing a bathroom.

Rooms: 2 twin rooms and 4 double rooms, all with bathrooms.

Price: 225-250 Frs for two, including breakfast.

Price: 210 Frs for two, including breakfast.

Meals: Dinner 75 Frs, excluding wine.

Meals: Not available.

Open: All year.

Open: All year.

To get there: *From Dol, N176 towards Dinan; take Plouer exit to town centre. Right at lights, right again at church. After 200m, left at fork towards La Hisse. House on right after 1.3km.*

To get there: *From St Brieuc, N12 towards Brest. At Morlaix, right on D58 for Roscoff. At 1st roundabout, follow signs to St Sève. At next roundabout, last exit; signposted.*

Map Ref No: 4

Map Ref No: 3

John ROBINSON
La Renardais, Le Repos
22490 Plouer-sur-Rance
Côtes-d'Armor
Tel: 96 86 89 81
Fax: 96 86 89 81 (tel first)

Christian & Marie Noëlle ABIVEN-GUEGUEN
Kerelisa
29600 St Martin-des-Champs
Finistère
Tel: 98 88 27 18

The sea breeze wafts over this 100-year-old manor and its large park. It is a family house with a richly furnished 'salon' and sea-view terrace. Each of the 1st-floor rooms rejoices in old 'armoires' and tables. Delightful Carentec, 1km away, has seven beaches, tennis courts, a coastal path, crêperies and seafood restaurants. Beyond, there are châteaux, typical Breton stone shrines and the Parc d'Armorique to discover. Kervezec is an ideal base for visitors to this fascinating area.

Rooms: 4 double rooms with own bathrooms.

Price: 250-350 Frs (July & Aug), 180-280 Frs (rest of year) for two, including breakfast.

Meals: None (7-8 restaurants in village).

Open: All year.

The rustic village farmhouse is owned by a dynamic young couple. They do not live on site – instead the grandparents do. Madame, however, is always there to greet guests and ensure everyone is settled and happy. Large, neat bedrooms, colourful curtains, immaculate bathrooms. Breakfast of homemade jams, gâteaux, etc. served in guests' own dining room.

Rooms: 2 double rooms with hand-basins and shared bathroom.

Price: 200 Frs for two, including breakfast.

Meals: Not available.

Open: Easter to 31 October.

To get there: *From Morlaix, D58 towards Roscoff. At Henvic turn right to Carantec; signposted at entrance to village.*

Map Ref No: 3

To get there: *From Châteaulin, take the D7 south-west to Cast and Kergoat. Take the 1st left turn after Kergoat and follow signposts.*

Map Ref No: 3

Famille BOHIC
Manoir de Kervezec
29660 Carantec
Finistère
Tel: 98 67 00 26

Henri BOURVEAU
Penfrout
Kergoat
29180 Quéméneven
Finistère
Tel: 98 92 21 58

Privacy is encouraged in this peaceful old house and garden close to the picturesque fishing port. Wood-panelled bedrooms vary in taste from the 1960s to modern rustic. Breakfast, with fresh juice and homemade yoghurt, is eaten at separate tables. Monsieur is chatty and a mine of local information. Not suitable for children. Beach 3 km.

Rooms: 2 double rooms and 2 twin rooms, all with bathrooms.

Price: 300 Frs for two, including breakfast. (Minimum of 2 nights' stay.)

Meals: None.

Open: Easter to 1 November.

The Cazucs, true Breton farmers, produce artichokes, onions and cauliflowers ("Prince de Bretagne") with hard work and much good humour. They love children and animals; all are made welcome in their converted 150-year old cowshed where the rooms are large, clean and functional. Madame bubbles with infectious gaiety and serves crêpes for breakfast to set you up for a day by the sea (8 km away). A simple – and favourite – address in Finistère.

Rooms: 2 double rooms, 1 twin room, each with own shower & wc.

Price: 200 Frs for two, including breakfast.

Meals: None (self-catering possible).

Open: All year.

To get there: *From Quimper, N165 to Pont Aven, then D783 towards Concarneau, then D77 to Kerdruc. In village, right into Chemin des Vieux-Fours.*

Map Ref No: 3

To get there: *From St Pol, D75 through Plouenan; on towards Plovorn for 2km, then left towards Lopréden. Signposted.*

Map Ref No: 3

Mme BROSSIER-PUBLIER
Pen Ker Dagorn
Chemin des Vieux-Fours
29920 Kerdruc-en-Nevez
Finistère
Tel: 98 06 85 01

Allain & Sylvie CAZUC
Lopréden
29420 Plouenan
Finistère
Tel: 98 69 50 62
Fax: 98 69 50 02

Handed down through generations, this neat old farmhouse overlooks the bay. Both guestrooms are spotless, with excellent modern bathrooms and traditional floral wallpaper; one has a canopied bed. Another of the rooms is in a converted pigsty! Breakfast crêpes are served in the rustic, flagstoned dining-room. The charming and interesting young hosts farm 28 hectares of maize.

Rooms: 2 double rooms (one on ground floor), each with own bathroom.

Price: 230 Frs for two, including breakfast.

Meals: None.

Open: All year.

Madame is a darling, quiet but serene and immensely kind. The house is almost Cornish, long, low and granite, and is all that remains of a hamlet. Most of the building consists of gîtes; the chambres d'hôtes are squeezed into the far end... small but impeccably simple, like the dining room. Although it doesn't really feel like a home it's such a lovely area, with the charming little harbour of Port Manech and some handsome beaches nearby, that it is a wonderful place for a holiday...and the cliffs are only five minutes away across the fields.

Rooms: 1 double room and 3 twin rooms, all with bathrooms.

Price: 230 Frs for two, including breakfast.

Meals: None (walk to village).

Open: All year.

To get there: *From Douarnenez, D7 towards Locronan. House is before village, on first road on left after sign for "la plage du Ris"; signposted.*

Map Ref No: 3

M Henri GONIDEC
Lanévry
Kerlaz
29100 Douarnenez
Finistère
Tel: 98 92 19 12

To get there: *From Pont Aven, D77 towards Port Manech: right just before the signpost Port Manech and 1st left. Signposted "Chambres d'Hôtes".*

Map Ref No: 3

Yveline GOURLAOUEN
Kerambris
Port Manech
29920 Nevez
Finistère
Tel: 98 06 83 82

This is a most unusual home, full of warmth and life with a very personal style. Outside, the 1930s have left their own peculiar mark; inside is an Aladdin's cave of remarkable sculptures by the Guillons' artist son, Jean-Luc. The upstairs rooms are furnished with brightly-painted modern furniture and have wide views. Although the lush garden is an enticement to idleness remember that there are dozens of places to see and things to do in this very special corner of Brittany.

Rooms: 3 double rooms, each with own bathroom.

Price: 230 Frs for two, including breakfast.

Meals: Not available.

Open: All year.

Surrounded by farmland and woods, this magnificent ivy-clad manor-house is set in large, mature gardens. Open doors and windows beckon you in. Spacious bedrooms are delightful – soft pinks, whites and creams dominate, giving a light and airy feel. Madame, sociable and with a good sense of humour, is always willing to help. A hearty breakfast is served by the hosts.

Rooms: 2 double rooms and 1 suite, all with bathrooms.

Price: 240 Frs for two, including breakfast.

Meals: None (town very near).

Open: All year.

To get there: *From Quimperlé, D790 towards Le Faouët then left onto D49, through Querrien and follow signs for Gîte Rural/Chambres d'Hôtes La Clarté.*

Map Ref No: 3

To get there: *From Douarnenez, D765 towards Audierne. Approx. 400m after lights, right onto C10 following signs for Chambres d'Hôtes.*

Map Ref No: 3

M & Mme Jean GUILLOU
25 La Clarté
29310 Querrien
Finistère
Tel: 98 71 31 61

Mme Marie-Paule LEFLOCH
Manoir de Kervent
Pouldavid
29100 Douarnenez
Finistère
Tel: 98 92 04 90

This is a low, stone-walled Breton working farm with a courtyard and large garden, and breathtaking views over the forested hills that surround it. Guest accommodation is separate, except for two rooms in the family house, and is comfortable if functional. Madame is friendly and makes a superb traditional Breton breakfast: galettes, crêpes and homemade jam. A good stop-over for families with older children only (i.e. who can sleep alone).

Rooms: 4 double rooms and 2 twin rooms, all with bathrooms.

Price: 230 Frs for two, including breakfast.

Meals: Not available.

Open: All year.

There is something magical about this small stone Breton house in the lovely Montagnes Noires area. The rooms may be a trifle small and share a bathroom but the house oozes warmth and trust...as does Madame. The dining-room, where breakfast with crêpes and homemade jam is served, is a delight with its country-style furnishings and wooden floor. Over the years Madame's loving hands have created a garden that simply drips colour. House and surroundings are totally peaceful, almost out of time.

Rooms: 2 double rooms sharing bathroom & wc.

Price: 180 Frs for two, including breakfast.

Meals: None (many local eating places).

Open: All year.

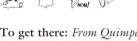

To get there: *From Quimper, D15 towards Gourin. D82 left towards Spézet. Just in Spézet, right before La Crémaillerie restaurant then follow Chambres d'Hôtes signs for about 1.5km.*

Map Ref No: 3

To get there: *From Quimper, D765 towards Quimperlé. At St Yvi turn left; signposted.*

Map Ref No: 3

Odile LE GALL
Kervren
29140 Saint Yvi
Finistère
Tel: 98 94 70 34

M & Mme LOLLIER
29540 Spézet
Finistère
Tel: 98 93 80 32

Miles of fascinating canal towpath to walk or bike along, the little-known beauties of inland Brittany, an exquisitely renovated house (old, old stones exposed and set off by plain white walls) with its own chapel, large oak-beamed guestrooms with antique furniture and modern beds, knowledgeable hosts who want to communicate their feel for the "real" Brittany and offer refined dinners using home-grown organic vegetables and organise fungus hunting holidays and... what more could one want?

Rooms: 2 double rooms, 1 twin room, all with own bath/shower & wc.

Price: 280 Frs for two, including breakfast.

Meals: Dinner available at variable prices.

Open: All year except Christmas.

A true Breton couple, the Ogors love their land and are delighted to guide guests towards real discoveries. Get up early and take the boat to Ile d'Ouessant, the wild westernmost point of France. Or visit one of the excellent beaches, come home to dry and make lunch in the small kitchen set aside for guests, then lounge in the garden for the afternoon. The rooms and furnishing are unpretentious, the welcome genuine – there may even be crêpes for breakfast.

Rooms: 1 double room with wc & shower, 2 double rooms with own showers, sharing wc.

Price: 170-200 Frs for two, including breakfast.

Meals: None (good restaurant and crêperie nearby).

Open: All year.

To get there: *From Brest, N165 towards Quimper. 45km on, left on N164 to Carhaix Plouguer. At "Districenter" shop on N164, follow signs to Prevasy, turn right at triangular green, straight on to house.*

Map Ref No: 3

To get there: *From Brest, D5 towards St Renan. Right into Guilers then immediately right at church towards Bohars. After 1km, signposted.*

Map Ref No: 3

Peter & Clarissa NOVAK
Manoir de Prevasy
29270 Carhaix
Finistère
Tel: 98 93 24 36

M & Mme OGOR
Kerloquin
29820 Guilers
Finistère
Tel: 98 07 61 97

Hospitality comes naturally to this Breton couple. They love children; there are ponies to ride and the dairy farm to explore. Copious breakfasts include crêpes, mixed in an enormous brass pot, and home-grown kiwi fruit when in season. Dinner is sometimes provided in winter when an open fire warms dining-room and lounge. Very large, country-style bedrooms.

Rooms: 3 double rooms and 1 twin room, all with bathrooms.

Price: 250 Frs for two, including breakfast.

Meals: Dinner 85 Frs, including wine (Nov-March only).

Open: All year.

Madame's attention to detail and evident kindness make this house a lot more special than its unexciting modernity and smallish rooms would lead one to imagine. Kergolay is just 8km from the sea, the surrounding area is peaceful farmland, there's an excellent crêperie nearby and Madame will help you in every possible way. A hearty breakfast is accompanied by advice on where to go and what to do.

Rooms: 2 double rooms, each with own bath or shower & wc.

Price: 230 Frs for two, including breakfast.

Meals: Not available.

Open: All year.

To get there: *From Scaër, D50 direction Coray-Briec; after 3km, left at "Ty Ru" and follow signpost for Kerloaï.*

Map Ref No: 3

Louis & Thérèse PENN
Kerloaï
29390 Scaër
Finistère
Tel: 98 59 42 60

To get there: *From Roscoff, D788 towards Lesneven. At Lanhouarneau, there are signs for 2 Chambres d'Hôtes; follow those for Kergolay (1km).*

Map Ref No: 3

Marie-France QUEGUINEUR
Kergolay
29430 Lanhouarneau
Finistère
Tel: 98 61 47 35
Fax: 98 61 69 34

This old farm, set in 25 hectares near a main road, produces cereals and rears pigs. A separate house provides simply furnished rooms which are clean and functional, with predominantly brown decor. After breakfast, guests can watch the pigs being fed. These kind hosts like chatting but are keen on peace and quiet – no noisy children! Kitchen facilities and small garden. The spectacular rocky landscape of Pointe du Raz is not to be missed.

Rooms: 1 twin room, 1 double room and 1 family suite for 3-5 people, all with private bathrooms.

Price: 200-220 Frs for two, including breakfast.

Meals: None (self-catering).

Open: 1 March to 31 November.

To get there: *From Châteaulin, D7 to Cast and D7 to Plonévez-Porzay. There, follow signposts.*

Map Ref No: 3

Angèle & Pierre RANNOU
Trévilly
29550 Plonévez-Porzay
Finistère
Tel: 98 92 52 25

Retired dairy farmers – they now only have a few donkeys - the Siohans are bright, welcoming, good-humoured .... the very best of hosts. They live in a modern house; you stay in an old part with simple, very pleasant rooms, sitting-room and use of a kitchen. A hearty Breton breakfast is served beneath the family portraits. The river runs by the house and Monsieur Siohan and his neighbour still operate the mill, fascinating for children to watch. Lovely walks directly from the farm. Altogether an ideal family holiday spot.

Rooms: 2 double rooms, each with own bathroom.

Price: 200 Frs for two, including breakfast.

Meals: None (self-catering).

Open: All year.

To get there: *From Roscoff, D788 towards Lesneven. In Lanhouarneau, signs for 2 Chambres d'Hôtes; go through village, left at signs "Chambres d'Hôtes Moulin", down hill 1km; mill on right by pond.*

Map Ref No: 3

Anne & Jean-Marie SIOHAN
Moulin de Coat-Merret
29430 Lanhouarneau
Finistère
Tel: 98 61 62 06

In a tiny Armorican village, this is a real Breton farmhouse, with low roof and small windows, closed in upon its secrets in stone – and a real country welcome inside where a generous breakfast with cheese and charcuterie can be taken at leisure in Madame's dining-room. She has renovated her house with simplicity and taste and loves to guide her guests through the long history of central Britanny, from standing stones to 19th-century roadside shrines.

Rooms: 1 double room with bathroom.

Price: 220 Frs for two, including breakfast.

Meals: None (crêperie and restaurants 3-15km).

Open: All year.

To get there: *From Morlaix, D785 towards Quimper. At La Croix Cassée, D42 to Botmeur; house is on right on leaving village towards La Feuillée.*

Map Ref No: 3

Marie-Thérèse SOLLIEC
Kreisker
29690 Botmeur
Finistère
Tel: 98 99 63 02

The old farm, in a secluded spot with views of woods and valleys, belonged to Madame's parents; she now continues their tradition of hospitality. In a separate building, the ground-floor guestrooms have a small kitchen and look out onto the flowered garden. The white rooms have old Breton and other locally-made furnishings and lino floors; it isn't luxurious but you are independent and redecoration is planned. Breakfast with crêpes in the farmhouse. Campsite nearby.

Rooms: 2 double rooms with own bathrooms.

Price: 180 Frs for two, including breakfast.

Meals: None (self-catering; in village).

Open: July & August only.

To get there: *From Morlaix, D785 towards Quimper. At Brasparts, D21 towards Le Faou; after 1km, 50m before stone cross on right; left down lane with wooden gate.*

Map Ref No: 3

Marie-Pierre TOUTOUS-JACQUEMET
Tuchennou, 29190 Brasparts
Finistère
Tel: 98 81 43 02
or (1)42 04 59 49 (Paris)

Fine for a family holiday: the sea is 5 minutes walk away and there are a games room, swings and a children's club run by the Williams' daughter who will even tell them a story and put them to bed. The coastal path passes near this modest house and there are sandy beaches, sailing and fishing in profusion. Terry and Jill, who teaches English, welcome their guests with enthusiasm; it all feels like an English seaside hotel, certainly too much so for some. Let us know.

Rooms: 5 double rooms & 1 twin room, all with own showeroom and wc.

Price: 250 Frs for two, including breakfast.

Meals: Dinner 90 Frs, excluding wine.

Open: March to October.

To get there: *From Pont-Aven, D783 to Riec then D24 to Moëlan-sur-Mer and on towards Clohars. At first roundabout, sharp right then follow signs.*

Map Ref No: 3

Terry & Jill WILLIAMS
Trenogoat
29350 Moelan-sur-Mer
Finistère
Tel: 98 39 62 82
Fax: 98 39 78 09

The sea is 3km from this dairy farm with its neatly converted stone farmhouse. The comfortable rooms include 2 with mezzanines; the other 3 are smaller. Jean, gentle and brighteyed, says he's tied to the farm but 'travels with his guests'. In cool weather. Marie-Madeleine is up before breakfast to lay the fire in the huge hearth where you can make your own toast! They both know and love their Breton music and walks and willingly share their enthusiasm.

Rooms: 5 rooms for 2-4 people, all with own shower-room & loo.

Price: 200-250 Frs for two, including breakfast.

Meals: Not available.

Open: All year.

To get there: *From Dol-de-Bretagne, N176 NE then D80 to St Broladre and D85 towards Cherrueix. Just before a small bridge, turn right; house is 200m along.*

Map Ref No: 4

Jean & Marie-Madeleine GLEMOT
La Hamelinais
35120 Cherrueix
Ille-et-Vilaine
Tel: 99 48 95 26

In a tiny hamlet, 100km from both north and south coasts of Brittany, this former dairy farm, built in 1700, has been beautifully converted by Claudine, an interior designer. She enjoys organising "weekends amoureux" with champagne and candles in the vast suite, but you don't feel pressured! Moreover, you can count on Beethoven and crêpes for breakfast. The Gomis treat their guests with huge care and the whole house wraps you in its warm embrace.

Rooms: 1 large suite, 1 triple room, both with own bathrooms.

Price: 250-300 Frs for two, including breakfast.

Meals: Dinner 50 or 100 Frs, excluding wine.

Open: All year.

To get there: *From Rennes, D163 towards Châteaubriant. After 28km, left on D92 and follow signs to Chambres d'Hôtes.*

Map Ref No: 4

Claudine & Raymond GOMIS
La Tremblais
35320 La Couyère
Le Sel de Bretagne
Ille-et-Vilaine
Tel: 99 43 14 39

Romantic Brittany at your feet: one of the last corsairs, the swashbuckling folk heroes of legend, lived here. The present owners live in the converted stable block; the guestroom is just beside the lake in the old wash-house where bread was also baked. A cosy sitting-room with open hearth and lovely little bedroom up a wooden stair, two exceptionally friendly, open hosts, soundless history-laden air all add up to an unforgettable place to stay... probably more than one day.

Rooms: 1 twin room with own shower & wc.

Price: 230 Frs for two, including breakfast.

Meals: Dinner 80 Frs, including wine.

Open: All year.

To get there: *From Dinan, D794 towards Combourg. Left onto N137 towards St Pierre-de-Plesguen. Right onto D10 to Lanhélin. 1km beyond this village follow signs to Le Pont Ricoul.*

Map Ref No: 4

Catherine & François GROSSET
Le Pont Ricoul
35720 St Pierre-de-Plesguen
Ille-et-Vilaine
Tel: 99 73 92 65
Fax: 99 73 94 17

A haven for travellers, this well-converted mill has a terrace over the river and a superb table d'hôte. Claude and Béatrice have seen the world and know what guests need: extremely comfortable rooms, hot water, flowers, good food (her father was in catering and she has inherited the touch) and tales to tell over dinner. The mill rooms have that solid feel of old stone built for work. The Krusts knew they could stop wandering and settle in this place. You too will want to stay...and stay.

Rooms: 1 double & 1 twin room, both with own shower and wc.

Price: 230 Frs for two, including breakfast.

Meals: 80 Frs "menu simple", 150 Frs "menu gastronomique", both including wine.

Open: All year.

To get there: *From Rennes, D177 towards Vannes. After 18km, right onto D776 (BIS to Vannes). After 5km, left onto D62 towards Guignen; house is 800m down on left.*

Map Ref No: 4

Claude & Béatrice KRUST
Le Moulin du Bignon
35580 Lassy
Ille-et-Vilaine
Tel: 99 42 10 04
Fax: 99 42 10 04

A fine 1620's water-mill, restored in the 19th century. The small guestrooms have stone walls, wooden ceilings, typical Breton furniture, some antiques and fittings...and lots of fluffy towels. Madame is the cook, specialising in Breton food (delicious galettes!), though she does have her off days. Dining with evening sunlight filtering through the spokes of the mill-wheel is a delight. There is a very pretty garden/orchard with swings and children's games.

Rooms: 2 double rooms and 2 triple rooms, all with bathrooms.

Price: 300 Frs for two, including breakfast.

Meals: Dinner 95 Frs, excluding wine (book ahead).

Open: All year, except 1 week in November.

To get there: *From Dinan, D794 towards Combourg; left to St Pierre-de-Plesguen, then D10 towards Lanhelin: right after sign "Clos Coq"; signposted.*

Map Ref No: 4

Annie MICHEL-QUEBRIAC
Le Petit Moulin du Rouvre
35720 St Pierre-de-Plesguen
Ille-et-Vilaine
Tel: 99 73 85 84

This fine old manor-house stands in forested grounds just 8 miles from St Malo. Brightly-painted furniture in the bedrooms (a different colour scheme for each), a very grand dining-room and candlelit breakfasts in the conservatory. Jean-François takes his guests along the pine-fringed beaches in a pony and trap. There are also mountain bikes and the lovely little fishing port of Briac is within riding distance. Your host's flair and flamboyance make this a unique (sic) experience.

Rooms: 4 double rooms and 1 suite, all with bathrooms.

Price: 350-500 Frs for two, including breakfast.

Meals: None (great choice 2.5km).

Open: 1 March to 30 November.

To get there: *From St Malo, D168 towards St Brieuc, then D603 towards St Briac-sur-Mer; first left on entering the town and follow signs.*

Map Ref No: 4

Jean-François STENOU
Manoir de la Duchée
St Briac-sur-Mer
35800 Dinard
Ille-et-Vilaine
Tel: 99 88 00 02

145

The 'marais' are the coastal marshes, much appreciated by bird-lovers, a lost world where farmers still move cows in flat-bottomed boats, a silent labyrinth of water, trees and pasture. This old farm has almost basic guestrooms under the eaves with touches of character: a wardrobe mirror painted by Madame or framed poems by guests, but the overall style is very mixed. Madame welcomes with her lilting, sing-song voice! A nice garden and the sea only a few kms away.

Rooms: 1 double room with extra bed and own bathroom.

Price: 180 Frs for two, including breakfast.

Meals: None (next-door auberge).

Open: All year.

To get there: *From Pornic, D751 towards Nantes; the house is 8km from Pornic; signposted.*

Map Ref No: 9

Jeannette BERTIN
Le Marais Mainguy
44210 Le-Clion-sur-Mer
Loire-Atlantique
Tel: 40 21 34 31

146

For 150 years this fine château has admired itself in the lake, surrounded by 100 hectares of magnificent park. The decor is utterly in keeping, the guestrooms superb, your hosts graceful and cultivated. Dinner with the family is a genuine taste of life with the French country aristocracy; dress for it and enjoy a game of billiards afterwards. Coët Caret is in the fascinating Brière Regional Park, where water and land are so inextricably mingled and wildlife abounds.

Rooms: 2 double rooms & 1 twin room, all with own bath or shower and wc.

Price: 400-450 Frs for two, including breakfast.

Meals: Dinner (candlelit) 220 Frs, including aperitif and wine.

Open: All year.

To get there: *From Nantes, N165 to Pontchâteau then Herbignac exit onto D33. At Herbignac, D47 left to Coët Caret.*

Map Ref No: 4

François & Cécile de la MONNERAYE
Château de Coët Caret
44410 Herbignac, Loire-Atlantique
Tel: 40 91 41 20
Fax: 40 91 37 46

The house is part of a much larger building, dated 1830, France's oldest agricultural college, grand and ivy-covered. Rooms, all on the 2nd floor, are comfortable (with canopied beds for extra elegance) but three share one wc. You are not far from a busy road so windows are double-glazed. Monique is kind and discreet and her dinner is very good value. The ponds ('plans d'eau') 500m away offer swimming, fishing, windsurfing...and pedalos.

Rooms: 1 triple with bathroom, 1 double, 1 twin, 1 triple sharing bathroom.

Price: 180-190 Frs for two, including breakfast.

Meals: Dinner 60 Frs, excluding wine.

Open: All year.

To get there: *From Rennes, N137 towards Nantes. Shortly before Nozay, left onto N171 towards Châteaubriand: after 2km, signs on right.*

Map Ref No: 4

Monique MARZELIERE
Grand Jouan
44170 Nozay
Loire-Atlantique
Tel: 40 79 45 85

One of the prettiest of houses: a long, low, thatched cottage that nestles in a field of flowers. There are even irises growing on the roof. The family were "in the colonies"; Madame has exquisite taste; the dining and drawing rooms are full of mementoes of their travels in exotic places. You can expect a large breakfast and beautiful guestrooms. Ask for the Blue Room where Madame's much-travelled trunk has pride of place among the stylish furniture.

Rooms: 2 double & 1 twin room, all with own shower or bath & wc (2 nights minimum).

Price: 330-360 Frs for two, including breakfast.

Meals: Not available.

Open: Easter to October, otherwise on request.

To get there: *From Vannes ringroad follow on D767 north towards Pontivy. After 11 kms, right on D767A, through Locqueltas and sharp left at first crossing. Follow signs.*

Map Ref No: 3

Mme CHEILLETZ-MAIGNAN
Chaumière de Kerisac
56390 Locqueltas
Morbihan
Tel: 97 66 60 13
Fax: 97 66 66 73

149

Bring your own rod, dig your own worms – and you can try your skills in the Collets' private pond. Otherwise, this is a fairly standard B&B conversion, recently done and a source of great pride to its owners. You can take your ease in the very large sitting-room and use the kitchen as much as you like. The stones are old (1780s), the landscape green and rolling and each room furnished with its own set of garden furniture. A warm welcome and generous breakfasts are guaranteed.

Rooms: 3 double rooms with own shower & wc, 2 double rooms sharing shower & wc.

Price: 220 Frs for two, including breakfast.

Meals: None (good restaurants nearby).

Open: All year.

To get there: *From Pontivy, D768 towards Auray. At roundabout just before Pluvigner, D16 towards Locminé. 3km on, turn left and follow signs.*

Map Ref No: 3

Marie-Claire COLLET
Kerdavid-Duchentil
56330 Pluvigner
Morbihan
Tel: 97 56 00 59

150

Built with old materials (400-year beams, 18th-century doors), this is the home of a charming, cultivated couple who have recently left Paris to live here, just 150m from the estuary. They love their adopted region and communicate their enthusiasm to their guests. There are standing stones and dolmens from prehistory and reminders of Caesar's Gallic Wars. Two delightful guestrooms with period furnishings and private bathrooms, an enormous, high living-room and a peaceful garden welcome you most warmly.

Rooms: 1 double room with shower & wc, 1 twin room with bath & wc.

Price: 400 Frs for two, including breakfast.

Meals: None (many possibilities locally).

Open: All year.

To get there: *From Vannes, N165 towards Lorient; left at Auray on D28 to St Philibert; right on D781. After 500m, left at Le Congre restaurant, left at next junction, left again rue des Peupliers. House at end on right – no signs!*

Map Ref No: 3

Mme Mylène CUZON du REST
Rue des Peupliers
Lann-Kermane
56470 St Philibert, Morbihan
Tel: 97 55 03 75
Fax: 97 30 02 79

151

The Henrios are so relaxed and friendly that you feel they run a B&B simply to meet new people – and guests-turned-friends who return year after year. A modern house, simple, comfortable rooms, a big Breton breakfast that you can have whenever you like ("people are on holiday, after all") and a good dinner (excellent value) are provided on top of the welcome. To all this must be added some magnificent countryside to explore. Vive la Bretagne!

Rooms: 2 double rooms with own shower or bath, sharing wc.

Price: 200 Frs for two, including breakfast.

Meals: Dinner 60 Frs, including wine (book ahead).

Open: All year.

To get there: *From Guingamp, D767 towards Pontivy. At Mur-de-Bretagne, D18 towards Cléguérec, cross canal and go 5km: house is on left (sign).*

Map Ref No: 3

Micheline & Jean-Claude HENRIO
Croix Even
Saint Aignan
56480 Cléguérec
Morbihan
Tel: 97 27 51 56

152

This converted farmhouse and stables were originally built with the stones from a château demolished after the French Revolution. The guestrooms are functional and comfortable. The dining-room still has its massive old beams and is high enough to house a mezzanine. Madame is very organised and her broad cheerful smile is engaging. This is a very attractive area of inland Brittany, all too often by-passed by travellers on their way to the coast.

Rooms: 4 double rooms & 1 twin room, all with own shower & wc.

Price: 250 Frs for two, including breakfast.

Meals: None (many local possibilities).

Open: April to October.

To get there: *From Lorient, D769 towards Morlaix. Pass Plouay; just before Meslan, left following signs to Roches du Diable and Roscalet.*

Map Ref No: 3

Jean & Marie-France JAMBOU
Roscalet
56320 Meslan
Morbihan
Tel: 97 34 24 13

153

The lawn slopes down to a peaceful inlet. The glassed-in veranda dining-room has lovely views. Copious breakfasts with crêpes are served on Breton pottery. Excellent seafood dinners merit old silver, porcelain and crystal. (Book dinner the previous day.) The rooms are comfortable and quiet. Nothing is too much trouble for your motherly, house-proud hostess.

Rooms: 2 twin rooms, 1 double room, 1 suite for 3-4 people, all with bathrooms. (1 ground floor room.)

Price: 270-320 Frs for two, including breakfast.

Meals: Dinner 80-120 Frs, excluding wine (book ahead).

Open: All year.

To get there: *From Vannes, N165 to Auray. There, D28 and D781 to la Trinité. After bridge, take road towards Chantier de Kervilor and follow signs.*

Map Ref No: 3

Nicole & Christian LE ROUZIC
La Maison du Latz
Le Latz
56470 La Trinité-sur-Mer
Morbihan
Tel: 97 55 80 91

154

The Maignans live and work in this most peaceful of places, a former dairy farm where the road ends beside the river Blavet. You are in the heart of Brittany. Two superbly-converted, big, uncluttered attic rooms, decorated with flair by the young owners, await their guests. You are welcome to try your hand at Philippe's wheel in his pottery workshop next door. Several long walks start from the house. Birds sing. The land is green. The welcome is genuine.

Rooms: 2 twin rooms each with own shower & wc.

Price: 200 Frs for two, including breakfast.

Meals: None (wide choice in St Nicolas, 3km).

Open: Easter to October; otherwise on request only.

To get there: *From Pontivy, D768 towards Lorient. At Port-Arthur, D1 right to St Nicolas-des-Eaux. Right immediately after bridge and follow signs for 3km (Chambres d'Hôtes and poterie).*

Map Ref No: 3

Philippe & Martine MAIGNAN
Lezerhy
Bieusy-les-Eaux
56310 Bubry
Morbihan
Tel: 97 27 74 59

It has turrets and a moat, it's 800 years old and has housed the same family since it was first built; this surely is the castle from one's childhood dreams of clanking knights and gallantry on the drawbridge. Three of the guestrooms are in the towers. The dining and drawing rooms are properly grand but your hosts are down-to-earth folk with a warm welcome. You are within easy reach of the Champagne cellars as well as the smiling angels of Reims Cathedral.

Rooms: 5 double rooms, all with own bath or shower and wc.

Price: 450 Frs for two, including breakfast.

Meals: None (20km).

Open: March to December.

Ardennes – Champagne

To get there: *From Reims, N46 then N47 towards Luxembourg; go through Vouziers to Buzancy, turn right onto D12 and follow signs.*

Map Ref No: 7

Jacques & Véronique de
MEIXMORON
Château de Landreville
08240 Bayonville
Ardennes
Tel: 24 30 04 39

An 18th-century farmhouse, very much still a working concern. Guestrooms, which have views over the farmyard full of agricultural implements and machinery, have been newly-decorated but equipped with old furniture. There is a patio/terrace with a barbecue. Madame warms to visitors and offers farmhouse cooking 'en famille' in the evenings. A good stopover.

Rooms: 2 double rooms, each with own bathroom.

Price: 190 Frs for two, including breakfast.

Meals: Dinner 70 Frs, excluding wine.

Open: All year.

In a small picturesque hamlet of only 18 inhabitants, this working farm, full of character and very rustic, is comfortable and peaceful. Children will love meeting the animals. Bikes for hire; picnics on request. The hosts give a warm welcome and meals are prepared using local farm produce. They don't all speak English...

Rooms: 2 double rooms, each with own bathroom.

Price: 245 Frs for two, including breakfast.

Meals: Dinner 95 Frs, excluding wine.

Open: All year.

To get there: *From Vitry-le-François, N4 towards Fère-Champenoise. 3km from N4/D2 crossroads; house on right, set back from road, opposite town hall; signposted.*

Map Ref No: 7

To get there: *From Epernay, D51 towards Sézanne. At Baye, just before church, right onto D343. At Bannay turn right. Farm is before small bridge.*

Map Ref No: 6

M & Mme Michel COLLOT
19 rue de Coole
51300 Maisons-en-Champagne
Marne
Tel: 26 72 73 91

Muguette & Jean-Pierre CURFS
Ferme de Bannay
51270 Montmort Lucy
Marne
Tel: 26 52 80 49
Fax: 26 59 47 78

Close by a beautiful forest, this farm rears cows and chickens. A fishing river runs through the grounds which include a campsite. The modern bedrooms (one with a piano!) have reasonable beds and adequate 50's-style showers. The busy hosts take time for a smile and a chat. Simple family meals include home-grown organic veg. Pétanque pitch.

Rooms: 2 double rooms, one with own bathroom and one sharing a bathroom.

Price: 180 Frs for two, including breakfast.

Meals: Dinner 70 Frs, including wine.

Open: All year.

A simple, unsophisticated and most welcoming pony-trekking centre with 4 B&B guestrooms and space for 19 trekkers and 15 horses! For the saddle-sore, pony-and-trap outings are also possible. The rooms are spotless. Breakfast is meticulously presented with superb brioche, fresh bread and first-class homemade jam. Lovers of country pursuits will find fishing, riding, swimming and tranquil walks all within easy reach. Memorable meals can be had 3km away at Anrosey where the chef is Madame le Maire. Honest and genuine.

Rooms: 3 double rooms, 1 twin room sharing bathroom & wc.

Price: 150 Frs for two, including breakfast.

Meals: None (good auberge 3km).

Open: All year.

To get there: *From Triancourt-en-Argonne, D151 to Senard then D54 to Les Charmontois.*

Map Ref No: 7

To get there: *From Langres, N19 towards Vesoul. Left on D460 towards Bourbonne; right on D34; 3rd left to Velles. Through village to grass triangle; house on left.*

Map Ref No: 7

M & Mme Bernard PATIZEL
51330 Les Charmontois
Marne
Tel: 26 60 39 53
Fax: 26 60 39 53

159

Alain & Christine ROUSSELOT
Les Randonneurs du Pré-Cheny
52500 Velles
Haute-Marne
Tel: 25 88 85 93

160

These delightful people (Madame is young, direct in manner and very talented) will feed you on wild boar raised on the estate and fish-of-the-day caught in their own lake. It is an irresistible spot for fishermen, water-sportsmen, ornithologists and architecture buffs; the local tour of half-timbered churches is considered one of the 100 most beautiful attractions in France. An elegant chandeliered dinner awaits you afterwards, as well as comfortable and attractive bedrooms.

Rooms: 2 double rooms, 2 twin rooms, 1 suite, all with own bathrooms & wc.

Price: 270 Frs for two, including breakfast.

Meals: Dinner 110 Frs, including wine.

Open: April to October.

To get there: *From Troyes, D960 to Brienne, D400 towards St Dizier. At Louze, D182 to Longeville then D174 towards Boulancourt; house on left at 1st crossroads.*

Map Ref No: 7

Philippe & Christine VIEL-CAZAL
Domaine de Boulancourt
Boulancourt
52220 Montier-en-Der
Haute-Marne
Tel: 25 04 60 18

The 18th-century manor-house and a smaller 16th-century house are surrounded by woods. Guestrooms are split between the two. Both have a strong period feel, with plenty of antique furnishings. Beds are excellent and bathrooms are being renovated. Cooked breakfast on request; bread is homemade. Madame is a sociable, open-minded hostess. Kitchen facilities available.

Rooms: 3 double rooms, 2 with bathrooms; 2 twin rooms, also with bathrooms.

Price: 180-250 Frs for two, including breakfast.

Meals: None (self-catering).

Open: All year.

Alsace – Lorraine

To get there: *From A4, St Menehould exit onto N3 towards Verdun-Chalons. House is signposted in La Vignette, the hamlet before les Islettes.*

Map Ref No: 7

M & Mme Léopold CHRISTAENS
Villa des Roses
La Vignette, Les Islettes
55120 Clermont-en-Argonne
Meuse
Tel: 26 60 81 91

Renovation may have hidden two centuries of history, here in what was once a hunting lodge for the neighbouring château, but it has produced very plush guestrooms. Dinner is a chance to sample some of the region's best dishes (terrines, magret, homemade pastries); your hosts will generally join you for desert. The area offers magnificent forests and very good fly fishing. A bit hotel-like but good value for a stopover between the ferries and Germany.

Rooms: 4 double rooms, all with own bathrooms.

Price: 250-300 Frs for two, including breakfast.

Meals: Dinner 120 Frs, including wine.

Open: All year.

To get there: *From Reims take A4, Voie Sacrée exit; take N35 towards Bar-le-Duc. At Chaumont-sur-Aire, D902 left to Longchamps-sur-Aire then D121 left to Thillombois. House is next to château.*

Map Ref No: 7

Lise & Eric DUFOUR
Le Clos du Pausa
Rue du Château
55260 Thillombois, Meuse
Tel: 29 75 07 85
Fax: 29 75 00 72

An unpretentious farmhouse with an old-fashioned approach to B&B. The rooms are imbued with a warm family atmosphere: comfortable, functional and with lots of knick-knacks on every available surface. Grand'mère is unforgettable, 88 and still talking proudly of her "liberated female" past (she was the first to drive a car in the village and ran the farm single-handed when her husband was a POW). There is a fine garden but the house is near the road.

Rooms: 1 twin & 1 triple room, sharing shower & separate wc.

Price: 160 Frs for two, including breakfast.

Meals: None.

Open: All year.

To get there: *From Nancy, A31/N4 east. At Void, D964 towards Vaucouleurs for 1km then right onto D10 to Rosières-en-Blois then D168 through Badonvilliers to Vouthon; house at end of village.*

Map Ref No: 7

Simone ROBERT
Le Bourg
55130 Vouthon-Bas
Meuse
Tel: 29 89 74 00
Fax: 29 89 74 42

Many will be very tempted to hang expense and stay a night at this grand and very stylish château now in the hands of a young and able couple. Two utterly French 'salons' with the right number of antiques, huge oils of the Napoleonic wars (French version), a library with a billiards table, dinner with candles and flowers and the unadulterated pleasure of dining like a 17th-century French aristo (there may be wild boar in season). Guestrooms and bathrooms are inevitably luxurious.

In a pretty corner of Lorraine, in the small village of Lidrezing, René and Cécile Mathis share their warm home with their visitors; home cooking, regional produce, an open hearth. Every possible French rural decorative touch is to be found here, plus modern extras (e.g.remote-control lighting). Close by is the Bride forest and an area of lakes with a bird sanctuary, to be explored after a vast breakfast including cheeses, charcuterie and, maybe, homemade cake.

Rooms: 3 double and 3 twin rooms, all with bathrooms.

Rooms: 2 double & 1 twin room, with own shower or bathroom.

Price: 580 Frs for two, including breakfast.

Price: 295 Frs for two, including breakfast.

Meals: Dinner 200 Frs, excluding wine (book ahead).

Meals: Dinner 100 Frs, excluding wine.

Open: 1 April – 31 October.

Open: 1 April – 31 October.

To get there: *From Nancy, N74 towards Château Salins. At Burthecourt crossroads D38 to Dieuzé, then D999 south; after 5km, left on D199F and D199G to the château.*

To get there: *From A31, exit 28 for St Avold (D910). At Han-sur-Nied, D999 towards Morhange and Dieuzé. 10km after Morhange, left to Lidrezing.*

Map Ref No: 8

Map Ref No: 8

Livier & Marie BARTHELEMY
Château d'Alteville
Tarquimpol
57260 Dieuzé, Moselle
Tel: 87 86 92 40
Fax: 87 86 02 05

René & Cécile MATHIS
La Musardière
2 rue le Faubourg
Lidrezing
57340 Morhange, Moselle
Tel: 87 86 14 05

Modern cereal-farming is practised here but parts of the building were elements of the circle of defence round Metz in the 1200s! Today, peace reigns. Children enjoy the goats and rabbits; adults like Brigitte's quiet caring manner and everyone loves her food, made with organic veg from the garden. Meals are served with local Moselle wines in the warm, tranquil dining-room under great beams. A wonderful family and a friendly village too.

Rooms: 1 triple room and 1 double, each with own bathroom; 1 triple and 1 double with 2 extra beds, with own bathrooms & sharing wc.

Price: 240 Frs for two, including breakfast.

Meals: Dinner 90 Frs, including wine (only during school holidays; on reservation).

Open: 1 March – 30 November.

To get there: *South of Metz on A31. At Féy, D66 towards Cuvry. Signposted in village.*

Map Ref No: 8

Brigitte & Jean-François
MORHAIN
Ferme de Haute-Rive
57420 Cuvry, Moselle
Tel: 87 52 50 08
Fax: 87 52 60 20

167

The house, on a hillside in a straggly hamlet, surveys the valley. This is a place to rescue the remnants of your idleness. Geraniums flow from every window-sill. The simple, comfortable bedrooms are quiet and tidy and you understand why old faithfuls return year after year. Organic fruits go into the jams and Alsace specialities (perhaps a spot of Kougelopf?) are served at breakfast. Madame Geiger's daughter now runs the house with the same warmth and enthusiasm as ever.

Rooms: 2 double and 1 twin room, each with a shower-room & wc.

Price: 210-230 Frs for two, including breakfast.

Meals: None (4km).

Open: 1 February – 31 December.

To get there: *From Colmar, A35 and N83 towards Sélestat (exit 11) then N59 and D424 to Villé. There, D697 to Dieffenbach-du-Val. Careful: ask for exact address as 2 other Engels do B&B!*

Map Ref No: 8

Doris ENGEL
Maison Fleurie
19 route de Neuve Eglise
Dieffenbach-au-Val
67220 Villé, Bas-Rhin
Tel: 88 85 60 48

168

Marlenheim produces rosé wine at the start of the Alsace 'route des vins' and this dairy farm manages to produce the 'pink drink' as well as milk. It is another old Alsatian house although it's on a busy thoroughfare. The guestrooms are at the back and quiet...smallish yet comfortable. Monsieur is an active farmer, Madame teaches German; they will welcome you in English and serve a generous breakfast in your room. A good stopover for those wanting to explore nearby Strasbourg.

Rooms: 2 double rooms, each with own shower-room.

Price: 220 Frs for two, including breakfast.

Meals: None (in village).

Open: All year.

To get there: *From Strasbourg, N4 towards Saverne. Farm is in middle of the village of Marlenheim, before post office.*

Map Ref No: 8

M & Mme Paul GOETZ
86 rue du Général de Gaulle
67520 Marlenheim
Bas-Rhin
Tel: 88 87 52 94

169

This beautiful 17th-century Alsatian house has been the heart of a wine-growing estate since it was founded in 1688 by a Ruhlmann forbear. Wine buffs will enjoy being shown round the wine cellar and non-drinkers can taste the spring water straight from the Vosges hills. Breakfast is served in a huge room full of relics: old barrels, a wine press, a grape basket, a china stove. The village is strikingly 'authentic' and the walks are worth the detour. The Ruhlmann couple love their life; it is seductive indeed.

Rooms: 2 double rooms, each with own shower, sharing wc.

Price: 230 Frs for two, including breakfast.

Meals: Not available.

Open: April to November.

To get there: *Dambach is about 8km north of Sélestat on D35. House in village centre, about equidistant between two gateways.*

Map Ref No: 8

Jean-Charles & Laurence
RUHLMANN
34 rue Mal Foch
67650 Dambach-la-Ville, Bas-Rhin
Tel: 88 92 41 86
Fax: 88 92 61 81

170

A large, comfortable house with its own courtyard, on the outskirts of the village, it has lots of character. The Dartois' is very much a family home, well-furnished and with a lived-in, easy-going feel; they are most hospitable hosts. A good base for walkers who might explore the nearby forest; there is also access to riding and fishing. Don't miss the source of the Douix that wells up most spectacularly in a grove near the charming little town of Châtillon.

Burgundy

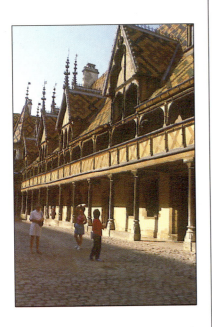

Rooms: 1 double & 1 twin, sharing a bathroom.

Price: 130-140 Frs for two, including breakfast.

Meals: Not available.

Open: All year.

To get there: *From Châtillon-sur-Seine, N71 towards Dijon. At Aisey-sur-Seine, D101 towards Chemin-d'Aisey; signposted.*

Map Ref No: 7

Simone & Jean DARTOIS
Chemin d'Aisey
21400 Châtillon-sur-Seine
Côte-d'Or
Tel: 80 93 22 51

A well-restored château in an idyllic setting; the River Coquille meanders through wooded parkland and meadows, murmuring at the feet of white stone turrets. Looks like a dream of old France but expect a more casual, 'modern' welcome. Rooms are comfortable with a lived-in once-elegant look. Dinner, served in the family dining-room, is superb, but make sure your booking is firm. Lovely gardens, fly-fishing heaven(!), a games room...

Rooms: 3 double rooms, 1 twin and 1 triple, all with bathrooms.

Price: 350 Frs for two, including breakfast.

Meals: Dinner 150 Frs, including wine (book ahead).

Open: 21 March to 1 November.

To get there: *From Dijon, N71 towards Châtillon-sur-Seine. Before St Marc-sur-Seine, right on D32 and D954 towards Aignay. Tarperon signposted on D954.*

Map Ref No: 7

Mme Soisick de CHAMPSAVIN
Manoir de Tarperon
Quemigny-sur-Seine
21510 Aignay-le-Duc
Côte-d'Or
Tel: 80 93 83 74

This is an endearingly higgledy-piggledy 18th-century house in an attractive hill-top village. The cheerful rooms are lent an artistic flourish by Madame's hand-decoration of some of the furniture. Breakfast features honey from Monsieur's own hives. You all eat together in the evening although Madame may remain up to cook before your eyes.

Rooms: 2 double rooms and 2 twin rooms, all with bathrooms.

Price: 200 Frs for two, including breakfast.

Meals: Dinner 80 Frs, including wine.

Open: 1 March – 30 November.

To get there: *From Dijon, N74 through Nuits-St-Georges towards Beaune. At Corgoloin, D115 to Magny-les-Villers. There, take road leading to Pernaud Vergelesses; house almost immediately on right as you leave Magny, going uphill.*

Map Ref No: 12

Françoise & Henri GIORGI
Magny-les-Villers
21700 Nuits-St-Georges
Côte-d'Or
Tel: 80 62 95 42

BURGUNDY

This is a modern house overlooking the river valley below the site of Roman Alesia. The Gounands have made every effort to make guests feel at home. Rooms are clean and comfortable. There is an outdoor kitchen and a barbecue in the well-kept garden. Breakfast is generous and delicious. Unpretentious hospitality and a good base from which to explore the Auxois.

Rooms: 1 double room and 1 twin, each with own bathroom.

Price: 170-220 Frs, including breakfast.

Meals: Available on special request – 60 Frs including wine.

Open: Easter to 31 October.

A pretty, turn-of-the-century house, in the heart of the Vosne-Romanée vineyard. Guestrooms are modern and elegant, very much 'grand confort'; two are on the ground floor with relatively easy access. The Grimms are charming and epitomise discreet hospitality. They also provide an excellent breakfast. There is a lovely sitting-room with views over the surrounding countryside. Not suitable for children. Better as a stop-over than a base, largely because the road is nearby.

Rooms: 1 double and 2 triple rooms, all with bathrooms.

Price: 450-500 Frs for two, including breakfast.

Meals: Not available.

Open: 1 April – 31 October.

To get there: *From Dijon, N71 towards Châtillon-sur-Seine. After Courceau, D6 left and follow signposts.*

Map Ref No: 7

To get there: *From A31 Nuits-St-Georges exit, N74 towards Dijon. In Vosne-Romanée, house is on left as you leave village; signposted.*

Map Ref No: 12

Claude GOUNAND
Villa Le Clos
Route de la Villeneuve D194
21150 Darcey
Côte-d'Or
Tel: 80 96 23 20

Jean-Paul & Claude GRIMM
La Closerie des Ormes
21 rue de la Grand-Velle
21700 Vosne-Romanée, Côte-d'Or
Tel: 80 61 20 24
Fax: 80 61 19 63

Gevry-Chambertin is a famous wine-village in the heart of Burgundy's Côte-d'Or, ideal for visiting vineyards and the area capital of Beaune whose Hospices run the world's most famous wine auction. Your hosts have a large and unusual 'maison bourgeoise' in the village, a solid, comfortable and very French house. Plenty of restaurants nearby.

Rooms: 2 double rooms and 1 twin, all with bathrooms.

Price: 220 Frs for two, including breakfast.

Meals: None; restaurants nearby.

Open: All year.

An attractive, secluded ferme-auberge from the mid-19th century, in lush farmland at the end of a valley. Rooms, including a suite big enough for a family of five, are pleasant with exposed beams. There are games for children and horse-riding on site. You may be greeted by an enormous shaggy dog but any stories will be told by the women of the house: 3 generations meet here. Deservedly popular with walkers and riders.

Rooms: 2 double rooms with showers, sharing wc.

Price: 230 Frs for two, including breakfast.

Meals: Dinner on request – 100 Frs including wine.

Open: All year.

To get there: *From Dijon, N74 towards Nuits-St-Georges; right into Gevrey-Chambertin; signposted.*

Map Ref No: 12

To get there: *From Nevers, D977 towards Auxerre. At Guérigny, left onto D8 towards Pougues-les-Eaux; 2nd right onto D110 for 2km: signposted.*

Map Ref No: 11

Mme SYLVAIN
14 rue de l'Eglise
21220 Gevrey-Chambertin
Côte-d'Or
Tel: 80 51 86 39

Bernadette BARBARIN
Ferme de la Maure
58320 Parigny-les-Vaux
Nièvre
Tel: 86 60 40 12

A charming, romantic 'maison de maître', elegant with white shutters and a terrace with a curved double staircase to the lawn, in a beautiful hillside position. The rooms reflect the atmosphere of secluded comfort: open fires and antique beds and sympathetic period decoration. Madame Bürgi is hospitable and good-humoured. A delightful house.

Rooms: 3 double rooms with own bathrooms; 1 double & 1 twin sharing a bathroom.

Price: 250-380 Frs for two, including breakfast.

Meals: Not available.

Open: All year.

To get there: *From Nevers, D977 to Prémery. There, D977 towards Corbigny; St Révérien is 15km along; signposted.*

Map Ref No: 11

Mme Bernadette BURGI
La Villa des Prés
58420 St Révérien
Nièvre
Tel: 86 29 04 57

178

A secluded 19th-century farm with a lovely, tranquil garden and a rural setting. Rooms are comfortable, with somewhat functional bathrooms. The family living-room is, however, delightful with a long table, oak furnishings, books and a log fire. There is also a barbecue for guests' use. The hosts, retired farmers, are open and easy to be with.

Rooms: 2 double rooms with bathrooms & 1 twin with wc.

Price: 215-250 Frs for two, including breakfast.

Meals: None (barbecue facilities).

Open: All year.

To get there: *From Nevers, D978 towards Château-Chinon. At Châtillon-en-Bazois, D945 towards Corbigny; left on D259 towards Mont-et-Marré; farm is 500m along.*

Map Ref No: 11

Paul et Nicole DELTOUR
Ferme Semelin
Mont-et-Marré
58110 Châtillon-en-Bazois
Nièvre
Tel: 86 84 13 94

179

A lovely 19th-century farmhouse with masses of character and a charming, enthusiastic hostess, committed to providing her guests with authentic country hospitality. Rooms are traditionally decorated and comfortable. There is a pleasant living-room with books and games. Breakfast (homemade jams) and dinner, if requested, are eaten with the family.

Rooms: 2 double rooms with own bathrooms.

Price: 270 Frs for two, including breakfast.

Meals: Dinner 120 Frs, including wine (book ahead).

Open: 1st March – 31st October.

In gorgeous undulating countryside, a very pretty, old farm complex, parts of it built in the 13th century, with a fairy-tale atmosphere. Guestrooms, in a converted outbuilding, are modern and comfortable. Farm produce is used at the breakfast and dinner table. A lovely flower garden, indoor and outdoor games and access to riding and bicycling. There is also a wealth of lovely monuments to see in the area.

Rooms: 4 doubles, 2 twins and 1 family room for 3-4 people, all with bathrooms; 1 family room for 3-4 people, shared bathroom.

Price: 250 Frs for two, including breakfast.

Meals: Dinner 80-150 Frs, excluding wine.

Open: All year.

To get there: *From Auxerre, N151 to Clamecy, then D977 and D957 towards St Amand. At Dampierre, D114 left towards St Loup. Second on left after 'les Bouillons'.*

Map Ref No: 6

Mme Elvire DUCHET
Chez Elvire
Chauffour
58200 Saint Loup
Nièvre
Tel: 86 26 20 22

To get there: *From Nevers, D977 through Guérigny to Prémery. Just past Prémery, right on D977 towards Corbigny; signposted.*

Map Ref No: 11

Famille FAYOLLE
Ferme Auberge du Vieux Château
Oulon
58700 Prémery
Nièvre
Tel: 86 68 06 77

Beside a huge, tranquil lake (free fishing for guests), this unusual farmhouse epitomises rural calm and hospitality. Spacious and comfortable guestrooms look out over water and rolling countryside and there are kitchen facilities. The excellent breakfast includes home-produced honey. There is a tennis court and windsurfing nearby.

Rooms: 2 double rooms with bathrooms.

Price: 170-230 Frs for two, including breakfast.

Meals: None (self-catering).

Open: All year.

In beautiful countryside, this 'grand rustic' château-farm has a comfortable chambre d'hôte for guests and gîte accommodation nearby. The farm produces poultry, ducks and eggs which, together with other produce, are sold on site. There are horses for hire and opportunities for cycling and walking.

Rooms: 1 double room with bathroom (2 extra beds available).

Price: 200 Frs for two, including breakfast.

Meals: Not available.

Open: All year.

To get there: *From Nevers, D975 to Rouy. There, D132 to Tintury; right on D112 to Fleury and first right after village; signposted.*

Map Ref No: 11

To get there: *From Prémery, D38 towards Châtillon-en-Bazois and St Saulge; signposted 'Gîte d'étape' at junction of D38 and D181 to St Martin.*

Map Ref No: 11

Michel & Marie-France GUENY
Fleury La Tour
58110 Tintury
Nièvre
Tel: 86 84 12 42

J-Patrick & Marie-Hélène JANDET
Basse-Cour de St Martin
58330 Sainte Marie
Nièvre
Tel: 86 58 35 15

This is a fine classic French manor gazing at itself in its own lake, surrounded by the beautiful Morvan National Park. There are spiritual highlights like Vézelay and Autun nearby and secular pilgrimages to be made to the wine cellars of Beaune and Sancerre. Come back to Lesvault for dinner before the great fireplace and a night in a superb room. Bibbi, a delightful American now well-rooted in France, creates an easy-going artistic atmosphere. Far too large for a Chambre d'Hôte, but we love the place.

Rooms: 6 double rooms with own bathrooms, 4 twin (or single) rooms sharing bathrooms.

Price: 450 Frs for two, including breakfast.

Meals: Dinner 130 Frs, excluding wine.

Open: All year.

To get there: *From Moulins-Engilbert, D18 towards Onlay for 5km. Château on left, well signposted.*

Map Ref No: 12

Bibbi LEE & Charles SIMONDS
Château de Lesvault
58370 Onlay
Nièvre
Tel: 86 84 32 91
Fax: 86 84 35 78

184

A lovely country house, warm stone and white shutters, built in 1690, set in 115 hectares of magnificent parkland. The property has been immaculately restored; rooms have good antique furniture and are tastefully decorated. The hosts are hospitable and well-organised, happy to suggest activities, from watching the goats being milked to visiting local châteaux.

Rooms: 4 double rooms with bathrooms.

Price: 250-300 Frs for two, including breakfast.

Meals: None (self-catering).

Open: All year, except January.

To get there: *From Château-Chinon, D978 through Châtillon-en-Bazois towards Nevers. 4km along, after service station, right on D112 towards Bernière; house on left after 1.5km.*

Map Ref No: 11

Colette & André LEJAULT
Bouteville
58110 Alluy
Nièvre
Tel: 86 84 06 65
Fax: 86 84 03 41

185

This is a 19th-century manor-house, with a courtyard framed by long barns and old outbuildings, in the rich, arable fields of the Loire valley. Rooms have tastefully uncluttered modern decor; there are separate living and dining-rooms, with tempting 'plats régionaux' in the evening. Those not tempted by genteel sloth may ride horses/bikes or play croquet/badminton or swim in the lake.

Rooms: 3 double rooms, all with private bathrooms.

Price: 280 Frs for two, including breakfast.

Meals: Dinner 150 Frs, including wine (book ahead).

Open: All year.

This young farming couple have done a very successful conversion of their old farmhouse next to the château. The rooms are modern and comfortable, the whole house has a lovely country atmosphere. There is a large garden with games for children. Madame is an excellent cook and enjoys introducing visitors to the delights of "la cuisine nivernaise", specializing in chicken dishes.

Rooms: 2 double & 1 triple room, all with bathrooms.

Price: 220 Frs for two, including breakfast.

Meals: Dinner (except Sundays) 80 Frs, including wine.

Open: All year except 20 December – 3 January.

To get there: *From Montargis, N7 through Briare towards Cosne-sur-Loire. 2km after Neuvy-sur-Loire; signposted.*

Map Ref No: 6

To get there: *From Avallon, D957 to Vézelay, then D958 towards Corbigny to Bazoches: house in village, below castle.*

Map Ref No: 6

Bernard PASQUET
Domaine de l'Etang
58450 Neuvy-sur-Loire
Nièvre
Tel: 86 39 20 06

Philippe & Nadine PERRIER
Ferme Auberge de Bazoches
58190 Bazoches-de-Morvan
Nièvre
Tel: 86 22 16 30

This former 17th-century convent has lots of original detail. There is nothing convent-like, however, about the impeccable rooms, with period furnishings, which overlook the large garden. Breakfast in a cheerful room with hand-painted furniture. Excellent regional dinners are served in the sumptuous dining-room with log fire. Madame, a welcoming hostess, lives next door. Sitting-room, library and bikes available.

Rooms: 4 twin and 2 double rooms, 1 room for four and 2 suites for four; all with private bathrooms.

Price: 450-650 Frs for two, including breakfast.

Meals: Dinner 200 Frs, including wine.

Open: All year.

To get there: *From Roanne, D482 and D982 towards Paray-le-Monial. House is in the town.*

Map Ref No: 12

Mme Josette BADIN
Les Recollets
71110 Marcigny
Saône-et-Loire
Tel: 85 25 03 34
Fax: 85 25 06 91

A genuine 'maison bourgeoise' with a welcoming, comfortable air; it was a Parisian taxman's summer residence in the 18th century. An English garden, relaxed English hosts who know and love the good things their adopted region has to offer (wine, good food, Cistercian abbeys, Romanesque architecture), a cushion-filled interior and perfect bathrooms, antique furniture and old fireplaces and a fine wine cellar make La Roseraie a good place to stay. To cap it all Roz can lay on vegetarian dinners.

Rooms: 4 double rooms, 2 twin rooms, all with own bathrooms.

Price: 320 Frs for two, including breakfast.

Meals: On reservation only. 200 Frs, including aperitif, wine, coffee, liqueurs.

Open: All year.

To get there: *From Cluny, D980 towards Montceau-les-Mines. 21km after Cluny, left on D27; through St Bonnet-de-Joux; 8.5km beyond, right to La Guiche. In village, left of Mairie; signposted.*

Map Ref No: 12

John & Roz BINNS
La Roseraie
71220 La Guiche
Saône-et-Loire
Tel: 85 24 67 82
Fax: 85 24 61 03

Canoe trips on the Loire and forays into the countryside are big attractions here. The unpretentious old farmhouse has a fine stone staircase and solid oak doors. A wood-burning stove provides glowing warmth. Modern bedrooms in beige with blue curtains and electric heaters. Madame, calm and hospitable, serves breakfast in the conservatory.

Rooms: 1 double room and 1 twin room, each with own bathroom.

Price: 240 Frs for two, including breakfast.

Meals: Not available.

Open: All year.

The young hosts use B&Bs themselves when they go to Ireland and they know all the do's and don'ts. Their beautiful old red-brick farmhouse has two suites converted for family use with stunning views over the rolling countryside. The rooms are simple and effective and the small luxuries provided, such as bathrobes in each room, show generous attention to detail. Home-made cheeses and local wines sold in the farmyard.

Rooms: 2 double rooms, 2 twin rooms ; 2 family suites with shower, wc and kitchen.

Price: 160-290 Frs for two, including breakfast.

Meals: None (self-catering possible in two of the rooms).

Open: All year.

To get there: *From Roanne, D482 and D982 towards Paray-le-Monial. 5km after Marcigny, left for Reffy. Next to church; signposted.*

Map Ref No: 12

M Daniel CHEVALLIER
Le Cèdre Bleu
Reffy, Baugy
71110 Marcigny
Saône-et-Loire
Tel: 85 25 39 68

To get there: *From Tournus, D14 towards Cluny. At Chapaize, D314 towards Bissy-sous-Uxelles. House next to church.*

Map Ref No: 12

Pascale & Dominique de la BUSSIERE
La Ferme
71460 Bissy-sous-Uxelles
Saône-et-Loire
Tel: 85 50 15 03

Another fabulous view and such silence! The house, a typical 'mâconnaise', has looked out over this valley for 300 years now, solid and enduring; it used to be a wine-growing estate. Monsieur speaks good English and shares his enthusiasm for local lore and culture, including viticulture. Following an excellent night in one of the large, comfortable rooms, breakfast is a feast of local pâtés, cheeses, honeys and breads that will give you strength for tramping round the local "caves de Bourgogne".

Rooms: 2 double rooms, each with shower or bath & wc.

Price: 250 Frs for two, including breakfast.

Meals: Not available.

Open: All year.

To get there: *From Tournus, D14 towards Cormatin. After 10km, left onto D163 towards Gratay and Chardonnay then right to Grévilly. Follow signs.*

Map Ref No: 12

Claude DEPREAY
Le Pré Ménot
71700 Grévilly
Saône-et-Loire
Tel: 85 33 29 92
Fax: 85 33 29 92

Keen to maintain their farmhouse home, this friendly and cheerful couple have converted the barns into large chambres d'hôtes. The cream, pink or blue rooms with simple matching bathrooms have parquet floors and rugs, country-style beds with good mattresses, old armoires and wood-burning stoves. The house, with its large flower-decked terrace and unobtrusive campsite, stands 500m from the road.

Rooms: 2 twin rooms with private bathrooms and extra bed or cot available + 1 suite for 5.

Price: 250 Frs for two, including breakfast.

Meals: Not available.

Open: All year.

To get there: *From Roanne, D482 and D982 towards Paray-le-Monial for about 30km. Enter Marcigny; signposted.*

Map Ref No: 12

Maïssa & Alain GALLAUD
La Thuillère
71110 Marcigny
Saône-et-Loire
Tel: 85 25 10 31

This is a grand old 19th-century manor-house which has a lovely 'worn round the edges' feel to it. Set up in the hills, it is ideal for hikers. Madame Gauthier has put a lot of effort into maintaining the original style of the house. Here you feel very much at home and there is even a piano room available.

Rooms: 1 double room with own bathroom and 1 suite for 4 with kitchen and bathroom.

Price: 240 Frs for two, including breakfast.

Meals: None (self-catering).

Open: All year.

This 18th-century townhouse has a large walled garden which shuts off any traffic noise. Inside the house, the bedrooms and bathrooms, with traditional furniture from the region, have been decorated in coordinated colours. An unusual feature here is Simone's large collection of antique flat-irons. Her husband paints in oils and several of his paintings adorn the house.

Rooms: 2 double rooms with own bathroom; 1 double room with shared bathroom. Spare beds and cot available.

Price: 250 Frs for two, including breakfast.

Meals: Not available.

Open: All year except 1 week in May and in September.

To get there: *From Mâcon, N79 towards Cluny. At Berzé-le-Châtel, N79 on towards Charolles, then D987 to Trambly. Left past church; house on left.*

Map Ref No: 12

To get there: *In Charolles, take street opposite church towards Sous-Préfecture. Turn first right; house is a little way along.*

Map Ref No: 12

François & Florence GAUTHIER
Les Charrières
71520 Trambly
Saône-et-Loire
Tel: 85 50 43 17

Mme Simone LAUGERETTE
3 rue de la Madeleine
71120 Charolles
Saône-et-Loire
Tel: 85 88 35 78

This enthusiastic and chatty young couple are renovating their old village house. Garden roses add a personal touch to the modest rooms where authenticity has been maintained, with traditional tiled floors and green and pink decor. Homemade bread at breakfast and simple dinners with home-grown veg (not 'en famille") in a dining-room with pretty English wallpaper. Parking next door.

Rooms: 1 double room and 1 twin room, each with own bathroom.

Price: 200 Frs for two, including breakfast.

Meals: Dinner 70 Frs, excluding wine.

Open: All year.

A quiet 19th-century house with a walled garden near the town centre (lively farmers' market on Mondays). The small, modern rooms are heated and well-insulated, with fresh, flowery decor and traditional beds. Two have kitchenettes; one has a separate entrance. The helpful young hosts have a small child and are willing to babysit.

Rooms: 2 double rooms and 1 twin room, each with own bathroom & two with kitchenettes.

Price: 250-280 Frs for two, including breakfast.

Meals: None (self-catering; restaurants in town).

Open: All year.

To get there: *From A6, Mâcon exit onto N79 towards Moulin, then D79 towards Beaubery. After a small lake, right on D168 to Ozolles. There, first left, over bridge; first house on right.*

Map Ref No: 12

To get there: *From Roanne, D482 towards Paray-le-Monial. At Marcigny, D989 towards la Clayette and Semur-en-Brionnals; second turning on right; signposted.*

Map Ref No: 12

Jean-François MONCORGER
Le Bourg
71120 Ozolles
Saône-et-Loire
Tel: 85 88 35 00

196

Andrée & Jean-Pierre RICOL
La Musardière
50 rue de la Tour
71110 Marcigny
Saône-et-Loire
Tel: 85 25 38 54

197

BURGUNDY

Living in an old farmhouse, practising one of most ancient of rural arts – wine-growing – the Sallets have elected to be utterly modern in their conversion; and very relaxing it is too, with clean-cut furniture, good bathrooms and a generous beamed living-room. Their wine is also praiseworthy, both red and white AOC. Madame, who now has 5 grandchildren, is as kind a hostess as you could imagine. The area is flat and quiet, excellent for a family stay.

Rooms: 2 double roms, 1 twin room, 1 triple room, all with own bath or shower & wc.

Price: 260 Frs for two, including breakfast.

Meals: None (self-catering).

Open: All year.

To get there: *From Tournus, N6 towards Mâcon. After 10km, right on D163 to Uchizy. Signposted.*

Map Ref No: 12

Annick & Gérard SALLET
71700 Uchizy
Saône-et-Loire
Tel: 85 40 50 46

A lovely, secluded Burgundian manor-house, in the family for 400 years, white-shuttered, covered in creeper and with a lovely gravel courtyard. The Brunots offer an impressive degree of luxury and genuine hospitality. Guestrooms are big and beautifully furnished, with prettily tiled bathrooms; there is a comfortable guest sitting-room. Madame is an accomplished cook and Monsieur has a superb wine cellar. Our readers have sent glowing reports.

Rooms: 2 double rooms and 1 twin, each with own bathroom; extra bed available.

Price: 350 Frs for two, including breakfast.

Meals: Dinner 160 Frs, including wine.

Open: All year.

To get there: *From A6, Auxerre-Nord exit on N6 towards Joigny; right on D48, left on D84 towards Brienon for 9km, past turning to Mont-St-Sulpice and right down small road by river; house is 0.5km on left.*

Map Ref No: 6

Didier & Françoise BRUNOT
Domaine des Morillons
89250 Mont-St-Sulpice
Yonne
Tel: 86 56 18 87
Fax: 86 43 05 07

The hosts at this working farm are entirely genuine in their welcome. The bedrooms are delightful and warm, true to the spirit of an old-fashioned French farmhouse; bathrooms are clean and modern. Isabelle serves good country fare at breakfast and dinner. A peaceful, rural location; the village is 2km away.

Rooms: 1 double room with own shower-room; 2 double rooms sharing a bathroom.

Price: 190 Frs for two, including breakfast.

Meals: Dinner 80 Frs including wine (book ahead).

Open: All year.

A lovely 19th-century manor-house conveniently close to Chablis and Auxerre, set in wooded grounds where truffle-hunting is a popular pursuit. The Chonés offer warm and comfortable (centrally-heated) bedrooms and those on the top floor are approached by a stone spiral staircase in a tower. Vineyards nearby and plentiful sporting and cultural activities in Auxerre.

Rooms: 5 double rooms, all with bathrooms.

Price: 250-300 Frs for two, including breakfast.

Meals: None (Auxerre 10km).

Open: All year.

To get there: *From Châtillon-sur-Seine, D965 towards Tonnerre and Laignes. At Pimelles, D12 to Cruzy-le-Châtel; house is 2km to north; signposted.*

Map Ref No: 7

To get there: *From Auxerre, N65 towards Chablis for 10km; signposted.*

Map Ref No: 6

Henri & Isabelle CHERVAUX
Les Musseaux
89740 Cruzy-le-Châtel
Yonne
Tel: 86 75 24 03

François & Françoise CHONE
Domaine de Montpierreux
89290 Venoy
Yonne
Tel: 86 40 20 91

Sleep safe and sound in your own four-poster bed in this fortified 12th-century château. The superb bedroom has an authentic mediaeval atmosphere, heaps of historical features and an open fire (also central heating). Martine is a talented cook; delicious breakfasts and bounteous dinners are served in the baronial kitchen/dining-room. A stylish and romantic retreat but not suitable for children.

Rooms: 1 double room with own bathroom.

Price: 450 Frs for two, including breakfast.

Meals: Dinner 120-200 Frs, excluding wine.

Open: All year.

Very grand and so very French! Lime trees shade the square by the 19th-century manor. Persian carpets on parquet floors, some antiques and good, firm beds grace the large, luminous guestrooms. Well-fitted bathrooms. In winter a wood fire burns in the sitting-room. Madame has taken great pains over her immaculate home; both hosts put you at your ease in their rather formal surroundings and enjoy talking to guests.

Rooms: 1 double with own bathroom; 1 double and 1 twin sharing a bathroom.

Price: 250-350 Frs for two, including breakfast.

Meals: Dinner 90 Frs, including wine (book ahead or restaurant next door).

Open: All year.

To get there: *From Avallon, N6 towards Saulieu. As you enter Ste Magnance, first house on right.*

Map Ref No: 7

To get there: *From A6, Joigny exit onto D943 towards Joigny then very shortly right onto D89 to Senan.*

Map Ref No: 6

Martine & Gérard COSTAILLE
Château Jacquot
RN6
89420 Sainte Magnance
Yonne
Tel: 86 33 00 22

Mme Paule DEFRANCE
4 place de la Liberté
89710 Senan
Yonne
Tel: 86 91 59 89

Madame creates a most wonderful atmosphere with her relaxed Bohemian manner, her love of jazz and her delightful family. After a delicious meal round the vast table in her generous sitting/dining room with its beams and tiled floor, she will go to the piano and sing for you. The rooms are soberly decorated and comfortable. There is a leafy garden to sit in and one understands why people return year after year to bask in the glow.

Rooms: 2 double rooms sharing a bathroom, 1 studio flat with own bathroom.

Price: 190-260 Frs for two, including breakfast.

Meals: Dinner 95 Frs, including wine.

Open: All year.

To get there: *From Joigny, D943 towards Migennes. At Laroche, left on D181 towards Brion then D47 to Bussy. In village, right on D140 towards Brienon. House 500m on left.*

Map Ref No: 6

Maud DUFAYET
Relais de la Forêt d'Othe
46-48 rue St Julien
89400 Bussy-en-Othe
Yonne
Tel: 86 91 93 48

The little village of Venouse nestles among orchards and vineyards close to the small town of Pontigny with its vast Cistercian abbey where Thomas-à-Beckett once took refuge. This fine village house has a large, shady garden where guests can enjoy Madame's home cooking, washed down with a glass of wine from nearby Chablis.

Rooms: 1 double room with bathroom.

Price: 240 Frs for two, including breakfast.

Meals: Dinner 90 Frs, including wine. Picnic on request – 40 Frs.

Open: All year.

To get there: *From Auxerre, N77 to Pontigny. House in village centre, near church.*

Map Ref No: 6

Magda & Philippe GARNIER
Place de l'Eglise
Venouse
89230 Pontigny
Yonne
Tel: 86 47 75 15

This 15th-century village house has a superb location next to the wonderful Basilica in the mediaeval town of Vézelay. A stone spiral staircase goes up to the bedrooms; one has a terrace overlooking the Basilica. The owner serves breakfast (flexible times) in her own dining-room, and likes to chat. A special place, for Vézelay is a 'must'.

Rooms: 1 double room and 1 twin, sharing bathroom.

Price: 260 Frs for two, including breakfast.

Meals: None (in Vézelay).

Open: All year.

To get there: *From Avallon, D957 to Vézelay. In town, 100m from Basilica – identifiable from turret on house.*

Map Ref No: 6

Mme Bertrand GINISTY
La Tour Gaillon
89450 Vézelay
Yonne
Tel: 86 33 25 74

This period farmhouse is set in splendid isolation, in a river valley deep in the countryside. Superb for experienced horse-riders; hire a mount and a guide from the hosts' stables and explore the surrounding woods and hills on horseback. Guestrooms are basic but comfortable and breakfast may be a bit basic too. Also, beware of scalding hot water. Dinner is available on reservation. A wonderfully peaceful and unspoilt place.

Rooms: 1 double room with own bathroom; 2 double rooms sharing a bathroom.

Price: 200 Frs for two, including breakfast.

Meals: Dinner 80 Frs, including wine (book ahead).

Open: All year.

To get there: *From Avallon, N6 towards Saulieu. In St Magnance, right 300m after lights to Bussières. After 1km, right on small road signposted 'Equitation, Chambres d'Hôtes'. Farm is down hill, on left.*

Map Ref No: 7

Christian & Nelly VINET
Ferme des Ruats
89630 Bussières
Yonne
Tel: 86 33 16 57

Fields of sunflowers stretch away from the farmhouse. The guestrooms are clean and cosy with traditional country furniture and lovely views. This comfortable old farmhouse has been in the family for years and has a homely, lived-in feel to it. Initially rather shy, the Chambrins are affable hosts. Guests' sitting-room with plenty of books.

Rooms: 2 double rooms and 1 twin room, each with own bathroom.

Price: 200 Frs for two, including breakfast.

Meals: Not available.

Open: All year.

The Loire Valley

To get there: *From Bourges, N144 to Levet; then D28 towards Dun-sur-Auron. After 2km turn right. House 300m from junction.*

Map Ref No: 11

Marie-Jo & Jean CHAMBRIN
Bannay
18340 St Germain-des-Bois
Cher
Tel: 48 25 31 03

208

At the heart of the Sancerre vineyards stands this 15th-century manor-house, with its turret and spiral stone staircase. The large guestrooms, with huge beams and tiled floors, are modern. If asked, the amiable, down-to-earth hosts will help out with a meal on the first night. Do try the 'pain d'épices' in the morning. (Cooked breakfast upon request.) Bikes available.

Rooms: 2 double rooms with bathrooms, 2 double rooms sharing bathroom. Extra beds available.

Price: 300 Frs for two, including breakfast.

Meals: Dinner 80 Frs, excluding wine.

Open: Easter to 31 October.

This house retains traces of its original use as a convent; ask for the large room in the converted chapel, which has vestiges of the Confessional and Sacristy. There's also an enchanting garden in which Madame grows her own vegetables. An imaginative, spontaneous person, she trusts to spur-of-the-moment inspiration for the evening meal – we gather it's always a success!

Rooms: 1 double room with own bathroom; 2 double rooms with shared bathroom.

Price: 200-290 Frs for two, including breakfast.

Meals: Dinner 85 Frs, including wine.

Open: All year.

To get there: *From Bourges, N151 and D955 towards Sancerre. Left on D86 to Briou. After 0.7km, left to Vauvredon.*

Map Ref No: 11

To get there: *From Bourges, N151 towards la Charité-sur-Loire. At St Germain, D155 to Ste Solange.*

Map Ref No: 11

M & Mme CIROTTE
Manoir de Vaudredon
Briou-de-Crézancy-en-Sancerre
18300 Sancerre
Cher
Tel: 48 79 00 29

Martine FROGER
Le Couvent
18220 Ste Solange
Cher
Tel: 48 67 43 05

The long old building is part of a tiny hamlet near the Sancerre vineyards. Guests have their own entrance, large sitting-room with fireplace and corner kitchen. Decoratively-themed rooms – poppy (all red checks!), bindweed and blueberry – with modern touches. Local farm produce goes into light regional dinners served in the family dining-room. Madame is cultured, helpful and welcoming.

Rooms: 2 double rooms and 1 twin (2 on ground floor), all with bathrooms.

Price: 250 Frs for two, including breakfast.

Meals: Dinner 80 Frs, excluding wine.

Open: All year.

A working farmer, Monsieur Manssens likes hunting and excellent game dishes are a speciality; the whole place is very French. Passionate about food, he is a shrewd, zealous host who is proud to be Berrychon. Girls serve in a dining-room with rustic charm. The comfortable guestrooms, newly decorated with good fabrics, are a cut above average, clean and well-kept.

Rooms: 2 double rooms with bathrooms.

Price: 200-230 Frs for two, including breakfast.

Meals: Lunch & dinner 75-90 Frs, excluding wine.

Open: All year except Wednesdays and 2 weeks in Sept.

To get there: *From Sancerre, D958 towards Bourges. At les Salmons, left on D93 to Montigny. Take D44 for 5km; signposted.*

Map Ref No: 11

To get there: *From Bourges, N144 to Levet and D940 towards Lignières. 3km before Lignières, right on D129 to La Celle Condé.*

Map Ref No: 11

Jean-Louis & Elizabeth GRESSIN
La Reculée
18250 Montigny
Cher
Tel: 48 69 59 18
Fax: 48 69 52 51

M Alain MANSSENS
Ferme-Auberge de Pont Chauvet,
La Celle Condé
18160 Lignière-en-Berry
Cher
Tel: 48 60 22 19

THE LOIRE VALLEY

The 1940s manor-house is furnished entirely in art deco style and houses an eclectic collection of modern art. Monsieur paints and also runs an antique shop. Guests find original art and good beds in the rooms and may breakfast whenever they want. Dine, upon request, with the spontaneously hospitable, down-to-earth hosts (both named Claude!) in a congenial Bohemian atmosphere.

Rooms: 2 double rooms and 1 twin room, all with own bathrooms.

Price: 350-400 Frs for two, including breakfast.

Meals: Dinner 80-150 Frs (book ahead).

Open: All year.

This early 20th-century house stands in 125 hectares of wheat and maize. The Proffits are typical farmers; they are big-hearted, friendly and caring hosts. The renovated guestrooms are spotless, with good beds and their own entrance. Modern rustic decor. Flexible breakfast times; dinner sometimes available. (Kitchen for longer stays.) Garden and bikes.

Rooms: 1 double room and 2 twin rooms, all with bathrooms.

Price: 200-230 Frs for two, including breakfast.

Meals: Dinner 60-70 Frs, excluding wine.

Open: All year.

To get there: *From St Amand-Montrond, D951 towards Sancoins and Nevers. At Charenton Laugère, D953 towards Dun-sur-Auron; house is 300m along on left.*

Map Ref No: 11

To get there: *From Bourges, N151 towards la Charité. At St Germain-du-Puy, D955 towards Sancerre. At Les Aix-d'Angillon, D12 to Rians; there, take road opposite church; signposted.*

Map Ref No: 11

M & Mme Claude MOREAU
La Serre
18210 Charenton Laugère
Cher
Tel: 48 60 75 82

Odile & Yves PROFFIT
La Chaume
18220 Rians
Cher
Tel: 48 64 41 58
Fax: 48 64 29 71

Water flows from the mill pond in the tranquil garden. Lots of originality and flair have gone into the restoration of the house. The guestrooms are big, cosy and comfortable, with antique furnishings and good quality bedding. Madame is a bustling, proud hostess. Meals are copious – breakfast will keep you going all day!

Rooms: 3 double rooms, all with bathrooms.

Price: 350 Frs for two, including breakfast.

Meals: Dinner 120 Frs, excluding wine.

Open: All year.

A large, rather austere courtyard opens out in front of the old farmhouse and adjacent small guests' house. This is charmingly decorated and is centrally heated. On the ground floor is a sitting-room (sofa-bed) and corner kitchen; the bedroom is upstairs. Children can play in the lovely garden behind the main house. Madame is welcoming but prefers to allow guests their privacy. Garage.

Rooms: 2 double rooms with bathrooms.

Price: 240 Frs for two, including breakfast.

Meals: None (self-catering).

Open: All year.

To get there: *From Bourges, N144 towards St Amand-Montrond. At Levet, D940 to Châteauneuf-sur-Cher; there, D14 to Lignières, then D219 to La Celle Condé; on through village, signposted on right.*

Map Ref No: 11

To get there: *From Chartres, D921 towards Illiers Combray. After 5.5km, at le Pont Tranchefêtu, right towards St Georges-sur-Eure. After level crossing, left towards Chauffours. Farm is on left after village.*

Map Ref No: 5

Mme Véronique SOUCHON
Le Moulin
18160 La Celle-Condé
Cher
Tel: 48 60 02 01

215

M Denis HASQUENOPH
Bailleau le Pin
3 rue des Gémeaux
28120 Chauffours
Eure-et-Loir
Tel: 37 26 89 15

216

This fine old farmhouse has been furnished and decorated in impeccable taste. Bedrooms with exposed timbers and excellent beds overlook the garden. There's a small guest kitchen and a salon with fireplace. Prettily presented breakfasts. The Lothons are proud of their home with its refined, rather exclusive air, and like appreciative guests. (Monsieur is an antiques dealer.)

Rooms: 2 double rooms with bathrooms.

Price: 350 Frs for two, including breakfast.

Meals: None (self-catering).

Open: All year.

These amiable farmers are renovating their house. The beamed bedrooms are modest but comfortable. The elderly Maréchals lead a sociable life; their grand-children are often around, so children are welcome. Expect meals (with, maybe, some fresh farm petit pois), eaten 'en famille', to be just that, i.e. no-frills basic family fare. The farm buildings include a gîte. A good stop-over.

Rooms: 2 double rooms with own bathrooms.

Price: 190-200 Frs for two, including breakfast.

Meals: Dinner 65 Frs.

Open: All year.

To get there: *From Houdan, D61 towards Bourdonné; right on D115 to Dannemarie. There, follow D101 to Faverolles.*

Map Ref No: 5

To get there: *From Dreux, N12 to Houdan; D115 to Boutigny; D101 to Prouais; signposted "Chambres d'Hôtes".*

Map Ref No: 5

Mireille & Jean-Claude LOTHON
4 rue des Fontaines
28210 Faverolles
Eure-et-Loir
Tel: 37 51 47 67

M Serge MARECHAL
La Ferme des Tourelles
11 rue des Tourelles
La Musse, 28410 Boutigny-Prouais
Eure-et-Loir
Tel: 37 65 18 74

The farmhouse is built on the site of the great-grandfather's mill. It is quite ordinary and accommodation is basic and functional but the Martins' warmth and hospitality outshine their surroundings. Breakfast is available in the kitchen from 6.30-11am! Simple, honest suppers made from farm produce (they cultivate maize, poultry and rabbits) are eaten in the family dining-room.

Rooms: 2 triple rooms with hand-basins; shared bathroom.

Price: 225 Frs for two, including breakfast.

Meals: Dinner 40 Frs, including wine.

Open: All year.

A beautiful painted sign leads to a stone-walled enclosure and garden. The old house has been well restored and retains a certain quaintness. Cosy, white rooms with excellent bedding. Madame is matronly and trusting and the house has a warm family atmosphere. Her cooking combines simple and refined dishes and her 5-course meals are eaten with the family. She will do vegetarian dishes on request.

Rooms: 3 double rooms, all with bathrooms.

Price: 195-225 Frs for two, including breakfast.

Meals: Dinner 75 Frs, including wine, coffee & digestif.

Open: All year.

To get there: *From A10, Allaine exit on D927 towards Châteaudun. At La Maladrerie, D39 to Loigny. Signposted opposite church.*

Map Ref No: 6

Solange & Robert MARTIN
8 rue Chanzy
28140 Loigny-la-Bataille
Eure-et-Loir
Tel: 37 99 70 71

To get there: *From Châteaudun, N10 towards Chartres. At Bonneval, D17 to Moriers; there, D153 to Pré-St-Martin; signposted.*

Map Ref No: 5

M & Mme VIOLETTE
Le Carcotage Beauceron
8 rue St Martin
28800 Pré-St-Martin
Eure-et-Loir
Tel: 37 47 27 21

Built in the 16th century as a monastery and converted to a family house at the beginning of the century, the house is in a quiet corner of the village, close to the church. Madame has an elegant dining-room with Chippendale furniture and a drawing-room that looks out across carefully-tended lawns. The family will help those wishing to bicycle or ride horses in this gently natural area whose woods and waters are teeming with birdlife. This is the Brenne Regional Park.

Rooms: 1 double room with bathroom.

Price: 250 Frs for two, including breakfast.

Meals: Dinner 100 Frs, including wine (book ahead).

Open: All year.

A fabulous late-19th-century château, built in elegant Renaissance style, set in 11 hectares of parkland with pretty gardens and a swimming-pool. Guestrooms, including apartments suitable for families, are beautifully decorated and furnished, with individual, sumptuously rich colour-schemes. There is a library with masses of information on the area. Magnificent surroundings.

Rooms: 1 double, 2 twin, 3 triple rooms and 1 suite for 2-4 people, all with bathrooms; 1 twin and 1 single sharing a bathroom.

Price: 370-475 Frs for two, including breakfast.

Meals: Dinner 140 Frs, excluding wine.

Open: 1 February – 24 December.

To get there: *From Châteauroux, D925 towards Mézières-en-Brenne. At Bois d'Ars, D27 to Méobecq; house is behind church.*

Map Ref No: 10

To get there: *From Châteauroux, N143 towards Châtillon-sur-Indre. At Buzançais, D926 towards Levroux for approx. 2km; signposted.*

Map Ref No: 10

Mme Cécile BENHAMOU
Logis des Moines
Le Bourg
36500 Méobecq
Indre
Tel: 54 39 44 36

Yves et Sylvie du MANOIR
Château de Boisrenault
36500 Buzançais
Indre
Tel: 54 84 03 01
Fax: 54 84 10 57

A very special 18th-century 'grange' (barn) that Solange Frenkel has turned into one of the friendliest, most charming of chambres d'hôtes. In George Sand country, it has high ceilings, huge beams and pretty, floral bedrooms with their own entrances onto the garden. One can apparently have unlimited breakfast while dinner with the family is always memorable, though vegetarians are not catered for. Guests can sometimes use the sister's swimming pool next door.

Rooms: 2 double rooms with bathrooms.

Price: 260 Frs for two, including breakfast.

Meals: Dinner 85 Frs, including wine.

Open: All year.

To get there: *From Bourges, N144 towards Monluçon. At Levet, D940 towards la Châtre. At Thevet-St-Julien, D68 towards St Chartier. After 2km, left and left again.*

Map Ref No: 11

Mme Solange FRENKEL
La Garenne
36400 Thevet-St-Julien
Cher
Tel: 54 30 04 51

A turreted, 17th-century mansion with an elegant grey-stone façade. Bedrooms are comfortable and decorated with Second Empire furniture inherited from Madame's great-grandmother. There are lovely gardens with tables, chairs and a barbecue. The hosts are quiet but helpful (binoculars for ornithologists) and clearly take delight in their own home. Walkers will enjoy being close to the Parc Régional de la Brenne.

Rooms: 2 double rooms, each with own bathroom.

Price: 260-280 Frs for two, including breakfast.

Meals: None.

Open: All year.

To get there: *From Argenton-sur-Creuse, N151 towards Poitiers. At Le Blanc, D975 towards Martizay; then D27 towards Rosnay. After 2km right to Les Chézeaux; signposted.*

Map Ref No: 10

Alain JUBARD
Les Chézeaux
36300 Le Blanc
Indre
Tel: 54 37 32 17

An English couple who have chosen to come and farm in France... and import their sheep! The nearest town, Argenton, is called the "Venice of the Indre" – well, it **is** a lovely little place, unjustly neglected by tourists. The Mitchells have preserved old beams, an original terracotta floor and a fine stone fireplace in the living-room. They have created an aura of tranquility, a resting-place for travellers, a memorable holiday for those who stay longer.

Rooms: 1 double room with own bathroom, 1 double, 1 twin, 1 triple room sharing a bathroom.

Price: 220-250 Frs for two, including breakfast.

Meals: Dinner 70 Frs, including wine (book ahead).

Open: April – December.

To get there: *N20 from Châteauroux; exit to Tendu taking 1st left into village. Pass Mairie then fork left at church towards Prunget. House signposted before Château de Prunget.*

Map Ref No: 10

Robin & Alison MITCHELL
La Chasse
36200 Tendu
Indre
Tel: 54 24 07 76

An old house set in a tiny hamlet. Monsieur, retired, keeps the garden in order and looks after guests. Madame teaches natural sciences. They are proud of the standard of comfort in their two country-style guestrooms. Breakfast in the family living-room-cum-kitchen. Madame likes to practise her good English, perhaps over a cup of English-style tea.

Rooms: 2 twin rooms, each with own bathroom.

Price: 250 Frs for two, including breakfast.

Meals: Dinner 80 Frs, including wine (advance booking).

Open: All year.

To get there: *From la Châtre, D940 towards Guéret. At junction for Pouligny St Martin, right to le Montet; signposted.*

Map Ref No: 11

Mme PESSEL
Le Montet
36160 Pouligny-St-Martin
Cher
Tel: 54 30 23 55

A magnificent, rambling château, rebuilt in the early 19th century, with 10 hectares of wooded grounds. Outside is a fairy-tale of turrets and topiary; inside, a picture of baronial splendour. Guestrooms are delightful, sparsely furnished for elegant, uncluttered comfort, with lovely fabrics and open stone fireplaces. The host, whose family has owned the property since 1858, is friendly and hospitable. Children are welcomed.

Rooms: 1 double and 2 twin rooms, all with bathrooms.

Price: 300-350 Frs for two, including breakfast.

Meals: None (self-catering facilities.)

Open: Easter to 15 November.

An old flour mill, built in 1383, has been sympathetically restored to provide 'grand confort' guestrooms without sacrificing character. Rooms are beautifully decorated and furnished with originality; 'Country Living' devoted an eight-page feature to the property. The hosts care enormously about the overall atmosphere; dinner is served by candlelight in the conservatory overlooking the lake.

Rooms: 2 double rooms and 1 twin, all with bathrooms.

Price: 350-450 Frs for two, including breakfast.

Meals: Dinner 160 Frs, excluding wine (book ahead).

Open: 1 March – 31 October.

To get there: *From Châteauroux, D943 towards la Châtre. After Vic, D918 to St Chartier. Château is just before village.*

Map Ref No: 11

To get there: *From Châteauroux, N20 south towards Argenton-sur-Creuse. At Lothiers, N151 to 2.5km past St Gaultier; D46 towards Migné. Right to les Chezeaux; signposted.*

Map Ref No: 10

M & Mme Hubert PEUBRIER
Château de Saint Chartier
36400 Saint Chartier
Indre
Tel: 54 06 30 84

Renze RIJPSTRA
Le Moulin des Chezeaux
Rivarennes, 36800 St Gaultier
Indre
Tel: 54 47 01 84
Fax: 54 47 10 93

By the forest of Bourgueil, this imposing lodge was built in the style of the 17th century, using materials from the château next door. An unusual and refreshingly natural place, it reflects the family's intention to return to country simplicity. Delightful rooms and living-dining area, terracotta tiles and scrubbed rafters. A bosky sanctuary with amiable, engaging hosts.

Rooms: 2 twin rooms with own shower-rooms.

Price: 280-295 Frs for two, including breakfast.

Meals: None.

Open: All year (except 20 December-5 January).

Near the troglodyte cave-dwellings of the Loire this modern house, designed by the architect-husband, is an elegant combination of the old and the new, with a fantastic view over the surrounding vineyards and woodland. This is in fact a well-reputed wine-growing estate; Madame will happily guide you round. Guestrooms are luxurious with warm fabrics and pleasant furnishings. There is a very Provençal swimming-pool. Madame is welcoming, humorous and anxious to please.

Rooms: 1 double and 1 suite for 3-4 people in the main house; 1 double in poolside cabin; all with bathrooms.

Price: 420 Frs for two, including breakfast.

Meals: Not available.

Open: All year.

To get there: *From Tours, N152 towards Saumur. At St Patrice, D35 to Bourgueil. There, D749 to Gizeux; D15 to Continvoir. In village, left on D64; signposted.*

Map Ref No: 5

To get there: *From Chinon, D21 to Cravant-les-Coteaux. Continue towards Panzoult; the Domaine de Beauséjour is on left after 2kms.*

Map Ref No: 10

Michel & Claudette BODET
La Butte de l'Epine
37340 Continvoir
Indre-et-Loire
Tel: 47 96 62 25

Marie-Claude CHAUVEAU
Domaine de Beauséjour
37220 Panzoult
Indre-et-Loire
Tel: 47 58 64 64

Where better than the Loire valley to have a deliciously watery home on an island? A carefully restored mill-house and restful shady garden, private sandy beach and the added temptation of 300 paperbacks. Its English owners want guests to feel at home but not invaded. One reader has said that nothing was too much trouble for Sue, another that Andrew's cooking was superb – but then he is a French-trained chef. They feel their island home is not really suitable for young children.

Rooms: 4 double & 1 twin, all with own bathrooms.

Price: 280 Frs for two, including breakfast.

Meals: Dinner 110 Frs, including wine.

Open: All year except Christmas & January.

To get there: *From Loches, N143 towards Châteauroux; pass Perusson then left at sign to St Jean-St Germain; house is last in village on right.*

Map Ref No: 10

Sue HUTTON & Andrew PAGE
Le Moulin
St Jean-St Germain
37600 Loches, Indre-et-Loire
Tel: 47 94 70 12
Fax: 47 94 77 98

(231)

Items in this lovely 17th/18th-century manor, formerly a silkworm farm, have featured in 'Marie-Claire Maison'. The interior epitomises simple, period comfort in a mixture of refinement and informality, with discerning use of natural materials and authentic colours: slightly austere, certainly not over-smart. Guestrooms are spacious; the garden is rambling and romantic, overgrown with roses and old fruit trees. Madame is relaxed, informal and an old B&B hand.

Rooms: 2 double rooms and 1 twin, all with bathrooms.

Price: 360 Frs for two, including breakfast.

Meals: Not available.

Open: Easter – 31 October.

To get there: *From Chinon, D749 towards Bourgueil. Little road to Montour is first on left; house easily found behind imposing gates. (2km off D749, 8km from Chinon.)*

Map Ref No: 10

Mme Marion KREBS
Manoir de Montour
37420 Beaumont-en-Véron
Indre-et-Loire
Tel: 47 58 43 76

232

French modern history in a nutshell! Richelieu, ultimate upholder of absolutism, invented the concept of the New Town, built from scratch to a deliberate plan. This house was sold by the Cardinal to a member of his entourage, became a convent, was sold during the French Revolution and is now a timelessly refined town house. Your hostess is a charmer, her smallish guestrooms some of the loveliest we know, immaculate and stylish like Madame. House and owner are a study in French elegance.

Rooms: 2 double & 1 twin room, each with own bathroom; 1 double & 1 single sharing a bathroom.

Price: 250-340 Frs for two, including breakfast.

Meals: None (good choice in town).

Open: 1 February – 31 December.

Set above the Loire (there are bicycles for exploring riverside paths) but also very near the main road, this is a well-worn family château set in its own parkland. Guestrooms are large and simply furnished, comfortable and clean. Monsieur, with 30 years' experience, is proud of his delicious regional cuisine. Madame is the costumier for the annual spectacle at Amboise, 'A la cour du Roy François'.

Rooms: 1 double, 1 triple and 1 room for four, all with private bathrooms; 1 suite for 4 people, with private sitting-room & bathroom.

Price: 400 Frs for two, including breakfast.

Meals: Dinner 150 Frs, including wine.

Open: All year (advance bookings only in winter).

To get there: *From A10, Ste Maure exit, D760 to l'Ile-Bouchard and D757 to Richelieu. There, rue du Collège to junction of rue Jarry and place des Religieuses.*

Map Ref No: 10

To get there: *From Tours, D751 towards Chaumont-sur-Loire. Mosnes is about 8km after Amboise.*

Map Ref No: 5

Mme Marie LE PLATRE
Les Religieuses
24 place des Religieuses
37120 Richelieu
Indre-et-Loire
Tel: 47 58 10 42

233

M & Mme MARLIERE
Château de la Barre
Mosnes
37530 Amboise
Indre-et-Loire
Tel: 47 57 33 40

234

A grand château, built from the mid 17th century and once a hunting lodge, now with a relaxed and deliberately informal atmosphere. Big bedrooms, some with wonderful old tiled floors. Madame organises gastronomic tours of the Loire (with La Huberdière as the point of departure); try her delectable dinners, overlooking the valley from the austere grandeur of the dining-room. Unpretentious, authentic and very easy-going.

Rooms: 4 double and 2 triple rooms, all with bathrooms.

Price: 390-570 Frs for two, including breakfast.

Meals: Dinner 170 Frs, including wine (book ahead).

Open: All year.

To get there: *From Amboise, D5 to Nazelles-Négron. Left on D1. At Vaubrault-la-Bardouillère, right to Vaugadeland; signposted.*

Map Ref No: 5

Mme Béatrice SANDRIER
Château de la Huberdière
Vallée de Vaugadeland
37530 Nazelles, Indre-et-Loire
Tel: 47 57 39 32
Fax: 47 23 15 79

235

A working dairy farm from the mid 19th century, with a comfortable, homely atmosphere. Rooms are pleasantly decorated; some have beams and stone walls. The garden has tables and chairs for picnics, swings and table-tennis. Breakfast includes goat's cheese and saucisson from the village. In the evening, Madame offers wholesome country cooking. Simple, warm, caring and ideal for families.

Rooms: 1 double and 3 triple rooms, all with bathrooms.

Price: 220-250 Frs for two, including breakfast.

Meals: Dinner 90 Frs, including wine.

Open: All year (except Christmas).

To get there: *From A10, Ste Maure-de-Touraine exit onto D760, then D59 towards Ligueil. At Sepmes turn left; signposted.*

Map Ref No: 10

Anne-Marie & Joseph VERGNAUD
La Ferme les Berthiers
37800 Sepmes
Indre-et-Loire
Tel: 47 65 50 61

236

A small Italianate château beside the Loire river, named after Marie de Médicis who came to take the waters here. Much care has been lavished upon room decorations and furnishings; the rooms are charming and peaceful. In summer you may dine outside, in some style, on a terrace overlooking the grounds of the château.

Rooms: 6 double rooms, all with bathrooms.

Price: 350-500 Frs for two, including breakfast.

Meals: Dinner 200 Frs (book ahead).

Open: All year.

An elegant Renaissance-style country house in the lovely Cher valley, just outside the rather unpromising village of Noyers-sur-Cher. A good base for exploring the caves, abbeys and museums of this fascinating region. Dine in a quiet shady garden in summer, or by the open fire when the weather changes. The family keeps horses, so riding is easily arranged. Genial hosts who enjoy a drink and a joke ...

Rooms: 5 double rooms, 4 with own bathrooms.

Price: 250 Frs for two, including breakfast.

Meals: None (good restaurant nearby).

Open: All year.

To get there: *From Blois, D956 to Contres, then D675 towards St Aignan. At Noyers-sur-Cher, right just before intersection of D675 and N76; rue de la Mardelle is 1st street after railway line.*

Map Ref No: 5

To get there: *Macé is 3km north of Blois along N152 towards Orléans. 500m on right before church.*

Map Ref No: 5

Baronne Véronique BAXIN de
CAIX de REMBURES
La Villa Médicis, Macé
41000 St Denis-sur-Loire
Loir-et-Cher
Tel: 54 74 46 38
Fax: 54 78 20 27

Mme CHOQUET
La Mardelle
68 rue de la Mardelle
41140 Noyer
Loir-et-Cher
Tel: 54 71 70 55

The château perches on a hillside over the Loire valley and the village. There were once troglodyte dwellings on the site. The furnishings of each room were carefully chosen to re-create a particular style, from Louis XIII onwards. From the care lavished on both rooms and guests one knows that the owners are passionate about their house. Not suitable for children.

Rooms: 2 double and 2 twin rooms, with bathrooms.

Price: 370-550 Frs for two, including breakfast.

Meals: None.

Open: All year.

Madame Langlais has dubbed her pretty ivy-covered 18th-century farmhouse 'le petit trésor caché' – a little jewel in rather ordinary surroundings. Its shutters open onto a rambling 'jardin de curé' which leads down to a small river (the Cisse) and water meadows. The ambience is warm and homely; roaring fires and comfortable furnishings. Rooms are beautifully decorated in a country style. A charming place.

Rooms: 3 double and 2 twin rooms, all with bathrooms.

Price: 330 Frs for two, including breakfast.

Meals: None.

Open: All year.

To get there: *From Vendôme, D917 through Montoire-sur-le-Loir to Troo. Château is signposted in the village.*

Map Ref No: 5

To get there: *From Blois, N152 towards Tours. At Chouzy-sur-Cisse, D58 to Onzain; house is 3km beyond village centre.*

Map Ref No: 5

Messieurs CLAYS et VENON
Château de la Voûte
41800 Troo
Loir-et-Cher
Tel: 54 72 52 52

Martine LANGLAIS
46 rue de Meuves
41150 Onzain
Loir-et-Cher
Tel: 54 20 78 82
Fax: 54 20 78 82

Behind tall white gates, this 18th-century house stands in 7 acres of wooded parkland that effectively cut out all sight of the power station. It is ideally placed for Chambord and the hunting and walking country of Sologne. The children of this welcoming family home will greet yours, take them riding on their ponies, fishing in the pond or play ping-pong with them. Guests have their own living-room with books. Dinner may feature game as well as vegetables from the Libauts' kitchen garden.

Rooms: 3 triple rooms with own bathrooms.

Price: 250 Frs for two, including breakfast.

Meals: Dinner 80 Frs, including wine (on reservation only).

Open: All year.

To get there: *From Orléans, D951 towards Blois. On entering St Laurent, follow signs to 'Chambres d'Hôtes'.*

Map Ref No: 5

Catherine & Maurice LIBEAUT
L'Ormoie
26 rue de l'Ormoie
41220 St Laurent-Nouan
Loir-et-Cher
Tel: 54 87 24 72

A traditional and charmingly dilapidated country farmhouse. The cosy bedrooms have quilts and typical country furnishings. The old-fashioned bathroom has a big bathtub. The manifestly kind and welcoming hosts keep free-range chickens and their vegetable patch provides the ingredients for their delicious soups. Wicker chairs under the fruit trees. Bikes for rent. Wonderful value.

Rooms: 5 double rooms; shared bathroom.

Price: 160 Frs for two, including breakfast.

Meals: Dinner 70 Frs, including wine (book ahead).

Open: All year, except Christmas to New Year.

To get there: *From Châteauneuf-sur-Loire, N60 to Bellegarde. There, D44 towards Lorris. 1km beyond Beauchamps-sur-Huillard, right following signs.*

Map Ref No: 6

Mme DHUIT
Le Bangin
Beauchamps-sur-Huillard
45270 Chatenoy
Loiret
Tel: 38 26 10 17

This vast estate by the Loire includes a private hunting reserve. Trees and garden surround the manor-house. The interior is carefully decorated and the rooms have lovely old furnishings. Breakfast in the salon (games and hi-fi) or on the flowered terrace. The young hosts – he is a vet and she looks after the house and their two small children – make it feel friendly despite the grand appearance. They themselves live in another house just nearby. Children welcome.

Rooms: 3 double rooms, all with own shower or bath & wc..

Price: 230-250 Frs for two, including breakfast.

Meals: Not available.

Open: All year.

To get there: *From A6, Dordives exit onto N7 to Briare then D952 towards Gien. Signposted by the nurseries, midway between Briare and Gien.*

Map Ref No: 6

Mme Bénédicte FRANÇOIS
Domaine de la Thiau
45250 Briare
Loiret
Tel: 38 38 20 92

243

You will soon warm to Madame Hatte's gentle manner. She has two very different rooms. One is in her own modern house; the other, which she affectionately refers to as 'la Maison des poupées' (the dolls' house) is where Madame Hatte's daughter lives and has a little walled garden. The furnishings are in a time-warp, in the 60's and 70's and the scale is miniature throughout.

Rooms: 2 double rooms, each with own bathroom.

Price: 250 Frs for two, including breakfast.

Meals: Not available.

Open: All year.

To get there: *From Sully-sur-Loire, D59 south-west to Isdes. In village take Route de Clémont; signposted.*

Map Ref No: 6

Mme Renée HATTE
30 route de Clémont
45620 Isdes
Loiret
Tel:

244

The canal de Briare flows past this attractive old village house, in which your youthful hosts take great pride. We liked the loft-like bedroom with its exposed beams. In the garden there's a small self-contained cottage, with a fireplace in the kitchen. An ideal place for a weekend; there's even the village bar next door! Don't miss the great 19th-century canal bridge over the Loire in Briare itself, a stupendous and handsome alliance of engineering and nature.

Rooms: 2 double rooms with own bathrooms and 1 single room.

Price: 250 Frs for two, including breakfast.

Meals: Dinner 110 Frs, including wine.

Open: All year.

To get there: *From Sancerre, D955 towards Cosne-sur-Loire. At les Fouchards (don't cross into Cosne), D751 to Léré where it becomes D951. Continue to Châtillon-sur-Loire.*

Map Ref No: 6

M et Mme Gilbert LEFRANC
La Giloutière
13 rue du Port
45360 Châtillon-sur-Loire
Loiret
Tel: 38 31 10 61

Five children enliven this large family house. Madame, natural and kind, likes guests to feel at home while still giving them privacy. They have their own entrance, dining-room and sitting-room. A 19th-century dressing table complements Laura Ashley paper and exposed timbers in the bedroom. Franglais breakfasts with eggs and bacon and croissants! More traditional dinners. Garden. Tennis court.

Rooms: 1 triple room with adjoining bathroom in main house; 1 double and 1 twin with shared bathroom in separate cottage.

Price: 320 Frs for two, including breakfast

Meals: Dinner 85-100 Frs, excluding wine.

Open: 1 March – 30 November

To get there: *In Gien follow directions for Gien Nord, then D44 towards Lorris. After sharp bend, take small left turning; property is just past a tennis court.*

Map Ref No: 6

Mme Annie LE LAY
Sainte Barbe
Route de Lorris
Nevoy
45500 Gien, Loiret
Tel: 38 67 59 53

The Nicourts are restoring their 200-year-old family house and extensive gardens. The bedrooms, if rather small, are cosy and well decorated with discreet florals. The sombre, rustic sitting-room comes into its own in winter. Your warm-hearted hosts are keen on hunting; upon request, guests can join the family in simple traditional dinners, of which game is often the highlight.

Rooms: 2 double rooms and 1 twin room, each with own bathroom.

Price: 220 Frs for two, including breakfast.

Meals: Dinner 80 Frs, excluding wine.

Open: All year.

To get there: *From Orléans, N60-E60 to Châteauneuf-sur-Loire; then D11 to Vannes-sur-Cosson. House on left as you enter village.*

Map Ref No: 6

M et Mme Aleth & Gérard
NICOURT
6 rue de la Croix Madeleine
45510 Vannes-sur-Cosson
Loiret
Tel: 38 58 15 43

247

A good place for families: there are ponies to ride, a basketball hoop, a slide and swings and a well-kept flower garden. Photo's fail to do justice to the handsome house. The comfortable ground-floor rooms are elegantly simple, with old farmhouse furniture and good beds. If asked, the friendly owners will provide cooked breakfast and farmhouse dinners.

Rooms: 3 double rooms with shared bathrooms and 1 large room for 2-4 people, with own bathroom.

Price: 220-310 Frs for two, including breakfast.

Meals: Dinner 80 Frs (book ahead).

Open: All year.

To get there: *From Gien, D940 towards Bourges; 6km along at top of hill – signposted.*

Map Ref No: 6

Jean-Luc RAFFIN
Ferme de Gault
45720 Coullons
Loiret
Tel: 38 67 59 77

248

THE LOIRE VALLEY

Surrounded by vineyards, sunflower, barley and wheat fields, the ivy-clad farmhouse also has a windmill. Guests are warmly greeted with a glass of home-made wine. Rooms have natural, muted tones, with plenty of interesting information on the area. Traditional, copious breakfasts (cooked, upon request). If staying in late September do not miss the Artichoke Fair in Coutures.

Rooms: 2 double rooms with shared bathroom.

Price: 180 Frs for two, including breakfast.

Meals: None.

Open: 1 February to 31 October.

This handsome Directory-period manor-house has been done up with an emphasis on traditional comfort. Guestrooms are big and bright with luxurious new bathrooms. The atmosphere is formal, though children are welcomed. There is a large garden stretching down to the banks of the Mayenne, a tributary of the Loire, where there are boats for hire. Easy access to tennis, horse-riding, boules, golf and swimming.

Rooms: 2 double, 1 twin room, each with own bathroom.

Price: 340 Frs for two, including breakfast.

Meals: Not available.

Open: Easter to 31 October.

To get there: *From Saumur, D751 to Coutures, through Gennes. 2km after Coutures, left on rue des Allends, following signs to Chambres d'Hôtes.*

Map Ref No: 5

Marcel & Thérèse ARNAULT
Fredelin
Coutures
49320 Brissac
Maine-et-Loire
Tel: 41 91 21 26

To get there: *From Angers, N162 towards Lion d'Angers. At Grieul (20km) right on D291 to Grez-Neuville. At church, rue de l'Ecluse towards river.*

Map Ref No: 4

Jacqueline & Auguste BAHUAUD
La Croix d'Etain
2 rue de l'Ecluse
49220 Grez-Neuville
Maine-et-Loire
Tel: 41 95 68 49

Corn and vibrant sunflower fields surround this impressive family home set in its own grounds on the banks of the Loir. Remains of a chapel, dovecote and watermill are reminders of more self-sufficient times. Friendly, approachable hosts make all ages feel welcome. Rooms, traditional style, decorated in natural colours, contain lovely antiques. Traditional French dishes enlivened by fresh vegetables from Madame's 'potager'.

Rooms: 2 double rooms, each with own bathroom.

Price: 330 Frs for two (60 Frs for children).

Meals: Dinner 110 Frs, including wine.

Open: Easter to 31 October.

To get there: *From Angers, N23 north. At Seiches-sur-Loir, D74 to Châteauneuf/Sarthe. Chateau is on right as you leave the village.*

Map Ref No: 5

Jacques & Marie BAILLIOU
Château de Montreuil
49140 Montreuil-sur-Loir
Maine-et-Loire
Tel: 41 76 21 03

251

A manor-house only 5 minutes from the centre of Saumur, yet peaceful with a lovely large garden. Restored by a young, energetic couple with four children it is attractively decorated and furnished. The hosts run a wholefood shop in town – Madame is a naturopath. Delicious organic produce served for breakfast, eaten in the large family kitchen. An ideal base for visiting the surrounding area.

Rooms: 2 self-contained suites (with bathrooms) for 2-3 people.

Price: 200-350 Frs for two, including breakfast.

Meals: None (wide choice in Saumur).

Open: All year.

To get there: *From Saumur centre, N147 towards Angers. Cross Loire and railway, left on Ave des Maraichers towards St Lambert-des-Levées. House on right-hand corner of junction with rue Grange Couronne (300m from Saumur station).*

Map Ref No: 10

Catherine & Emmanuel BASTID
La Bouère Salée
Rue Grange Couronne
St Lambert-des-Levées
49400 Saumur, Maine-et-Loire
Tel: 41 67 38 85

252

On the banks of the winding Thouet stands this carefully modernised 500-year-old watermill. Tranquil views for those who eat breakfast on the sunny terrace or under the willow tree. Traditional rooms in the mill itself. Walk by the river or ride a horse to free wine-tastings at local cellars with your hosts (they will keep wines you buy for collection on your way back). Excellent local wines with dinner in the on-site restaurant. It may seem rather like an hotel to some.

Rooms: 7 double rooms and 2 suites (2-4 people) all with bathrooms.

Price: 265-500 Frs for two, including breakfast.

Meals: Dinner 90-205 Frs (4 menus), excluding wine.

Open: All year, except February.

Overhanging trees shade the grassy approach to this rambling 19th-century château set in 4 hectares of mature gardens (with Judas trees that flower prolifically in spring). Chaises-longues encourage guests to picnic in the evenings. Bedrooms are elegantly sparse but comfortable, furnished with antiques; the suite would be ideal for a family. Madame Calot is warm and informal. Children are welcome.

Rooms: 1 double, 1 triple & 1 suite for 5, all with bathrooms.

Price: 290-420 Frs for two, including breakfast.

Meals: Not available.

Open: All year.

To get there: *From Montreuil-Bellay, D938 towards Thouars. After about 4km, right on D158 to Passais. Take D178 towards Le Puy Notre Dame; blue and yellow signs on the left.*

Map Ref No: 10

To get there: *From Saumur, N147 towards Longué. At la Ronde, D767 towards Vernantes; left on D129 towards Neuillé. 1km before Neuillé take Fontaine Suzon road; signposted.*

Map Ref No: 5

Anny et Jean BERGEROLLE
Le Moulin du Couché
49260 Le-Puy-Notre-Dame
Maine-et-Loire
Tel: 41 38 87 11
Fax: 41 38 86 99

Mme Monique CALOT
Château du Goupillon
49680 Neuillé
Maine-et-Loire
Tel: 41 52 51 89

You'll feel quickly at home in this 200-year-old farmhouse. The young owners are exceptionally friendly, as are their dogs (!). Remarkable food, vegetarians catered for and the choice of eating it in a lovely dining-room or on a terrace by the pool. A reader writes: "We received the most wonderful welcome with a cool drink beside the pool; the house is immaculate and imaginatively furnished; the table d'hôte superb; the setting... too beautiful for words". Arrive 4pm onwards.

Rooms: 2 double rooms and 2 twin rooms, all with bathrooms.

Price: 220 Frs for two, including breakfast.

Meals: Dinner 100 Frs, excluding wine.

Open: 15 April to 31 October.

Pine, chestnut and walnut trees line the lane up to this grain-growing farm where three families – father and two sons – work their 37 hectares of fertile land on the edge of the Loire valley. Jean-Claude and Martine are real country folk and like direct, simple contact with their guests. They have given each guestroom, in a wing of their superb old farmhouse, a personal touch. This is rural hospitality at its best; it is a privilege to stay among people so rooted in the land.

Rooms: 2 double, 1 twin room, all with own shower, sharing wc.

Price: 200 Frs for two, including breakfast.

Meals: None (restaurants 3 or 7km).

Open: All year.

To get there: *From Angers, N162 towards Laval. At Le Lion-d'Angers, D770 towards Candé. Left after 1.5km; signposted.*

Map Ref No: 4

To get there: *From Angers, N260 towards Cholet, then D748 towards Poitiers. After Brissac, D761 towards Poitiers. Continue for 2km; house signposted on left, at end of avenue of chestnut trees.*

Map Ref No: 5

M & Mme Patrick CARCAILLET
Le Petit Carqueron
49220 Le Lion d'Angers
Maine-et-Loire
Tel: 41 95 62 65

Jean-Claude COLIBET
La Pichonnière
49320 Charcé
Maine-et-Loire
Tel: 41 91 29 37 (mealtimes)

This mediaeval abbey farm lies on the pilgrim route to Spain. The monks' woods and fishponds still remain as does the 13th-century tithe barn and the farm is almost self-sufficient. Classical music accompanies dinner served on silver and English china. The father cooks and the daughter – elegant, charming and efficient – welcomes. The rustic-style bedrooms are large and sumptuous. Perhaps more a private hotel than Chambres d'Hôtes. What do you think?

Rooms: 2 double rooms, 4 twin rooms, 1 triple room, 3 single rooms and 1 family suite, all with bathrooms. (2 rooms on ground floor.)

Price: 365 Frs for two, including breakfast.

Meals: Dinner 135 Frs, excluding wine.

Open: All year, except January.

To get there: *From Saumur, D947 to Montsoreau; then D147 towards Loudun. About 2km after Montsoreau, right to 'Mestré'.*

Map Ref No: 10

Rosine & Dominique DAUGE
Le Domaine de Mestré
49590 Fontevraud-l'Abbaye
Maine-et-Loire
Tel: 41 51 72 32
Fax: 41 51 71 90

257

This noble château, in the family for seven generations, stands in peaceful farmland and woodland. Fine views from comfortable guestrooms. Book the one with 4-poster bed and private terrace. Guests can relax in their own day-room; children kept amused by many outdoor toys. Once a Benedictine Abbey, this is an exciting, almost eccentric place. One loo for three bedrooms is a small price to pay for an experience like this. (We'd welcome reports on the breakfasts.)

Rooms: 3 double rooms, each with own shower or bath, sharing wc.

Price: 260-280 Frs for two, including breakfast.

Meals: None.

Open: 1 April to 31 October.

To get there: *From Ancenis, N23 towards Angers. At Varades, D752 through St Florent-le-Vieil towards Beaupréau. Signposted from La Boutouchère.*

Map Ref No: 4

Mme de BONFILS
Le Château de Montmoutiers
La Boutouchère
49410 St Florent-le-Vieil
Maine-et-Loire
Tel: 41 72 51 53

258

A converted farm building, surrounded by meadow and orchard, in the grounds of the Château du Teilleul. The room is charmingly decorated, beamed with a sloping roof, and has views of the château's gardens and lake. The young hosts are relaxed and friendly and obviously enjoy having guests in their splendid home. Breakfast can be served in your room.

Rooms: 1 twin room with own bathroom.

Price: 210 Frs for two, including breakfast.

Meals: Dinner 100 Frs, including wine.

Open: All year.

To get there: *Take D923 from St. Sauveur towards Segré. Driveway is on right, 200m after village.*

Map Ref No: 4

M & Mme de VITTON
Le Domaine du Teilleul
49500 St Sauveur-de-Flée
Maine-et-Loire
Tel: 41 61 38 84

Set in an orchard producing apples, pears, plums and cherries (so lots of homemade jams), a long, low, ivy-covered old house greets you. The magnificent Loire is just 7km away, you can visit architectural wonders such as troglodyte dwellings and aristocratic châteaux, or just idle in a deck chair in Madame's leafy garden. Simple, uncluttered rooms and a warm, kindly hostess complete the picture.

Rooms: 3 double rooms with bathrooms.

Price: 240 Frs for two, including breakfast.

Meals: Dinner 80 Frs, including wine.

Open: All year.

To get there: *From Angers, N761 towards Brissac and Doué. At les Alleuds, left onto D90 towards Chemellier. After 3km, hamlet on left.*

Map Ref No: 5

Eliette EDON
La Poirière
49320 Maunit-Chemellier
Maine-et-Loire
Tel: 41 45 59 50

The château, partly in bad repair but endearingly so, has been in the family since 1757. Monsieur is quiet; Madame is South American; both are superb hosts. The guestrooms have an engaging air of faded grandeur. The suite (summer only) has white walls and Mexican rugs. Dinner at a long table, with wooden settles, fireplace and copper pans on the walls. River Loir 2km. Peace and real atmosphere and your hosts go out of their way to give you a good time. A wonderful place.

Rooms: 2 double rooms, each with own bathroom; 1 double room with shared bathroom; 1 family suite.

Price: 400-500 Frs for two, including breakfast.

Meals: Dinner 120 Frs, excluding wine.

Open: All year.

This modern village house, minutes away from rolling hills and farmland, has dormer windows, an attractive garden and a mass of flowers providing plenty of colour. Rooms, centrally-heated, are comfortable – the sparkling clean bathroom is shared by guests. Madame, a genial host, is also an excellent cook and uses home-grown ingredients.

Rooms: 2 double rooms with shared bathroom.

Price: 170 Frs for two, including breakfast.

Meals: Dinner 75 Frs, including wine.

Open: All year.

To get there: *From Paris, A11, Durtal exit then D859 towards Châteauneuf for 2km, then D68 to Baracé.*

Map Ref No: 5

To get there: *From Ancenis, 7km SE on D763 then D751 towards St Florent-le-Vieil. At Bouzillé, first right after church; signposted.*

Map Ref No: 4

Michel & Lucia FRANÇOIS
Château de la Motte
49430 Baracé
Maine-et-Loire
Tel: 41 76 93 75

Mme Françoise GAUDIN
14 rue des Aires
49530 Bouzillé
Maine-et-Loire
Tel: 40 98 13 08

This 300-year-old mansion with a delightful courtyard is located centrally in a small town full of historical interest. Lovingly restored, spacious rooms with many antiques restored by Monsieur. The hosts are friendly and welcoming; Madame enjoys practising her English. Delicious breakfasts, beautifully presented, served in owners' dining-room (cooked breakfast on request). Restaurants nearby,

Rooms: 3 double rooms, all with bathrooms; 1 ground floor double with kitchenette & bathroom.

Price: 270 Frs for two, including breakfast.

Meals: None (self-catering).

Open: 1 March to 31 October.

This large 16th-century house stands close to the Mayenne river at the outskirts of Montreuil-Juigné. All the rooms – large and with their own entrances – have fine views. The dining-room is attractive with a huge open stone hearth. Guests can expect to be warmly greeted by their hosts who also welcome children.

Rooms: 2 double rooms, 1 twin room and 1 family room for three-four, all with bathrooms.

Price: 210 Frs for two, including breakfast.

Meals: None (in village).

Open: All year.

To get there: *From Saumur, D147 towards Poitiers. In Montreuil-Bellay, Place des Augustins is parallel to, and on the right of, Rue Nationale.*

Map Ref No: 10

To get there: *From Angers, N162 towards le Lion d'Angers. Take D768 towards Montreuil centre. Right onto Avenue Europe; left at next roundabout; signposted..*

Map Ref No: 4

M & Mme Jacques GUEZENEC
Demeure des Petits Augustins
Place des Augustins
49260 Montreuil Bellay
Maine-et-Loire
Tel: 41 52 33 88

263

Jean-Louis & Suzanne HUEZ
Le Plateau
Rue Espéranto
49460 Montreuil-Juigné
Maine-et-Loire
Tel: 41 42 32 35

264

There's a piano in the family sitting-room and the attractive guestrooms have exposed original beams and pretty wallpapers. Meals are served 'en famille' at a pine table in the homely kitchen (cooked breakfasts available). Food is based on produce from the garden and the small farm. Having chosen to leave urban England, the hosts now keep sheep, poultry and pigs. Children are welcome.

Rooms: 1 triple, 1 twin, 1 single room, with hand-basins; shared bathroom.

Price: 190 Frs for two, including breakfast.

Meals: Dinner 70 Frs, including wine.

Open: All year.

To get there: *From La Flèche, D308/D938 towards Baugé. There, follow sign for Tours and Saumur; right on D61 to Vieil Baugé. Signposted after 2km.*

Map Ref No: 5

John & Vanessa KITCHEN
La Chalopinière
49150 Le Vieil Baugé
Maine-et-Loire
Tel: 41 89 04 38

265

The old farmhouse burnt down a while ago: this is a modern house with swings and a lake at the bottom of the garden, wonderful for children. Annick is an engaging woman, greeting guests like old friends, and you can expect to meet at least a few of her 13 grandchildren. Rooms are modestly comfortable, with old furniture. Vaulted sitting area just off the kitchen. Spectacular 'Son-et-Lumière' at nearby Château du Lude (summer).

Rooms: 1 double room and 1 twin room; shared bathroom.

Price: 160 Frs for two, including breakfast.

Meals: Dinner 60 Frs, including wine.

Open: All year.

To get there: *From A11, Seiches exit onto D766 to Baugé and D817 towards Le Lude. After Parnay, D138 to Genneteil; house 2km before village.*

Map Ref No: 5

Annick LARUE
La Loge
49490 Genneteil
Maine-et-Loire
Tel: 41 82 10 07

266

Yet another magnificent château, in its own grounds on the edge of a village. The river is only a three-minute walk away and there are river-views from the bedrooms. The rooms are huge and traditional, full of 'château furniture' (which you may find full of 20th-century clothes). The dining-room is beautifully furnished in period style, with lots of antiques. Breakfast is served on the terrace in the summer. Altogether a splendid, much-lived-in place.

Rooms: 2 double rooms and 1 suite for 2, all with bathrooms.

Price: 300-400 Frs for two, including breakfast.

Meals: None.

Open: All year.

In the centre of the village, this is a substantial ivy-clad house. Rooms are modern in style, centrally heated and sparkling clean. Excellent access for anyone physically disabled. Traditional breakfast served in the homely kitchen. Madame, grandmother of eight, loves children – there are dolls waiting to be played with.

Rooms: 1 room with 1 double & 2 single beds and own bathroom.

Price: 150 Frs for two, including breakfast – 50 Frs supplement for extra bed.

Meals: Not available.

Open: All year.

To get there: *From la Flèche, N23 towards Angers. At Durtal, left towards Gouis; signposted.*

Map Ref No: 5

To get there: *From Nantes, N23 to Ancenis; D763 to Liré, then D751 towards St Florent-le-Vieil. House in centre of Bouzillé.*

Map Ref No: 4

Mme Monique LINOSSIER
Château de Gouis
Grande Rue
49430 Durtal
Maine-et-Loire
Tel: 41 76 03 40

Mme MORINIERE
2 rue de l'Hermitage
49530 Bouzillé
Maine-et-Loire
Tel: 40 98 17 72

O'Neill is a fine Irish name for a very French family. Madame is an interior decorator and a gifted cook and often mingles at dinner time. The dining-room has elaborate panelling and old paintings. The bedrooms, furnished with period pieces, writing-tables and canopies, have matching bathrooms. Things to do? Fishing on the private lake; Gregorian chant at Solesmes Abbey (a magical experience); son-et-lumière at Le Lude (one of the best), troglodytes all around. Main road rather close by.

Rooms: 2 double rooms & 2 suites, all with bathrooms.

Price: 350 Frs for two, including breakfast.

Meals: Dinner 120 Frs, including wine.

Open: 1st March – 31st October.

This delightfully easy-going young couple runs a market garden from their 'maison bourgeoise'. Guests settle in easily, enjoying views of the river or fruit orchards from comfortable, attractive rooms full of old, mellow furniture. Simple French home cooking, using delicious local produce. Traditional breakfasts include homemade juice, jams and honey. Plenty of distractions for children.

Rooms: 2 double and 2 twin, each with own bathroom.

Price: 250-300 Frs for two, including breakfast. Reduction for 3 nights or more.

Meals: Dinner 105 Frs, including wine.

Open: All year.

To get there: *From Angers, N23 towards Durtal and la Flèche; signposted.*

Map Ref No: 5

To get there: *From Angers, D952 to Saumur. House is on left (signposted) as you enter St Mathurin-sur-Loire.*

Map Ref No: 5

Mme Marie O'NEILL
Préfontaine
49430 Lézigné
Maine-et-Loire
Tel: 41 76 97 71

269

M et Mme Claudine & Christian PINIER
Verger de la Bouquetterie
118 rue du Roi René
49250 St Mathurin-sur-Loire
Maine-et-Loire
Tel: 41 57 02 00
Fax: 41 57 31 90

270

Set atop a steep rise, with gardens sloping down to the river, this manor-house is built in the local stone ('tuffeau') which was used for St Paul's in London. The huge guestrooms overlook the Loire and are furnished with a mix of old and new, with rugs strewn over bare floorboards. One has a marble fireplace. No sitting-room.

Rooms: 1 suite for 3-4 people, with own bathroom.

Price: 350 Frs for two, 450 Frs for three and 550 Frs for four, including breakfast.

Meals: None.

Open: Easter to 31 October.

Built in 1830, the Logis du Ray has always been connected with horses. The Lefebvres came here to live and play and work with them. Their rooms are top of the B&B league, the house is all elegance and light touch; you may feel inspired to dress for dinner among the beautiful furniture, a reminder of cabinet-makers and antique-collecters in the family past. The welcome is warm, the food excellent and Monsieur's horse-and-trap drive with well-stocked picnic hamper very tempting.

Rooms: 2 double & 1 triple rooms, all with own shower and wc.

Price: 300-350 Frs for two, including breakfast.

Meals: Dinner 150 Frs, including aperitif, wine, coffee, digestif. Fantastic picnics also available.

Open: All year.

To get there: *From Saumur, D751 towards Gennes. House signposted 300m before Cunault – look for large cedar in front.*

Map Ref No: 5

To get there: *From Angers, D107 and D191 to Feneu. There, D768 towards Sablé-sur-Sarthe. St Denis-d'Anjou is 28km from Feneu.*

Map Ref No: 5

François & Fanny TONNELIER
22 rue Beauregard
Cunault
49350 Chênehutte-les-Tuffeaux
Maine-et-Loire
Tel: 41 67 92 93

271

Martine & Jacques LEFEBVRE
Le Logis Du Ray
53290 St Denis-d'Anjou
Mayenne
Tel: 43 70 64 10
Fax: 43 70 65 53

272

Enjoy real quiet in a green river-run, squirrel-scampered garden then dine with your hosts, sharing delicious food and wide-ranging conversation about their time as foreign correspondents. They have now settled here as free-lance translators and converters of old French houses. The guestrooms are fine rooms with beams, bathrooms, sitting-room with open fireplace and masses of atmosphere, though no hint of any priestly ghosts lurking in this old presbytery.

Rooms: 2 double rooms with own bathrooms.

Price: 230-260 Frs for two, including breakfast.

Meals: Dinner 65 Frs, including wine (book ahead).

Open: All year.

To get there: *On N12 from Mayenne towards Alençon; after 5km, D34 to Montreuil-Poulay. In village, left on D160; house is 700m along.*

Map Ref No: 5

Denis & Patricia LEGRAS-WOOD
Le Vieux Presbytère
53640 Montreuil-Poulay
Mayenne
Tel: 43 00 86 32
Fax: 43 00 81 42

273

"Old stones" indeed! as they say in French. A 15th-century manor with staircase tower – you will climb it if you have the upstairs bedroom – bread-oven and a fine dining-room where breakfast is served to the ringing of the church bells.
This is the Nays' family home, carefully restored and really lived in (they have two small sons). Their enthusiasm is catching, the countryside delectable and the tiny village does offer its own cheap and cheerful restaurant (there is a better one 3km away).

Rooms: 1 double room, 1 triple room, both with own bathrooms.

Price: 180 Frs for two, including breakfast.

Meals: Not available.

Open: All year.

To get there: *From Laval, N157 towards Le Mans. At Soulgé-sur-Ouette, D20 left to Evron then D7 towards Mayenne. In Mézangers, signposted.*

Map Ref No: 5

Léopold & Marie-Thérèse NAY
Le Cruchet
53600 Mézangers
Mayenne
Tel: 43 90 65 55

274

All of 'deep France' is here: rugged Brittany and lush Mayenne meet at Pontmain where the Virgin appeared in 1871; the pilgrimage trade still flourishes. Madame willingly provides information on the hidden delights of the area. The Pinots belong to a local produce group and there is a shop with honey, cheeses, wools, etc. Mixed-style guestrooms, in a separate building, have a kitchenette, a sitting-room and flowers everywhere. This is indeed good value.

Rooms: 2 double, 1 twin & 2 triple rooms, all with own shower & wc.

Price: 190 Frs for two, including breakfast.

Meals: None (self-catering).

Open: All year.

To get there: *From Fougères, D806/D33 towards Gorron. At La Tannière, D31 to St Mars. Through village; after 1km, signs on left.*

Map Ref No: 4

Jeannyvonne PINOT
"Aussé"
53220 St Mars-sur-Futaie
Mayenne
Tel: 43 05 01 55

For 500 years this fine old manor has stood in a loop of the Vègre. Its present owner has restored it with flair and a sense of history. Two rooms are reached by a spiral stone staircase; the tone of subdued elegance suggests that interior design and all things cultural are Monsieur's home ground. He greets you affably, talks fascinatingly about the mediaeval history of the area (don't miss Gregorian chant at Solesmes Abbey) and serves a banquet – and music – at breakfast.

Rooms: 1 double room, 1 twin room, 1 suite, all with own bathrooms.

Price: 420 Frs for two, including breakfast.

Meals: Dinner 120 Frs, including wine.

Open: Beginning April to 5th September.

To get there: *From Sablé-sur-Sarthe, D22 to Solesmes; go through Asnières. First right after village then keep going left.*

Map Ref No: 5

Jean ANNERON
Manoir des Claies
72430 Asnières-sur-Vègre
Sarthe
Tel: 43 92 40 50

Have you dreamed of owning a French château? Nothing overwhelming, just something lovely like this. It is surrounded by farmland and woods, is on the edge of a village with good shops, and has a big garden and a private drive. The interior is gratifyingly untidy in corners but just what one would expect from a proper family home, and there is much un-selfconscious good taste about. Big windows and satisfying views.

Rooms: 2 suites, with bathrooms, for 4-6 people.

Price: 280 Frs for two, including breakfast.

Meals: Dinner 85 Frs, including wine.

Open: All year except 16-29 July.

Expertly restored by its 'interior architect' owner, this lovely, pale-stone manor, dating from the 17th century, now provides guests with privacy and rural tranquility. Rooms are delightfully simple, light and spacious, with independent kitchen and living areas. A peaceful country retreat with good food and a super-efficient, friendly hostess.

Rooms: 1 suite for 3-4 people, with bathroom; 1 flat for 3-4 people, with kitchen and bathroom.

Price: 350-450 Frs for two, including breakfast.

Meals: Not available.

Open: All year, except 1st week in January and all February.

To get there: *From Le Mans, N23 towards La Flèche. At Cerans-Foulletourte, D31 to Oizé; left onto D32; signposted on right.*

Map Ref No: 5

To get there: *From Le Mans, D304 towards Le Grand-Lucé. At Parigné-L'Evêque, D90 towards Volnay. About 1km before Volnay, turn right; signposted.*

Map Ref No: 5

M & Mme David DUBOIS
Château de Montaupin
72330 Oizé
Sarthe
Tel: 43 87 81 70

Mme Anne EVENO-SOURNIA
Le Domaine du Grand Gruet
Route de Challes
72440 Volnay
Sarthe
Tel: 43 35 68 65

A 14th-century farmhouse 2km from the village, in the heart of the countryside. The owners are artists and the exhilarating profusion of colours shows this. The doors and furniture are painted, as are the bathrooms; delightful! Each room, cosy rather than 'spacious', has its own terraced area with tables and chairs; one has a canopied bed. Colourful and/or artistic visitors will love it. (Art classes available.)

Rooms: 3 double rooms with bathrooms.

Price: 320 Frs for two, including breakfast.

Meals: None.

Open: All year.

To get there: From la Flèche, N23 towards Le Mans. At Clermont-Créans, D13 towards Mareil-sur-Loir. The farm is 2km from village; signposted.

Map Ref No: 5

Josy HERE
Ferme de Semur
72200 Mareil-sur-Loir
Sarthe
Tel: 43 45 44 24

Just about everything that appears on Christine's table is home-produced and dinner can last several hours. This is a wonderful address for lovers of French family cooking. The Langlais are a lively, active couple with a large farm to run (70ha) and three children to care for but they still find time to hand-paint lampshades, take visitors to watch the milking or search for freshly-laid eggs. For landscape lovers the lovely but little-known Sarthe deserves every minute you can give it.

Rooms: 2 double, 1 twin, 1 triple room plus 1 suite in "La Petite Maison", all with own shower & wc.

Price: 220-250 Frs for two, including breakfast.

Meals: Dinner with family 90 Frs, including wine.

Open: All year.

To get there: *From Alençon south on N138. After 4km, left onto D55, through Champfleur towards Bourg-le-Roi; farm signposted 1km after Champfleur.*

Map Ref No: 5

Denis & Christine LANGLAIS
Garencière
72610 Champfleur
Sarthe
Tel: 33 31 75 84

Set back from the town square this old townhouse from the 1850s is remarkably quiet at the back, noisier in the front. One of the rooms has fine views over the oldest part of town. The feel inside is of freshness and cleanliness, with well co-ordinated colour scheme and a near-professional touch. Our inspector wrote: "squeaky clean, bright and hospitable." Madame is English, most helpful and friendly and runs cycling tours.

Rooms: 1 double room with shower & wc; 1 double room with wash-basin & shared bathroom; 2 family rooms with own bathrooms.

Price: 255-275 Frs for two, including breakfast.

Meals: None (good eating places very near).

Open: From 1 March to 30 September.

To get there: *From Le Mans, N138 towards Tours. Situated in town centre, set back from town square.*

Map Ref No: 5

Mme LE GOFF
22 rue de l'Hôtel de Ville
72500 Château-du-Loir
Sarthe
Tel: 43 44 03 38

It looks like a fairy-tale cottage: mellow old stone, white shutters, green ivy all over, a large leafy garden and a 12th-century castle round the corner. And the lovely Sarthe countryside, its gentle hills, bosky woods, streams and châteaux, simply crying out to be discovered and appreciated. A quiet welcoming house where guests can be as independent as they like (separate entrance).

Rooms: One 3-room suite for 5 with bathroom.

Price: 240 Frs for two, including breakfast.

Meals: Dinner 70 Frs, excluding wine.

Open: April – October.

To get there: *From Le Mans, N138 towards Tours. After Dissay/Courcillon, left onto small road on the bend and follow signs to "Chambres d'Hôtes".*

Map Ref No: 5

Mme Michèle LETANNEUX
La Châtaigneraie
72500 Dissay-sous-Courcillon
Sarthe
Tel: 43 79 45 30

The Lorieux are tenant farmers on this 60-acre holding in the ravishing Sarthe countryside. Madame is an utterly delightful hostess and the atmosphere of the house is one of simple, unaffected hospitality. Of the two rooms, one is ideal for a family with a large double bed and two singles tucked into a corner of the tower. Parquet floors, period furnishings; both rooms and Madame's excellent table d'hôte are very good value.

Rooms: 2 double rooms, one with extra beds for children, sharing bathroom & wc.

Price: 210 Frs for two, including breakfast.

Meals: Dinner 80 Frs, including cider (wine extra).

Open: All year.

To get there: *From Mamers, D3 towards Le Mêle for 6km. Do not go into Allières. Farm on left.*

Map Ref No: 5

Marie-Rose & Moïse LORIEUX
La Locherie
Aillières
72600 Mamers
Sarthe
Tel: 43 97 76 03

'Perray' means 'built in stone'. Only a tower remains of the mediaeval fortress – the rest is 18th century; the Thibaults have owned the château since 1930. Rooms, varying in size and decor, are furnished with antiques. Simple, classic dinners are served in the dining-room furnished with 18th-century pieces and paintings. Salon and library and an air of relaxed "laisser-aller". Although there's a lift and lots of rooms, we think the house is special enough to be included

Rooms: 4 double rooms, 3 twin and 2 triple rooms, all with private bathrooms.

Price: 370-490 Frs for two, including breakfast.

Meals: Dinner 100-130 Frs, including wine (book ahead).

Open: All year.

To get there: *From Le Mans, N138 towards Tours. 3km past Château-du-Loir (at La Croix-de-Bonlieu), D11 towards La Bruère-sur-Loir; signposted.*

Map Ref No: 5

Mme Genevieve THIBAULT
Château le Grand-Perray
72500 La Bruère-sur-Loir
Sarthe
Tel: 43 46 72 65

Right in the village and fronting the street, this is a really ancient house dating from the 14th century. The modest exterior hides a most attractive interior, with a good garden behind. The accommodation is self-contained in restored buildings at the rear and around the garden, so you can be as independent as you wish. A simple house but honest, comfortable and hospitable.

Rooms: 1 double room with bathroom; 1 family suite with bathroom and small kitchen.

Price: 240-270 Frs for two, including breakfast.

Meals: Dinner 60-80 Frs, excluding wine.

Open: All year.

Henry Court Mantel, son of Henry II and crowned Henry III of England, is buried in the chapel of this château which still has its 1023 drawbridge. There is much more history, told at length and in detail by your host; the family has been here for generations. The house has fireplaces, antiques mixing with 60s furniture and vast grounds. Madame will provide a hearty breakfast to set you up for cycling or châteaux-visiting.

Rooms: 2 double rooms, 2 triple rooms and 1 suite for 2-3 people, all with bathrooms.

Price: 340 Frs for two, including breakfast.

Meals: None (large choice nearby).

Open: All year.

To get there: *From Saumur, D947 towards Chinon. At Montsoreau, D947 towards Loudun. Entrance to château 4km after Fontevraud; signposted.*

Map Ref No: 10

To get there: *From Le Mans, D147 to Arnage, then D307 to Pontvallain. House in town centre; signposted.*

Map Ref No: 5

Mme Michèle VIEILLET
Place Jean Graffin
72510 Pontvallain
Sarthe
Tel: 43 46 36 70

Jacqueline MOREAU
Château de la Roche Marteau
86120 Roiffé
Vienne
Tel: 49 98 77 54
Fax: 49 98 98 30

The house stands alone on the brow of a hill and is surrounded by oak forest. Rooms are in a very well-converted stable-block and overlook a lawn and a small swimming pool. There is also a tennis court. The owners, who breed horses, will provide a picnic hamper of local goodies if you want to venture into the countryside. Delightfully quiet, although the village is less than half a mile away, this is a good centre for a holiday and guests often stay several days.

Rooms: 1 double & 1 twin, with bathrooms.

Price: 275 Frs for two, including breakfast.

Meals: None (self-catering possible & new restaurant to open in village).

Open: All year.

The Atlantic Coast – Poitou

To get there: *From Angoulême, N141 to la Rochefoucauld and D13 towards Rochechouart. After about 5km, D62 left towards Chasseneuil and D162 to St Adjutory.*

Map Ref No: 10

Sylviane & Vincent CASPER
La Grenouille
16310 Saint Adjutory
Charente
Tel: 45 62 00 34

A visit here would be especially enjoyable between December and February when distillation takes place at the family Cognac distillery. The traditional bedrooms, with parquet floors, are centrally heated. Dinner, eaten in the friendly family kitchen, is a bargain, with appetising regional cooking and wines from the Chainier estate. After dinner, a visit to the distillery ...

Rooms: 2 triple rooms with bathrooms. 2 double rooms and 1 twin room, all with hand-basins, but sharing a bathroom.

Price: 170-200 Frs for two, including breakfast.

Meals: Dinner 70 Frs, including wine.

Open: All year.

To get there: *From A10, Pons exit on D700 towards Barbezieux Archiac. After Echebrune, D148 (1st left) towards Lonzac-Celles. Left onto D151, then follow signpost "Le Chiron".*

Map Ref No: 10

Micheline & Jacky CHAINIER
Le Chiron
16130 Salles d'Angles
Charente
Tel: 45 83 72 79
Fax: 45 83 64 80

288

The Legons are a friendly English couple, proud of their restoration of this lovely 18th-century farmhouse/distillery. In a slightly hotel-like (Costa del Sol?) atmosphere, it has comfortable, modern rooms (partitions may be thinnish), in a converted stable-block, some with stone walls and beams, overlooking an enclosed courtyard. An appetising evening menu is served in the dining-room where the original copper stills can be seen, glowing like the general ambience here.

Rooms: 3 double rooms, 1 twin and 2 family rooms for 4-6 people; all with bathrooms.

Price: 270-350 Frs for two, including breakfast.

Meals: Dinner 50-200 Frs, excluding wine.

Open: All year.

To get there: *From Jarnac, D736 towards Sigogné. After 2.5km, pass turnings for Les Métaires and Luchac; after 1km take next right. Maison Karina down road on right (5km from Jarnac).*

Map Ref No: 10

Austin & Nikki LEGON
Maison Karina
Bois Faucon
16200 Sigogne, Charente
Tel: 45 36 26 26
Fax: 45 81 10 93

289

A delightful old house (it once produced cognac) in the country surrounded by its lovely gardens. The owners are keen to do the job perfectly and are extremely proud of their house, having done all the restoration work themselves. They are emigrés from Paris, where they owned a grocery store. They now live in rural bliss, with forest, the River Dordogne and the sea close by.

Rooms: 1 double, 1 triple and 2 twin rooms, all with own bathrooms.

Price: 250 Frs for two, including breakfast.

Meals: Dinner 90 Frs, including wine.

Open: All year, except October.

The Logis is a grand 18th-century house in a quiet, leafy garden near Saintes. Alix and Jacques, genuine gentlefolk, have received guests for over 20 years (their nephew now runs the farm). In summer, groups of painters and musicians come for inspiration and one can see why. The charming guestrooms have not a hint of 'hotel' about them. Add the cultural attractions for all tastes (cognac, wine, exquisite Romanesque churches or the sea 20km away) and you may stay a while.

Rooms: 1 double room with own bathroom; 2 twin rooms, sharing a bathroom.

Price: 260-290 Frs for two, including breakfast.

Meals: None (next-door auberge).

Open: 1 March – 30 November.

To get there: *From Paris, A10 Mirambeau exit onto D730 towards Montlieu-la-Garde; then N10 towards Angoulême. After Pouillac, first left after (closed) petrol station; signposted after 800m.*

Map Ref No: 10

To get there: *From Saintes, N137 towards la Rochelle. After 10km, D119 to Plassay; house on right as you enter village; signposted.*

Map Ref No: 9

Denise & Pierre BILLAT
La Thébaïde, Pouillac
17210 Montlieu-la-Garde
Charente-Maritime
Tel: 46 04 65 17
Fax: 46 04 65 26

Alix & Jacques CHARRIER
Le Logis de l'Epine
17250 Plassay
Charente-Maritime
Tel: 46 93 91 66

With a fine old exterior, this house exudes light and elegant informality inside. Guestrooms are well furnished, with comfortable beds and pastel decor. Breakfast can be served in the rooms. At dinner refined professional cooking with estate wines is served at individual tables. Run by a friendly mother and daughter who go out of their way to make their B&Bs a success.

Rooms: 2 double rooms and 3 twin rooms, all with own bathrooms.

Price: 500-550 Frs for two, including breakfast.

Meals: Dinner 160 Frs, excluding wine.

Open: From Easter until 31 September.

To get there: *From A10, Mirambeau exit on D730 to Royan. Château is between Lorignac and Brie-sous-Mortagne; signposted at D730/D125 junction.*

Map Ref No: 9

Mme Sylvie COUILLAUD
Château des Salles
17240 St Fort-sur-Giron
Charente-Maritime
Tel: 46 49 95 10
Fax: 46 49 02 81

292

The Deschamps are wonderful hosts for whom nothing seems too much trouble: they'll even delay a friend's party to dine with you. Their farmhouse is set in spacious grounds overlooked by the traditional guestrooms. Breakfast times allow for a long lie-in. Good regional cooking at dinner may include duck or chicken from the farm, which also produces tobacco and cereals. Tennis court, ping-pong, and bikes to rent.

Rooms: 3 double rooms and 2 twin rooms; shared bathrooms.

Price: 200-240 Frs for two, including breakfast.

Meals: Dinner 80 Frs, including aperitif, wine & coffee.

Open: From Easter to 30 October.

To get there: *From St Jean d'Angély, D939 towards Matha. 3km after crossroads to Varaize, D229 towards Aumagne. House 0.8km on left.*

Map Ref No: 10

Mme Eliane DESCHAMPS
Le Treuil d'Aumagne
17770 Aumagne
Charente-Maritime
Tel: 46 58 23 80

293

This large Charentais cottage (with windmill) has been converted by your English hosts using simple light colour schemes and English antiques. A faint scent of old pine and dried flowers pervades. You are welcome to join the family – or be independent; the guestroom has its own entrance. A log fire brightens cooler evenings and a croquet lawn beckons in summer. Don't miss the treasures of Romanesque architecture in this area. Not for very young children.

Rooms: 1 room for 2-4 with bathroom.

Price: 250 Frs for two, including breakfast.

Meals: Dinner 50 Frs, including wine (book ahead).

Open: All year except Christmas.

To get there: *From St Savinien, D124 towards Rochefort. After 2km, 2nd left after "Le Pontreau" sign; house 200m on right.*

Map Ref No: 9

John & Jenny ELMES
Le Moulin de la Quine
17350 Saint Savinien
Charente-Maritime
Tel: 46 90 19 31
Fax: 46 90 19 31

A mill-stream runs through the extensive grounds of this very large, 400-year-old house next to the 100-hectare cereal farm. The guestrooms have period furnishings, good bedding and central heating. There are cooking facilities, but it would be a shame to miss Madame's excellent regional cooking. Vegetarian dishes upon request.

Rooms: 2 double rooms with bathrooms; 1 twin room with shared bathroom.

Price: 240 Frs for two, including breakfast.

Meals: Dinner 85 Frs, including wine.

Open: All year.

To get there: *From Gendarmerie in St Jean d'Angély, D127 towards Dampierre-Antezant. In Antezant, first right.*

Map Ref No: 10

Pierre & Marie-Claude
FALLELOUR
Les Moulins
17400 Antezant
Charente-Maritime
Tel: 46 59 94 52

Here are the endless, flat oyster beds that produce those tons of shellfish consumed by the French at Christmas. Here also is a quiet garden brimming with flowers where a comfortable room awaits you (don't be put off by a rather drab-looking village). There are lovely beaches 10 minutes away, 6000h. of forest to walk in and the hinterland has an astounding variety of birdlife. Your hosts are a quiet, kind couple who will soon make you feel genuinely at home.

Rooms: 1 double room with own bathroom.

Price: 200-250 Frs for two, including breakfast.

Meals: Not available.

Open: All year except October.

A neat farmhouse with four very welcoming beamed bedrooms (one especially adapted for people with physical disabilities). They have old furniture, good new bedding and central heating and are named after flowers with matching decor. Farmhouse dinners are eaten with the friendly retired hosts who still keep some poultry, rabbits and a pig. In short, a genuine country family atmosphere. There are bikes for rent and swings.

Rooms: 1 double room, 2 twin rooms and 1 triple room, all with own bathrooms.

Price: 210-250 Frs for two, including breakfast.

Meals: Dinner 80 Frs.

Open: All year.

To get there: *Take D123 towards Ile d'Oléron. At Marennes, right towards Château de la Gateaudière then follow signs.*

Map Ref No: 9

To get there: *From Saintes, N150 towards Niort. After 6km, D129 towards Ecoyeux; signposted (red and white).*

Map Ref No: 9

Jean & Jacqueline FERCHAUD
5 rue des Lilas
La Ménardière
17320 Marennes
Charente-Maritime
Tel: 46 85 41 77

Henri & Marie-Andrée FORGET
Chez Quimand
17770 Ecoyeux
Charente-Maritime
Tel: 46 95 92 55

Surrounded by woods this modern farm enjoys a peaceful rural setting. The simple rooms with contemporary furnishings are very clean, with good bedding and electric heating. Breakfast is served in the kitchen. Monsieur has retired from farming but Madame still works. Guests have use of kitchen facilities and a barbecue. There are a lake and pony club nearby.

Rooms: 3 double rooms: 2 with shared bathroom and 1 with own bathroom. Small extra room for a child.

Price: 190 Frs for two, including breakfast.

Meals: None (self-catering).

Open: From Easter to 31 October.

Mother and daughter, both charming, run this very special place. There is a splendid garden graced with many fine trees and a swimming pool with a little summer-house. Inside are a Louis XV dining-room and bedroom, a sculpted Louis XV fire-surround, and – of course – a little museum of old-fashioned toys, dolls and doll's furniture. There are two horses and a pony-and-trap if you prefer a wooden seat.

Rooms: 1 twin room and 4 double rooms (1 on ground floor), all with bathrooms.

Price: 260-390 Frs for two, including breakfast.

Meals: Dinner 100 Frs, including wine.

Open: All year.

To get there: *From Rochefort, N137 towards Saintes, then right on D117. Follow signpost for "Poney Club"; house is just after sign.*

Map Ref No: 9

Monique & Yves FOUGERIT
La Piègerie
17250 Trizay
Charente-Maritime
Tel: 46 82 03 08

To get there: *From A10, exit 24 for St Jean-d'Angély. There, left on N150 towards Niort. House signposted just after St Denis-du-Pin.*

Map Ref No: 9

Michèle & Florence FRAPPIER
Domaine de Rennebourg
St Denis-du-Pin
17400 St Jean-d'Angély
Charente-Maritime
Tel: 46 32 16 07

This is a very grand farmhouse, more like a small château but a working farm nevertheless (fruit and vegetables) with beautifully tiled out-buildings. Madame cooks with the freshest of her own produce and breakfast, served on the terrace or in the family dining-room, includes honey on the comb (in season). Nicely fitted rooms give the final touch of quality to this attractive place. There is lots to explore nearby (river, sea, Cognac and its cellars, Romanesque churches galore).

Rooms: 1 double, 1 triple (family) room, each with own shower & wc; 1 suite with 2 bathrooms.

Price: 230 Frs for two, including breakfast.

Meals: Dinner 70 Frs, including wine.

Open: All year.

This house is deep in the countryside and not far from the beach. The large garden, with well-kept lawns and flowerbeds, is available for croquet. Flowers and chocolates complete the attractively traditional rooms, centrally heated and spotless. Breakfasts include regional 'brioches'. Madame is a charming, if slightly formal, hostess.

Rooms: 2 double rooms, 1 twin room and 1 single room all with hand-basin. Shared bathrooms.

Price: 250 Frs for two, including breakfast (2 nights minimum).

Meals: Not available.

Open: 15 March – 15 September.

To get there: *Les Essards is 7km east of Saintes. From the village, D237 for 1km (signs to Le Pinier); farm is on left.*

Map Ref No: 9

To get there: *From La Rochelle, N11 towards Poitiers. After Zone Commerciale de Beaulieu, D9 towards Luçon. After St Xandre village, D202 to Sauzaie. There, take road for Usseau; 50m along, right into rue du Château: 2nd house on left.*

Map Ref No: 9

Jean-Claude & Francine JAMIN
Le Pinier
17250 Les Essards
Charente-Maritime
Tel: 46 93 91 43

Mme Annick LANGER
Aguzan, Rue du Château
La Sauzaie
17138 Saint Xandre
Charente-Maritime
Tel: 46 37 22 65

A fine 19th-century house set on the edge of the village. The traditional guestrooms have high ceilings, some good pieces of antique regional furniture and a good supply of books. Meals are served on the terrace in summer with dinner 'en famille'. The kind-hearted and charming hosts are farmers who rear Limousin cattle.

Rooms: 1 twin room on ground floor and 1 suite for 2-4, all with own bathrooms.

Price: 220-250 Frs for two, including breakfast.

Meals: Dinner 80 Frs.

Open: All year.

A bee farm! Charline and Jacky are indefatigable, eager hosts who encourage guests to take an interest in bees. The renovated building opposite the main house has one guestroom with Louis XV-style oak furnishings and another with more contemporary decor. A small shop in the courtyard is a hive of activity in summer. Guests make themselves breakfast from a well-stocked fridge. Lots of interest for children, plus games.

Rooms: 1 double and 1 twin, each with bathroom. (Extra beds available.)

Price: 220 Frs for two, including breakfast ingredients. (Children under 5 free.)

Meals: None (BBQ available; restaurant in St Savin).

Open: 15 February – 15 October.

To get there: *From A10, Saintes exit onto N137 towards Rochefort-la-Rochelle. After about 11km, D119 to Plassay. House on left on entering village.*

Map Ref No: 9

To get there: *From Chauvigny, N151 towards St Savin. 2km before St Savin, left to Siouvre; signposted.*

Map Ref No: 10

Michelle & Jacques LOURADOUR
La Jaquetterie
17250 Plassay
Charente-Maritime
Tel: 46 93 91 88

Charline & Jacky BARBARIN
Siouvre
86510 St Savin
Vienne
Tel: 49 48 10 19
Fax: 49 48 46 89

The Brémauds, who farm cattle and grain, have been welcoming guests for years. He is a jovial, brusque, rosy-cheeked farmer (as we may fondly imagine farmers should be), she quietly gets on with her cooking. They share dinner with their guests, enjoying the contact with people from elsewhere. The renovated house, 50m from the church, has a fine large doorway; the bedrooms are on the first floor. Chinon, châteaux and abbeys make this a fascinating area to explore.

Rooms: 2 double rooms, one with extra bed for child, each with own shower & wc.

Price: 185 Frs for two, including breakfast.

Meals: Dinner 70 Frs, including wine.

Open: All year.

A large and elegant 18th-century house in the centre of Chauvigny, just 20km from the Futuroscope. The exterior and hall are typically "French-dilapidated" but the guestrooms are full of antique furniture and there are flowers everywhere. Definitely not an hotel (no keys on doors, for example). Your hosts share their love of the area's history and culture with their visitors. From the peaceful walled garden there are fine views of the château up above.

Rooms: 4 double rooms, 1 triple and 1 single; all with bathrooms.

Price: 230-300 Frs for two, including breakfast.

Meals: Dinner 80 Frs, including wine.

Open: February – November. On reservation at other times.

To get there: *From Loudon, D60 towards Moncontour. At Mouterre-Silly, find the church; house is 50m along, signposted 'Chambres d'Hôtes'.*

Map Ref No: 10

To get there: *From Poitiers, N151 towards Le Blanc. On entering Chauvigny, second left turn after church.*

Map Ref No: 10

Agnes & Henri BREMAUD
Le Bourg
86200 Mouterre Silly
Vienne
Tel: 49 98 09 72
Fax: 49 22 33 40

304

Jacques & Claude de GIAFFERRI
8 rue du Berry
86300 Chauvigny
Vienne
Tel: 494 63081/14176
Fax: 494 76412

305

"It's out of this world it's so beautiful" (an authentic reader statement...). The house was the orangery, built in the 17th century for the château of Bois Dousset. It has been in the family for 200 years. There are 300 hectares of grounds for guests to walk in. This is really "vieille France" – make the most of a dying species! And base yourself for excursions to lovely old Poitiers, the Romanesque treasures of the Haut-Poitou and peaceful riverside walks.

Rooms: 2 double, 1 twin, 1 suite all with own bathrooms.

Price: 350 Frs for two, including breakfast.

Meals: None (forest inn 4km).

Open: All year.

To get there: *From A10, Poitiers Nord exit, N10 towards Limoges. After 7km, left to Bignoux; follow signs to Bois Dousset.*

Map Ref No: 10

Vicomte Hilaire de VILLOUTREYS de BRIGNAC
Logis du Château du Bois Dousset
86800 Lavoux
Vienne
Tel: 49 44 20 26

Wild flowers abound in the Vienne valley near this elegantly restored house. Richard teaches English; Deby looks after their young children and guests. Her parents sell antiques (and help decorate the house...) and her brother runs the 300-acre sheep farm. Produce from the kitchen garden, meat and eggs from the farm. This is a happy, energetic family who will make you feel welcome in French, Italian or English. The walled garden adds to the charm.

Rooms: 5 double rooms, all with bathrooms.

Price: 290 Frs for two, including breakfast.

Meals: Dinner 90 Frs, including wine (book ahead).

Open: All year.

To get there: *From Chauvigny, D54 to Montmorillon then D727 towards la Trimouille. House is 10km along on this road: signposted.*

Map Ref No: 10

Richard & Deby EARLS
La Boulinière
Journet
86290 La Trimouille
Vienne
Tel: 49 91 55 88

In 1791 an ancestor (secretary to Louis XVI) acquired the house, originally a mediaeval fortress then a fortified farm. The guestrooms, in a converted stable block, are furnished with high old beds and family pieces. The conversion was almost all Pierre-Claude's own work and his energy is contagious. He regales guests with family history over candlelit dinners at the huge kitchen table. Good value meals with mainly organic produce and Chantal's own recipes.

Rooms: 2 double rooms, 1 room for 3-6, each with own shower & wc. 1 double room, 1 room for 2-4 with own showers, sharing wc.

Price: 190 Frs for two, including breakfast.

Meals: Dinner 105 Frs, including wine and coffee.

Open: All year.

To get there: *From Saumur, D947 to Candes, then D147 to Loudun. There, D14 to Monts-sur-Guesnes; signposted.*

Map Ref No: 10

Pierre-Claude & Chantal FOUQUENET
Domaine de Bourg-Ville
86420 Monts-sur-Guesnes, Vienne
Tel: 49 22 81 58
Fax: 49 22 89 89

This attractive traditional French house, set among cornfields, sunflowers, melons and vineyards, is well placed for exploring the Loire Valley and the Vienne. Tim and Marion, well-integrated English 'immigrants', will tell you where to go wine-tasting, sailing, riding or swimming in the area. In summer, dinner is on the pretty leafy terrace, facing the sunset and Tim, a musician, insists on music at dinner... plus log fires in winter.

Rooms: 2 double rooms, 1 twin and 1 triple, all with bathrooms. (Extra beds & cots available.)

Price: 250 Frs for two, including breakfast.

Meals: Dinner 55-90 Frs, excluding wine.

Open: All year.

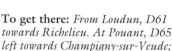

To get there: *From Loudun, D61 towards Richelieu. At Pouant, D65 left towards Champigny-sur-Veude; signposted.*

Map Ref No: 10

Marion & Tim LAWRENCE
Le Pin
Pouant
86200 Loudun
Vienne
Tel: 49 22 55 76

The atmosphere is 'vieille France': family trees, period pieces and portraits. A lovely château that has been occupied by the family for 5 centuries, apart from a short, German, break. Guestrooms are reached by a worn and winding staircase; one overlooks the 'cour d'honneur' while from the bed of another you can survey the lawns. Your hosts love talking to their guests. You share the family sitting-room and dine 'en famille', with good cooking by Madame.

Rooms: 2 double rooms with hand-basins; shared bathroom.

Price: 250 Frs for two, including breakfast.

Meals: Dinner 90 Frs, including wine.

Open: 1 March – 30 November.

The Lonhiennes moved to this 15th-century manor-house in 1948; it is a haven of peace and quiet. The downstairs room is a converted stable which still has its original hay-rack, and the other rooms are equally interesting. The owners' children now look after guests and they will utterly spoil you, bringing breakfast to your room if you wish. Readers have sent dazzling reports of the hospitality here.

Rooms: 2 double rooms and 1 triple room, all with bathrooms.

Price: 250 Frs for two, including breakfast.

Meals: Not available.

Open: All year.

To get there: *From Loudun, D759 towards Thouars. After 7km, left on D19 to Arçay.*

Map Ref No: 10

M Hilaire LEROUX de LENS
Château du Puy d'Arçay
86200 Arçay
Vienne
Tel: 49 98 29 11

To get there: *From Châtellerault, D9 towards La Puye and St Savin. After 20km, left on D3 towards La Roche-Posay. 2km on, left at very sharp bend; 1km to house.*

Map Ref No: 10

M Jacques LONHIENNE
La Talbardière
86210 Archigny
Vienne
Tel: 49 85 32 51

An impressive driveway leads to the farmhouse. Overlooking the garden with its large chestnut trees are the vast bedrooms. Good furnishings include handsome wardrobes. Sunlight streams into the huge sitting-room with its magnificent fireplace, beams, white walls and terracotta tiled floor. Breakfast on the terrace is a pleasure. The quiet, reserved but welcoming hosts are busy cereal farmers.

Rooms: 1 double room and 1 suite with double bed and twin beds, each with own bathroom.

Price: 180-250 Frs for two, including breakfast.

Meals: Not available.

Open: All year.

It is easy to get to this fine sheep farm and the views all around are of uninterrupted rolling countryside. All the farm produce is organic. Don't miss the chance to try some home-produced lamb, rabbit, chicken cooked in honey, vegetable pies, then a fresh-fruit dessert. Limousin specialities are Madame's pride and joy. Monsieur is well-travelled and enjoys chatting with guests. Superb place with simple natural values for children and adults alike.

Rooms: 1 triple room and 1 double, with showers and basins; shared wc.

Price: 180 Frs for two, breakfast included.

Meals: Dinner 80 Frs, including wine.

Open: All year.

To get there: *From Richelieu, D7 towards Loudun. After 4km, left onto a lane with linden trees on both sides.*

Map Ref No: 10

To get there: *From Poitiers, D741 to Civray. There, D148 east and D34 to Availles. There D100 towards Mauprévoir. After 3km, signposted.*

Map Ref No: 10

Jean & Marie-Christine PICARD
Le Bois Goulu
86200 Pouant
Vienne
Tel: 49 22 52 05

312

Pierre SALVAUDON
Les Ecots
86460 Availles-Limousine
Vienne
Tel: 49 48 59 17

313

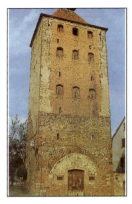

Ramshackle but romantic. A high room with a memorable if limited view through arrow slits over the sea, some fine vintage manure and a working railway. Find peace in the authentic rural bathroom on the other side of a courtyard full of organic thistles (Madame makes unforgettable coffee with these). Local gossip to be had with the clients for Monsieur's friendly offal auction, Rottweilers to be teased on their ancient chains and genuine farmyard children to be chased. Out of this world!

Rooms: 1 room with 7 beds.

Price: Negotiable.

Meals: None. Restaurant 98 kms away.

Open: Rarely, upon request.

To get there: *From UK, better not even try.*

Map Ref No: 14

Marquis et Marquise de SALCHER
EVIDE
La Tour Rista
97650 Outre-Tombe-en-Mer
Baie de Gascogne
Tel: 01 02 03 04

314

A 'Grand Cru St Emilion' is a name to brandish but wine won't be the only good memory of your stay. Madame's regional specialities are another. So, although the guestrooms have their own kitchen, be tempted by dinner. She cuts no corners in her rooms either: each has a different board game or original painting, stone walls, wood ceilings and good, old furniture. And the breakfast table is beautiful. A pleasant, conscientious hostess, she keeps a dictionary handy!

Rooms: 2 double rooms, 2 twin and 1 triple, all with bathrooms.

Price: 280 Frs for two, including breakfast.

Meals: Dinner from 85 Frs, excluding wine (book ahead).

Open: 1 February – 31 December.

Aquitaine – Bordeaux

To get there: *From Libourne, D243 towards St Emilion. 3km before St Emilion, D245 towards Pomerol; signposted.*

Map Ref No: 10

Claude et Jacqueline BRIEUX
Château Millaud-Montlabert
33330 St Emilion
Gironde
Tel: 57 24 71 85
Fax: 57 24 62 78

Built on the foundations of a mediaeval château, this 18th-century mansion surveys vineyards, fields and forest. The large, quiet, sunny rooms have their own entrance, kitchen and living room. For three of the rooms, the communal 3-bathroom/2-loo system has a somewhat institutional feel. In summer, guests may dine with the Chartiers. They breed horses; just one member of the family speaks English. Well-organised, unpretentious hospitality.

Rooms: 1 large room for 2-4 people, with own bathroom & w.c.; 2 large rooms for 2-4 people and 1 twin room, all with own bathrooms but sharing w.c.

Price: 180-240 Frs for two, including breakfast.

Meals: Dinner 80 Frs, including wine (summer only; self-catering & restaurants nearby).

Open: All year.

To get there: *From A10, Exit 28 on D132 and D115 to St Savin. There, D18 to St Mariens. Left just before village; signposted.*

Map Ref No: 10

Daniel & Yvonne CHARTIER
Château de Gourdet
33620 St Mariens
Gironde
Tel: 57 58 99 33

The refreshingly straightforward Lanneaus live in a large 18th-century 'maison paysanne' in the north of the Médoc wine area. In the garden created by Monsieur stands a small 1900s house. Originally built for grape pickers, it is now an excellent chambre d'hôte with modern pine furnishings. Come and visit at grape harvest time! Some 'old faithfuls' return to Mirambeau year after year. Useful nearby ferry to fashionable Royan. No children.

Rooms: 1 double room with bathroom.

Price: 220 for two, including breakfast.

Meals: None.

Open: All year.

To get there: From Bordeaux, N215 towards Le Verdon. After about 80km, right to St Vivien; in village, go towards Grayan (rue Gal de Gaulle): approx. 800m on right.

Map Ref No: 9

Pierre & Marguerite LANNEAU
Mirambeau
33590 St Vivien-de-Médoc
Gironde
Tel: 56 09 51 07

The room in the main house (2 others in a separate building) overlooks some of the world's most famous vineyards. Your hosts are slightly formal, as befits a small château in such a wealthy aristocratic area, though the estate now owns fewer vineyards (in classic French manner, it was divided up after an inheritance dispute); they are wine-lovers and will guide you expertly in your tastings. Dinner is refined too, naturally accompanied by a superb wine list. A quiet village position and a walled garden complete the picture.

Rooms: 1 double room, 2 suites, all with own bathroom.

Price: 330-430 Frs for two, including breakfast.

Meals: Dinner 100Frs, excluding wine (book ahead).

Open: All year.

The slopes of "Entre-Deux-Mers" vineyards run down into valleys criss-crossed by streams and orchards. The peaceful, renovated house offers numerous activities from wine-tasting and cookery courses to canoeing. Guestrooms, with armchairs and roomy cupboards, are superb. Large sitting area with books and records. Madame is a trained cook and used to run a restaurant, so book for dinner!

Rooms: 1 double and 1 triple room with bathrooms.

Price: 250 Frs for two, including breakfast.

Meals: Dinner 95-165 Frs, including wine.

Open: January to September.

To get there: *In St Estèphe, follow signs to "Pharmacie". House signposted to right on entering village, opposite chemist.*

Map Ref No: 9

To get there: *From Libourne, D670 through Sauveterre, then left on D230 to Rimons. At Rimons sawmill on the right, take first left; signposted.*

Map Ref No: 15

Françoise & Ivo LEEMANN
Au Bourg
33180 St Estèphe
Gironde
Tel: 56 59 72 94
Fax: 56 59 39 58

318

Mme Dominique LEVY
Grand Boucaud
Rimons
33580 Monségur
Gironde
Tel: 56 71 88 57

319

A miniature château, maybe – but a vastly gracious approach that is palpable as you turn into the avenue of fine oaks, admiring the 20-hectare park and long views. The châtelaine adds her own elegance by her flair for furnishing and her table settings. But this is still an unsmart family house and children love to roam the park in total freedom. All rooms have private bathrooms but some are rather far to reach. The less expensive rooms are the best value. The kiwi-orange jam for breakfast has been much admired.

Rooms: 1 double and 1 twin with private bathrooms; 2 large doubles with bathrooms en-suite.

Price: 300 Frs for two (600 Frs for the larger doubles), including breakfast.

Meals: None (1km).

Open: April to October (other times on request).

To get there: *D33 north from Peyrehorade. Right on D6. After St Lon-les-Mines, first left towards Orist. Château de Monbet is opposite at first crossroads, 1.5km from village.*

Map Ref No: 14

M & Mme Hubert de LATAILLADE
Château du Monbet
40300 St Lon-les-Mines, Landes
Tel: 58 57 80 68
Fax: 58 57 89 29

These easy-going people live in a calm, rambling country house that exudes rustic charm. The garden full of exotic trees (bamboo, banana, orange), the pond with ducks, moorhens and rowing boat, the sheep and the Shetland ponies lend a special character to the whole. Inside, there is an interesting assortment of styles – one room is all 1930s furniture. River trips and water sports are to be had at the harbour just down the road. A perfect place for family holidays.

Rooms: 1 double, 1 twin & 2 suites, all with own shower or bath & wc.

Price: 200-230 Frs for two, including breakfast.

Meals: Not available. Good auberge 200m.

Open: All year.

To get there: *From Bayonne, N117 towards Pau. After 29km, left into Port-de-Lanne. Just before the port, right as signposted; Au Masson on right.*

Map Ref No: 14

Philippe & Monique DURET
Au Masson
Route du Port
40300 Port-de-Lanne
Landes
Tel: 58 89 14 57

Madame Lajus exudes Gallic charm and joie de vivre. She has that ability to make you feel she's really glad to see you. Larroque is a lovely 18th-century gentleman's residence, in the family for generations, preserving 200 years' worth of family furniture and memorabilia. Each guestroom evokes the elegance and romance of its origins with the convenience of modern plumbing. Good breakfasts presented with style. Thoroughly recommended.

Rooms: 1 double (with extra single bed) and 1 twin, each with own bathroom.

Price: 240 Frs for two, including breakfast.

Meals: None (300m).

Open: All year.

To get there: *From Mont-de-Marsan, N124 towards Dax. After 4km, D3 to St Perdon; house on right as you enter village.*

Map Ref No: 14

Louis & Marguerite LAJUS
Larroque
40090 St Perdon
Landes
Tel: 58 75 88 38

Strangely urban in character for a farmhouse in deepest rural France, La Borde once housed missionaries; the dining-room was their chapel. Two generations of Bugé women now run the house in true chambres d'hôtes spirit: relaxed and practical. Hosts always dine with their guests and most of the meal is home-produced, including the foie gras (on Sunday). There is a games room upstairs and masses of space outside for children. A real French family house.

Rooms: 2 double & 3 twin rooms, all with own shower & wc.

Price: Half-board only: 400 Frs for two, including breakfast and dinner (and wine).

Meals: Dinner included.

Open: May – September.

Limousin – Dordogne

To get there: *From Brive, N20 towards Uzerche about 18km then left through Sadroc to St Bonnet; here, D156 towards Perpezac-le-Noir. Farm is 1km on left.*

Map Ref No: 10

Nadine BUGE
La Borde
19410 St Bonnet-l'Enfantier
Corrèze
Tel: 55 73 72 44

The Greenwoods have lovingly restored their small old farmhouse to give its original beams and stonework pride of place and it is now a very comfortable home. Savour the precious peace and the stunning countryside on foot, do the local cultural scene – there is a wealth of history and architecture here – or go canoeing on the Dordogne. Your hosts will give you all the advice you need.

Rooms: 1 double & 1 twin room sharing a bathroom.

Price: 180 Frs for two, including breakfast.

Meals: Dinner 70 Frs, including wine.

Open: All year.

To get there: *From Beaulieu-sur-Dordogne, D940 towards Tulle. After 5km, in Laroche de Nonards, left opposite bar towards Nonards and Puy d'Arnac. House is 400m on right.*

Map Ref No: 11

Paul & Jean GREENWOOD
Le Marchoux
19120 Nonards
Corrèze
Tel: 55 91 52 73

You may well wonder... This hacienda style was brought to the heart of France by a general of Napoleon III's, fresh from fighting in Mexico. Pass the gate and you enter the Henriets' very special world. To each room a theme – Provence, birds, Wild West (a small boy's dream...) or pure Art Deco. Add to this a tranquil, flower-filled courtyard, a huge drawing-room and Madame's gentle manner and you begin to get the measure of this very different home, with the softly serpentine Dordogne just yards away.

Rooms: 4 double rooms, 1 twin room, 1 suite, all with own bathroom.

Price: 250-300 Frs for two, including breakfast.

Meals: Dinner 80 Frs, including wine.

Open: May to October.

To get there: *From Tulle, D940 to Beaulieu. "La Maison" is in the centre of Beaulieu, next to the Gendarmerie.*

Map Ref No: 11

Jean-Claude & Christine HENRIET
"La Maison"
11 rue de la Gendarmerie
19120 Beaulieu-sur-Dordogne
Corrèze
Tel: 55 91 24 97

325

In the heart of rural France, the Lafonds grow walnuts and tobacco – constrained with seemingly mediaeval legalities by the state-owned monopoly – and raise beef cattle. Their village is in a listed area beside the Dordogne, a paradise for fishermen, walkers and canoeists. Their new house is furnished with period pieces and set in a garden full of old trees. The atmosphere is farming, family and friends.

Rooms: 3 double & 1 twin room, all with own shower & wc.

Price: 250 Frs for two, including breakfast.

Meals: None (self-catering; good choice 6km).

Open: All year.

These refugees from rainy England are the only people locally to boast a fine English lawn round their farmhouse. (They also, rather alarmingly, keep a distinctive tumbril in their drive). They offer their visitors a warm friendly base for a holiday. Visits to the nearby farm can be arranged and there are some excellent walking paths, well-marked but little-used. They offer a 4-course dinner with good-quality wine to end the day.

Rooms: One twin room with bathroom (extra room for children).

Price: 190 Frs for two, including breakfast.

Meals: Dinner 75 Frs, including wine.

Open: All year.

To get there: *From Tulle, N120 to Argentat then D12 along River Dordogne towards Beaulieu, through Monceaux to Saulières (6km from Argentat).*

Map Ref No: 11

To get there: *From Argentat, N120 towards Tulle then left onto N121 towards Brive. Pass sign to Albussac; 300m on, left to Le Prézat, through hamlet; house is on right with English lawn.*

Map Ref No: 11

Marie-Jo & Jean-Marie LAFOND
Saulières
Monceaux-sur-Dordogne
19400 Argentat
Corrèze
Tel: 55 28 09 22

Anne & Jim LARDNER
Le Prézat
19380 Albussac
Corrèze
Tel: 55 28 62 36

The green hills rise up behind the house, the river flows under the bridge, the trout doze and leap (1st-category fishing at the bottom of the garden) and you can have breakfast on the pontoon if you like. Your English host makes this a home from home, informal and relaxing. Perfect for families looking for a good basic service in a peaceful spot (l'Hospital used to be a leper colony, so well away from town) whence to explore the delights of a little-known region of France.

Rooms: 2 double rooms with own bathrooms, 6 double rooms sharing bathrooms.

Price: 210 Frs for two, including breakfast.

Meals: None (BBQ in summer 55 Frs; good choice in Argentat).

Open: March – October, otherwise on request.

To get there: *From Tulle, N120 towards Aurillac, past Argentat; after crossing river, 1st right off by-pass; right again, through l'Hospital and across bridge; house beside bridge.*

Map Ref No: 11

James MALLOWS
Au Pont de l'Hospital
19400 Argentat
Corrèze
Tel: 55 28 90 35
UK 01983 730797

Founded in the 1100s, this is a fairy-tale castle, all turrets and history, that sits four-square before its stunning views of Puy d'Arnac. You can hear the stream rushing past, the geese patrolling, the cock crowing, the bacon frying and not much else. The renovation is top-class, the guestrooms large with fresh flowers, the salon (where breakfast and dinner are served) incontestably French and the hospitality genuine...from an English couple utterly devoted to France.

Rooms: 2 double rooms & 1 suite, all with own bathrooms.

Price: 380-480 Frs for two, including breakfast.

Meals: Dinner 80 Frs, including wine.

Open: All year except Christmas.

To get there: *From Tulle, D940 towards Beaulieu for about 30km then right onto D106 to Nonards; signposted.*

Map Ref No: 11

Gill & Joe WEBB
Château d'Arnac, Nonards
19120 Beaulieu-sur-Dordogne
Corrèze
Tel: 55 91 54 13
Fax: 55 91 52 62

At the heart of La Creuse, an unsung region of small farms and pine forests, is the 18th-century farmhouse of La Borderie, quite literally at the end of the road – the last of just five houses in the hamlet. Such deep-country quiet is rare... and so valuable. Marc and Maryse and their four children welcome those wishing to share the tranquillity of an area whose history and walks they know intimately. Children love the room with the mezzanine...

Rooms: 2 double rooms with own bathroom; 1 twin room with shared bathroom.

Price: 170-230 Frs for two, including breakfast.

Meals: None (auberge 6km: advance booking).

Open: All year.

To get there: *From Royère-de-Vassivière, D8 towards Bourganeuf. Just before you reach le Compeix, right to "La Borderie"; signposted.*

Map Ref No: 11

Marc & Maryse DESCHAMPS
La Borderie
St Pierre Bellevue
23460 Royère-de-Vassivière
Creuse
Tel: 55 64 96 51

This big 18th-century house on the edge of the old town overlooks a valley dominated by a château. Madame is a painter and retired couturier's assistant. She now runs courses in patchwork and drawing. Bedrooms are comfortable and centrally-heated; one includes a useful corner kitchen. Children are welcome – there are games and a garden. Garage and restaurant nearby.

Rooms: 3 double rooms, all with bathrooms (1 with kitchenette).

Price: 220 for two, including breakfast.

Meals: None (self-catering possible).

Open: 1 March – 30 September.

To get there: *From Montluçon, D916 through Domérat, Huriel, Trégnat. In Boussac square, bakery to left of Town Hall; turn into Rue des Loges (by bakery).*

Map Ref No: 11

Françoise & Daniel GROS
3 rue des Loges
23600 Boussac
Creuse
Tel: 55 65 80 09

This typical farmhouse has traditional bedrooms opening onto a terrace and overlooking the countryside. The farm produces cereals, asparagus and poultry. Diffident at first, Madame becomes enthusiastic when discussing local cuisine – meals here are a must and can be served outside in warm weather. Also, Madame runs cookery courses in winter.

Rooms: 1 double, 1 triple and 2 twin rooms, all with showers.

Price: 200 Frs for two, including breakfast (2 nights minimum).

Meals: Dinner 80 Frs, including wine.

Open: From 21 January to 19 December.

Think of your dream house – you may just picture something like this. A 17th-century millhouse in the loveliest of settings with an island beyond the mill-race for solitary meditations (and an inspired cook for more worldly needs). The Armitages are justifiably proud of their conversion. John's gardening talent is underpinned by a few grass-cropping sheep and both he and Diana enjoy pointing their guests in the direction of the known and unknown treasures of the region. They are very English but have totally adopted their new country.

Rooms: 1 double room, 1 twin room, each with own bath or shower & wc.

Price: 500 Frs for two, including breakfast.

Meals: Dinner 150 Frs, including wine.

Open: All year.

To get there: *From Périgueux, N21 towards Limoges. About 2 km on, right over bridge towards airport. Left at next roundabout onto D5 towards Hautefort. 1.5km after Tourtoirac, left towards La Crouzille. Cross the Auvezère. 1st drive on right.*

Map Ref No: 10

To get there: *From Bergerac, D32 towards St Alvère. After 10km, look for signpost "Périgord – Bienvenue à la Ferme".*

Map Ref No: 10

Marie-Jeanne ARCHER
La Barabie – D32
Lamonzie-Montastruc
24520 Mouleydier
Dordogne
Tel: 53 23 22 47

332

John & Diana ARMITAGE
Le Moulin de la Crouzille
Tourtoirac
24390 Hautefort
Dordogne
Tel: 53 51 11 94

333

With its 13th-century tower (built by the English) this house is genuinely picturesque. The retired farming couple is friendly and Madame is proud of her home with its strong country atmosphere and simple style. Upstairs from the kitchen, the two guestrooms, with screened-off bathroom, are old-fashioned but comfortable. Perfect for a family which enjoys a bit of character.

Rooms: 2 connecting double rooms, each with own wc but shared bathroom. Apartment also available.

Price: 180 Frs for two, including breakfast.

Meals: Not available.

Open: From 1 March to 31 October.

Four miles from the village, this is a lovely country house in a woodland setting. A quiet, restful place, from where you can explore the Dordogne and nearby Périgueux. You are at the heart of the foie gras region and truffles are hunted here. Don't be worried about meeting hordes of immigrant English; they are a minority ... still. Children over seven welcome.

Rooms: 6 rooms with bathrooms. One of the rooms ideal for a family.

Price: 320 Frs for two, including breakfast.

Meals: Dinner 120 Frs, including aperitif, wine & coffee.

Open: All year.

To get there: *From Bergerac, N660 towards Port de Couze to Beaumont. Take D676 towards Villeréal; house is 500m on left after Nojal.*

Map Ref No: 15

Mme Georgette BERTHOLOM
Lapeyère
24440 Sainte Sabine
Dordogne
Tel: 53 22 31 07

To get there: *From Le-Buisson-de-Cadouin, D29 towards Lalinde-Bergerac. After 4km, V1 towards Cussac; signposted.*

Map Ref No: 1

M & Mme BOUANT
Domaine du Pinguet
Cussac
24480 Le-Buisson-de-Cadouin
Dordogne
Tel: 53 22 97 07

This enterprising young couple have chambres d'hotes in a château called La Pomarède, with fine views over rolling countryside. It has real character and is beautifully maintained. Off-season it is let to just one couple or family, so privacy is guaranteed. There are parquet floors, antique furnishings, open fireplaces and lots of books. They like guests to be independent and do their meals themselves. When booking, say you want rooms in La Pomarède.

Rooms: 1 double room with cot, 2 twin rooms, 1 room for 3 children. Shared bathrooms.

Price: 290 Frs for two, including breakfast.

Meals: Dinner 80 Frs on arrival; otherwise, self-catering.

Open: All year.

To get there: *From Périgueux, D170 to le Bugue; D51 towards le Buisson. Before crossing river, left on D51 to Coux-et-Bigaroque.*

Map Ref No: 10

Admire the authentic shape of the roofscape! This house was built as an orangery in the 18th century and still, with its later additions (including a much-appreciated pool), has an elegant, serene feel to it as well as a fine garden, Madame's pride and joy. A pleasant home to come back to after a day spent on the physical or cultural pursuits that abound in the Dordogne – watch out for the British colony playing cricket on the grass of Périgord.

Rooms: 1 twin room with bathroom (extra beds available).

Price: 340 Frs for two, including breakfast.

Meals: None (large choice in Bergerac, 5km).

Open: June – September.

To get there: *From Bergerac, D660 for 2km towards Lalinde; right across Dordogne river, right onto D19, left towards Cours de Pile, right towards La Conne and left, following signs to La Graulet.*

Map Ref No: 10

Christine & Michel BOURGES
La Carral
Le Coux-et-Bigaroque
24220 St Cyprien
Dordogne
Tel: 53 31 62 77 or 53 316149

Marie-Thérèse CAILLET
L'Orangerie de La Graulet
24100 Bergerac
Dordogne
Tel: 53 63 34 25

A charming couple. They have taken on this 250-year-old farmhouse and made it work exceptionally well. It stands in gentle rolling countryside, surrounded by fields of corn and sunflowers. Inside, the atmosphere is bright and welcoming, with stencilling on light-coloured walls. Your hosts organise Gourmet Weeks during the spring and autumn months.

Rooms: 2 double rooms with bathrooms.

Price: 400 Frs for two, including breakfast (minimum 3 nights).

Meals: None (village restaurant nearby).

Open: All year except February.

To get there: *From Angoulême, D939 towards Périgueux. At La Rochebeaucourt, D12/D708 to Verteillac, then D97 to Bouteilles. There, left at crossroads, past church to last house on right (200 m).*

Map Ref No: 10

Tom & Patricia CARRUTHERS
La Bernerie
Bouteilles
24320 Verteillac, Dordogne
Tel: 53 91 51 40
Fax: 53 91 08 59

Madame de Bosredon is a refined, well-travelled, energetic lady who enjoys receiving English people – she worked in England 'some time ago'. Now she shares this handsome country manor (of 17th and 18th-century origin) with her guests whom she likes 'to welcome as friends'. Her drawing room is full of fine antiques and flowers from the garden. Guests are welcome to picnic and barbecue outside. This is a house with no set rules and lots of charm.

Rooms: 2 double rooms with own bathrooms.

Price: 310 Frs for two, including breakfast.

Meals: None (use of barbecue).

Open: Easter to end October.

To get there: *From Bergerac, N21 south for 11km, then left on D14 to Issigeac, then D21 towards Castillonnes. At Monmarves, sign to Domaine du Petit Pey; turn into green gate.*

Map Ref No: 15

Annie de BOSREDON
Le Petit Pey
Monmarves
24560 Issigeac
Dordogne
Tel: 53 58 70 61

Guests can help out on this busy goose farm (2500 geese!) which, apart from foie gras, also sells goose down and walnuts. Trees provide shade in the yard by the house, rebuilt 20 years ago. The spotless rooms are decorated in modern rustic style. Périgourdin dishes are eaten 'en famille' in the evenings with the energetic Madame Dubois, who also runs cookery courses.

Rooms: 2 twin rooms and 3 double rooms. 2 rooms have own bathrooms and 3 share a bathroom but have handbasins.

Price: 200 Frs for two, including breakfast. (340 Frs half-board.)

Meals: Meals 125-175 Frs.

Open: All year.

To get there: *From Brive, N89 to Périgueux. At Larche, D60 to Chavagnac. Turn right to Ladornac – follow signposts.*

Map Ref No: 10

M et Mme Guy DUBOIS
Peyrenègre
Terrasson
24120 Ladornac, Dordogne
Tel: 53 51 04 24
Fax: 53 51 11 22

340

Wonderful 18th-century manor-house, lived in for a time by the de Laugeries, a grand, old Périgord family, and retaining the flavour and warm hospitality of old France. Simply furnished rooms, some with superb fireplaces, look out onto rolling countryside. Lunch and dinner are offered; Périgourdin menu on a beautiful antique dining-table. At the foot of the garden, a delightful Romanesque church.

Rooms: 2 double rooms and 2 twin rooms; shared bathrooms.

Price: 240 Frs for two, including breakfast.

Meals: Dinner 150-170 Frs.

Open: From Easter to 30 November.

To get there: *From Nontron, D675 towards Brantôme. At St Martial-de-Valette, right on D708 towards Mareuil. Left on D84 to St Front-sur-Nizonne; house behind church.*

Map Ref No: 10

Mme Micheline DUPIN
La Chouette Gourmande
St Front-sur-Nizonne
24300 Nontron
Dordogne
Tel: 53 56 14 70

341

This converted barn, just over a century old, is part of a working farm which produces foie gras, walnut oil and all kinds of vegetables. Expect to dine with your hosts in the evening; they are keen for you to get to know the hidden corners of this area. André, full of local history and lore, likes to accompany his guests on walks and visits to places of interest such as caves and châteaux. But he also guarantees peace and total freedom for all.

Rooms: 2 triple roms with showers and wash-basins, sharing a wc.

Price: 220 Frs for two, including breakfast.

Meals: Dinner 70 Frs, including wine.

Open: All year.

Another spot for wine-lovers...and for teetotallers too! An old house on the hillside; a spring rises just behind and falls into troughs beside the terrace overlooking the vineyards of the estate. The whole place revolves around wine. Monsieur produces it and Madame gives courses in growing and knowing about it. They are cheerful and active. Their rooms are rather small but who cares when there's true French tradition to be observed...and her fruits lovingly tasted?

Rooms: 2 twin rooms and 1 single, all with bathrooms. (Extra bed available.)

Price: 280 Frs for two, including breakfast.

Meals: None (in village).

Open: All year.

To get there: *From Angoulême, D939 south. After Dignac, D23 to Villebois-Lavalette; D17 to Gurat, then D102 towards Vendoire; house is 2km along, opposite petrol station.*

Map Ref No: 10

To get there: *From Bergerac, D933 towards Marmande. After 7km, restaurant "La Diligence" on right: 500m on, house signposted to left.*

Map Ref No: 10

M André DURIEUX
Le Bouchaud D17
24320 Vendoire
Dordogne
Tel: 53 91 00 82

342

Mme Liliane GAGNARD
Le Vieux Touron
Route de Marmande
24240 Monbazillac, Dordogne
Tel: 53 58 21 16
Fax: 53 61 21 17

343

This family raises dairy cows and grows walnuts; also plums which are dried and sold as prunes. In the evenings, Madame uses the farm produce to prepare succulent regional dishes that are eaten in the kitchen with the friendly family. The modest, heated bedrooms have kept their wooden beams and traditional decor. Simple, good-value rooms in an early 19th-century farmhouse.

Rooms: 1 double room with own bathroom; 2 double rooms with shared bathroom. (1 room on ground floor.)

Price: 180 Frs for two, including breakfast. Half-board 340 Frs for two.

Meals: Dinner 80 Frs, including wine.

Open: All year.

To get there: *From Beaumont-du-Périgord, D660 5km towards Montpazier; second farm on right after sign for Petit Brassac.*

Map Ref No: 15

Gilbert et Reine MARESCASSIER
Petit Brassac
Labouquerie
24440 Beaumont-du-Périgord
Dordogne
Tel: 53 22 32 51

344

A blissfully peaceful rural setting for this house, newly built in Périgord style using old stone. Beamed bedrooms have country furnishings with functional showers neatly curtained off. The hosts produce kiwi fruit and traditional crops. Home-grown veg, eggs and poultry are served at mouthwatering meals, sometimes eaten with the family. Monsieur makes his own aperitifs and liqueurs. Tours are available in a horse-drawn buggy.

Rooms: 2 twin rooms and 3 double rooms, all with own shower & wc.

Price: 200 Frs for two, including breakfast. July and August half-board only – 360 Frs for two.

Meals: Dinner 80 Frs, including aperitif, wine & coffee.

Open: 1 March to 30 November.

To get there: *From Périgueux, N89 towards Brive then D710 towards Cahors-Fumel. At "le Périgord en Calèche" sign, turn right. It is the first house.*

Map Ref No: 15

Jacqueline & Robert MARESCASSIER
Le Bourg
24550 Mazeyrolles
Dordogne
Tel: 53 29 93 38

345

The origins of Western man are nearby; you are a stone's throw from Lascaux and the Vézère flows practically at your feet. The Roussels keep a comfortable town house and also run a wine business; their inside knowledge will be invaluable if you hope to carry more than the odd prehistoric rock home. In this delightful merchant's house, ideally central for evening sorties, the guestrooms are smallish, prettily decorated with parquet floors, if a wee bit noisy for the night.

Rooms: 1 double room, 1 twin (plus adjacent single), both with own bathroom, sharing wc.

Price: 200 Frs for two, including breakfast.

Meals: Not available.

Open: March to October.

This renovated 18th-century manor-house with a garden and pool provides a setting of blissful peace. Guests sleep in a big separate building. White walls contrast with wooden beams in the spotless rooms, which have excellent beds and central heating. Breakfast is served until late and the Rubbens enjoy chatting to their guests. Well-behaved children are tolerated!

Rooms: 1 triple room with own bathroom; 3 double rooms with shared bathrooms.

Price: 360 Frs for two, including breakfast.

Meals: Not available.

Open: From Easter to 30 October.

To get there: *From Brive, N89 to Le Lardin-St Lazare; left on D704 to Montignac. House is on north side of river near bridge, at sign 'Maison du Vin'.*

Map Ref No: 10

To get there: *From Périgueux, D939 to Brantôme. There, D78 & D83 towards Champagnac-de-Belair; D82 & D3 to Villars and "Grottes de Villars". Left to Lavergne; signposted.*

Map Ref No: 10

Jean & Deborah ROUSSEL
2 rue du Professeur Faurel
24290 Montignac
Dordogne
Tel: 53 51 97 91

Mme Eliane RUBBENS
L'Enclos
Lavergne
24530 Villars
Dordogne
Tel: 53 54 82 17

A well-maintained 17th-century farmhouse in lovely wooded grounds (walnuts from the tree at the right time of year). Madame is French, Monsieur English; they run well-reputed language courses and are excellent company...when present! Rooms are extremely pleasant; stone walls and beamed ceilings make it a classic southern house, dark and restful. Breakfast is served in a guests' dining-room. A rural retreat whence to explore the Périgord.

Rooms: 3 double rooms and 2 twin rooms, all with shower-rooms (two share a separate wc).

Price: 240 Frs for two, including breakfast.

Meals: Not available.

Open: All year.

In a word: marvellous! The Belières have retained the 17th-century elegance without stiffness or formality; there are beams, stone walls, a huge open fire, gorgeous antiques, family mementoes, parquet floors – and the warmest of welcomes. Concessions to modernity include firm beds and new wool mattresses. DIY breakfast at all hours. Pool not available in July and August. The spirit of the house is real grandeur based on trust.

Rooms: 1 double & 1 twin room with shared bathroom; a suite for 3 and a flat for 4-6 people, with private bathrooms.

Price: 270-360 Frs for two, including breakfast.

Meals: None (2km).

Open: 1 April – 1 November.

To get there: *From Périgueux, D939 towards Angoulême. After Puy-de-Fourches, D106 to Bourdeilles; D78 towards Ribérac. In La Rigeardie – first house on left.*

Map Ref No: 10

To get there: *From St Céré, D673 for 3km towards Gramat; then D30 towards Carennac. After 4km, right after large house with dovecote; signposted.*

Map Ref No: 11

M & Mme TRICKETT
La Rigeardie
24310 Bourdeilles
Dordogne
Tel: 53 03 78 90
Fax: 53 04 56 95

348

Mme Annie BELIERES
Château de Gamot
46130 Loubressac
Lot
Tel: 65 10 92 03
or 65 38 58 50

349

The Bells, a South African couple, are obviously in love with the area which they consider one of the most beautiful of southern France. Their converted stone farmhouse is in the tiniest, quietest of hamlets near the jewel that is St Céré as well as the more touristy Rocamadour and Gouffre de Padirac. They have preserved the old beams, the enormous fireplace and an old stone sink. You will be offered walnuts from their trees ... and local lore galore. They also give pottery and art courses.

Rooms: 2 double, 2 twin rooms, all with own bathrooms.

Price: 215-290 Frs for two, including breakfast.

Meals: Dinner 80-100 Frs, including wine & coffee.

Open: All year.

This is an unusual place. Guests stay in typical, completely circular 'gariotte' houses. Made of stone, these are cool in summer and keep their warmth in winter. Spotless and comfortable, they suit people wishing to get away from it all and who don't mind preparing their own food. There are attractive walks in the oak forest around the house. (Don't forget to bring what you need for breakfast!)

Rooms: 3 double rooms with bathrooms, in converted shepherds' huts.

Price: 180 Frs for two. No breakfast.

Meals: Self-Catering. (Restaurant in village.)

Open: All year.

To get there: *From Cahors, N20 north; right onto D677 to Gramat then D14 to Pigeonnier; left onto D36 towards Rignac. Darnis is shortly on the right.*

Map Ref No: 11

To get there: *From Cahors, D6 south. 1km before entering Lalbenque, left at sign. OR telephone from the village – Monsieur is willing to come and show you the way!*

Map Ref No: 15

Gavin & Lillian BELL
Auberge de Darnis
46500 Rignac
Lot
Tel: 65 33 66 84
Fax: 65 33 71 31

M Daniel PASQUIER
L'Ermitage
46230 Lalbenque
Lot
Tel: 65 31 75 91

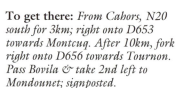

The mill-stream still runs past this typical old 'Quercynois' water-mill, parts of which date back to the Templars. The owners left Provence for a quieter life – and picked this wonderfully wild watery spot. The house has all its original character and is adorned with paintings, drawings and old tapestries hanging on stone walls behind the beds. Good, simply-decorated rooms. Memorable dinners. An inkling of 'hotel' dissolves in the warm atmosphere.

Rooms: 4 double rooms & 1 twin, all with bathrooms.

Price: 230-340 Frs for two, including breakfast (on reservation only).

Meals: Dinner 100 Frs, including wine.

Open: 15 March – 15 November.

To get there: *From Gramat, N140 towards Figeac; after 500m, left onto a small road leading to the mill.*

Map Ref No: 11

Gérard & Claude RAMELOT
Moulin de Fresquet
46500 Gramat
Lot
Tel: 65 38 70 60

"... an idyllic place to holiday", a reader enthused. Peter & Zoé have restored a 17th-century farmhouse and barn, built in the lovely pale local stone, and provide superb guestrooms in a rural paradise. Their house looks out over two valleys and some incomparable Lot views, plus clear starry hushed nights. The Scotts are enthusiastic and charming hosts.

Rooms: 1 double room with bathroom; 1 double & 1 single room sharing a bathroom.

Price: 200-300 Frs for two, including breakfast.

Meals: Dinner 80-85 Frs, including wine.

Open: 7 January – 14 December.

To get there: *From Cahors, N20 south for 3km; right onto D653 towards Montcuq. After 10km, fork right onto D656 towards Tournon. Pass Bovila & take 2nd left to Mondounet; signposted.*

Map Ref No: 15

Peter & Zoé SCOTT
Mondounet
46800 Fargues
Lot
Tel: 65 36 96 32
Fax: 65 31 84 89

In ten hectares of tranquil parkland (and a poultry farm with over 8000 free-range chickens!), this lovely 17th-century château has a warm, informal atmosphere ideal for families. As well as a swimming-pool, there are ponies, bicycles and table-tennis. Rooms are comfortable, with views over the gardens to meadows and woods beyond. Breakfast (home-produced breads and ... eggs!) and dinners are very much 'en famille'.

Rooms: 1 double room and 2 twin rooms, all with own bathrooms.

Price: 280-300 Frs for two, including breakfast.

Meals: Dinner 85 Frs, including wine.

Open: All year.

Chestnut trees line the approach to the 19th-century mansion, nicknamed Maison de la Prune; you will be able to sample Simone's home-made jams at breakfast. She is well-organised and very much the mistress of the house; and a most elegant house it is, with period furniture, billiards, table tennis and a pool. There is a fine garden, with a verandah where great dinners are served. Francis is active in the community, being a vet and regional councillor.

Rooms: 3 double rooms and 1 suite for 2-4 people, all with private bathrooms.

Price: 330-370 Frs for two, including breakfast.

Meals: Dinner 90 Frs, including wine (book ahead).

Open: All year (book in advance to be sure).

To get there: *From Marmande, D933 towards Casteljaloux. Château on right; signposted.*

Map Ref No: 15

To get there: *From Villeneuve-sur-Lot, N21 towards Bergerac. At Cancon, D124 towards Monbahus. Left after 150m; signposted.*

Map Ref No: 15

M & Mme de la RAITRIE
Château de Cantet
Samazan
47250 Bouglon
Lot-et-Garonne
Tel: 53 20 60 60

354

Francis & Simone LARRIBEAU
Chanteclair
47290 Cancon
Lot-et-Garonne
Tel: 53 01 63 34
Fax: 53 41 13 44

355

Madame is a real farmer's wife: big-hearted, strong, no-nonsense – and great fun! She runs her chambres d'hôtes well, yet you are aware that the farm continues to produce cereals, fruit and vegetables as it always has done, some of them for your scrumptious dinner. This is a fine 17th-century house (justifiably called "Le Château") with good guestrooms, one of which has its own fireplace, a boon for out-of-season travellers. Style in the architecture, simplicity in the atmosphere, hard work at the back of it all.

Rooms: 3 double rooms with bathrooms; 2 double rooms with shared bathroom.

Price: 180-220 Frs for two, including breakfast.

Meals: Dinner 70 Frs, including wine.

Open: All year.

To get there: *From A62 Aiguillon exit onto D8 and D666 towards Villeneuve-sur-Lot. At Bourran, D146 to Clairac then D911 for 2km towards Granges.*

Map Ref No: 15

Aimé & Gisèle MASSIAS
Caussinat
47320 Clairac
Lot-et-Garonne
Tel: 53 84 22 11

356

This farm, built during the desperate last decade of the 18th century, lies close to three famous 'bastides' and there's a château thrown in for the view. Two good bedrooms with country furniture in a converted pigeon tower. A high chair, bottle-warmer and games are kept on hand for children. Farm milk at breakfast. The farm also produces tobacco, maize and sunflower oil. Madame has an infectious energy, her affable husband is quieter...and they speak fluent English.

Rooms: 2 double rooms, each with own bathroom; 1 with kitchenette.

Price: 230-280 Frs for two, including breakfast.

Meals: Dinner 80 Frs, including wine.

Open: All year.

To get there: *From Villeneuve-sur-Lot, D676 to Monflanquin and D272 towards Monpazier. House is opposite "Dordogne" sign 1.5km after crossroads to Devillac.*

Map Ref No: 15

Michel PANNETIER
Colombié
47210 Devillac
Lot-et-Garonne
Tel: 53 36 62 34
Fax: 53 36 04 79

357

With its idyllic setting, overlooking the hills, and the hosts' commitment to creating a genuinely invigorating environment – complemented by natural therapy, yoga, tai chi and massage – this 200-year-old farmhouse has a uniquely restorative atmosphere. There is a swimming-pool and a sauna and access to fishing/boating. Organic meals are served on the panoramic terrace.

Rooms: 1 double room, 2 rooms for up to four people, and 1 family room for four to six people; all with private bathrooms.

Price: 320 Frs for two, including breakfast.

Meals: Dinner 100 Frs, including wine.

Open: All year.

To get there: *From Villeneuve-sur-Lot, N21 towards Agen. "Les Huguets" is signposted on the left – follow signs for 3km.*

Map Ref No: 15

Ward & Gerda POPPE-
NOTTEBOOM
Les Huguets
47300 Villeneuve-sur-Lot
Lot-et-Garonne
Tel: 53 70 49 34

358

An environment of calm natural beauty, 3 hectares of oak-trees and a centuries-old manor-house built around a courtyard. Monsieur has restored it most lovingly, with the old stone tiling, walls and beams exposed and, with a flourish, jacuzzis. You will certainly remember this lovely house and its amazing pool... ancient and modern well combined. Breakfasts are grand, dinners very refined, what Monsieur calls "cuisine inspirée". This is B&B with a difference!

Rooms: 4 double rooms and 1 suite for 4, all with own bathrooms.

Price: From 400-480 Frs for two (suite 750 Frs), including breakfast.

Meals: Dinner 130 Frs, excluding wine.

Open: All year.

To get there: *From Villeneuve-sur-Lot, D676 to Monflanquin, then D272 towards Laussou. After bridge, left to Envals. After 3km, left for Soubeyrac.*

Map Ref No: 15

Claude ROCCA
Manoir du Soubeyrac
Envals
47150 Monflanquin
Lot-et-Garonne
Tel: 53 36 51 34

359

A Dutch couple owns this ancient farmhouse (parts date from the 12th century) in the heart of the vineyards of the Côtes-de-Duras. The rooms are stone-walled and wooden-beamed; there is a dining-room, a living-room and a games room (with table-tennis) for guests. There is also a swimming pool, with tennis and horse-riding nearby.

Rooms: 5 double rooms, all with own bathrooms.

Price: 280 Frs for two, including breakfast.

Meals: Dinner 75 Frs.

Open: From 15 April to 31 October.

This lovely 18th-century house is, luckily, out of ear-shot of the autoroute nearby. In large grounds with its own lake, it has been beautifully maintained and furnished. Rooms have wooden floors and huge beds. Guests can use the family library, living-room and dining-room, decorated throughout with Madame's paintings. She serves dinner (regional specialities) in an informal, family atmosphere.

Rooms: 1 twin room and 1 double room, with bathrooms.

Price: 200 Frs for two, including breakfast.

Meals: Dinner 60 Frs, including wine.

Open: All year.

To get there: *From Bergerac, D936 to Ste Foy and D708 to Duras. There, D237 to Réole. At bottom of hill, D134 towards Baleyssagues. Turn right; signposted.*

Map Ref No: 15

To get there: *From Bordeaux, A62, Damazan exit. Enter Damazan; right at Renault garage on D108 towards Buzet/Nirac. "Balous" on right after 200m.*

Map Ref No: 15

M & Mme SCHAEPMAN CRAMER
Savary, Baleyssagues
47120 Duras
Lot-et-Garonne
Tel: 53 83 77 82

Mme Françoise TAQUET
Balous
47160 Damazan
Lot-et-Garonne
Tel: 53 79 42 96

North of Limoges are the Monts d'Ambazac. Andrée spent her childhood here and now returns each summer. The Chanudets normally live in Boulogne and yet still like meeting the English! The new guestroom, in an annexe, has a small adjacent salon. Careful attention has been paid to details, such as thick towels. Dinner if wished, with Limousin dishes. Good hiking country.

Rooms: 1 independent suite for 2 people (+ 2 children).

Price: 200 Frs for two, including breakfast.

Meals: Dinner 70 Frs, including wine (book 24hrs ahead).

Open: 25 June – 31 August.

In wooded ground above the River Vienne this splendid 17th-century manor is ideal for children and adults alike (all water sports on Lac de Vassivière). Monsieur is a jazz musician (if you're lucky he'll play the piano) and his house is full of antiques, curios, toy trains (museum), old cars and surprises. In a separate building, two of the guestrooms have an air of (delicious) decadence; the other two, on the 2nd floor, are 'smarter'. The courtyard is beautiful.

Rooms: 2 double, 1 triple and 1 suite, all with bathrooms.

Price: 250-300 Frs for two, including breakfast.

Meals: 65 Frs, excluding wine or 100 Frs at ferme-auberge next door (closed on Mondays).

Open: All year.

To get there: *From La Souterraine, D1 to Laurière. At Laurière, D28 towards St Goussaud. After 3km, right to La Bezassade.*

Map Ref No: 10

To get there: *From Limoges, D979 towards Eymoutiers; Fougeolles (name of house) is on left just before entering Eymoutiers, signposted Chambres d'Hôtes.*

Map Ref No: 11

Andrée & Robert CHANUDET
La Bezassade
87370 Laurière
Haute-Vienne
Tel: 55 71 58 07 (summer)

M & Mme J. du MONTANT
Fougeolles
87120 Eymoutiers
Haute-Vienne
Tel: 55 69 11 44

Two and a half acres of garden keep Madame busy, as does her beautiful home, which she has decorated herself. The bedroom is pretty and the whole house is crisp and clean with splashes of colour and imagination everywhere. It is also a gîte, so there is a sitting-room with fireplace and a kitchenette. There is an extra room available for spill-over. A most charming place and Madame, a wonderful hostess, will often accompany guests on local visits of discovery.

Rooms: 1 double room with bathroom and small kitchen.

Price: 200 Frs for two, including breakfast.

Meals: Self-Catering.

Open: All year.

The house stands almost alone in the hills east of Limoges. Adjacent, in a converted coaching inn, the guestrooms and sitting-room are decorated with Michel's paintings and lamps : he is a sculptor, Josette makes window blinds and the house is imbued with creative spirit. They are young, 'sympathiques', left Paris in search of peace of mind and enjoy having guests in their very special, off-the-beaten-track corner of France.

Rooms: 2 double rooms, each with own bathroom.

Price: 250 for two, including breakfast.

Meals: Dinner 80 Frs, including wine.

Open: All year.

To get there: *From Limoges, N241 to St Léonard de Noblat then D39 towards St Priest; after 5km right towards Lajoumard; first left and follow signs.*

Map Ref No: 10

Mme JANSEN de VOMECOURT
La Réserve
Bassoleil
87400 St Léonard-de-Noblat
Haute-Vienne
Tel: 55 56 18 39

To get there: *From Eymoutiers, D30 towards Chamberet. House in village of La Roche, 7km beyond Eymoutiers.*

Map Ref No: 11

Michel & Josette JAUBERT
La Roche
87210 Eymoutiers
Haute-Vienne
Tel: 55 69 61 88

Patrick and Mayder, who is Basque, raise goats (biodynamically) in this delectably quiet and pretty corner of the Limousin. The rooms have been lovingly restored and you soon understand why addicted guests return year after year. Children love going with Patrick to milk the goats and collect eggs. Good home cooking with, naturally, a Basque flavour and organic ingredients. Smiling hosts who get on with their lives and let you choose to share theirs or lead your own.

Rooms: 2 double rooms, each with own shower & wc.

Price: 220 Frs for two, including breakfast.

Meals: Dinner 70 Frs, including wine.

Open: All year.

To get there: *From A20, exit 41 to Magnac Bourg; take D215 southwest then follow signs to La Chapelle.*

Map Ref No: 10

Patrick & Mayder LESPAGNOL
La Chapelle
87380 Château-Chervix
Haute-Vienne
Tel: 55 00 86 67

366

Since January 1995
Ren RIJPSTRA
Le Clos de Paunat
24510 Ste Alvère
Dordogne
Tel: 53 63 19 79
Fax: 53 61 62 05

366A

Rooms: 4 double rooms with own bathrooms.

Price: 400-450 Frs for two, including (copious) breakfast.

Meals: None (good choice nearby).

Open: All year except Christmas.

To get there: *From Le Bugue, D703 to Cabrioles Funpark; continue D703 approx 4km towards Ste Alvère. Left at sign to Paunat. House in village opposite abbey.*

From October 1995
Xavière SIMAND
"La Maison des Bois"
Maison-Neuve
24510 Paunat, Dordogne
Tel: 53 22 75 74
Fax: 53 22 75 74

366B

Rooms: 1 double room, 1 suite for 2 or 3; each with own bathroom (with bath).

Price: For two, including breakfast: double 250-300 Frs; suite 350-400 Frs (3rd person 100 Frs).

Meals: 2-course dinner with wine 75 Frs (book ahead).

Open: All year.

To get there: *From Le Bugue, D703 towards Bergerac for 10 km. At crossroads, left to Maison-Neuve (signposted). Her house and curiosity shop are 1km down this road.*

This ancient village house has dramatic views from its mountain valley perch. The restored interior sports numerous beams and game trophies, from birds to a boar's head. The two small, heated rooms are traditionally decorated and have new bathrooms. There is a guest sitting-room. Monsieur Berdé is a most affable host and a chef, cooking regional dishes with local produce. His children are just as delightful.

Rooms: 1 double room and 1 twin room, each with own bathroom.

Price: 200 Frs for two, including breakfast.

Meals: Dinner 75 Frs, including wine.

Open: All year except 24/25 December.

The Midi – Pyrénées

To get there: *From Foix, N20 towards Andorra. At Luzenac, D2 to Unac. First right on entering village, then third right.*

Map Ref No: 16

M & Mme BERDE
09250 Unac
Ariège
Tel: 61 64 45 51

A big, incredibly rambling place with a certain character, stemming partly from the rustic features of the building and the simple country furnishings, and partly from the wall-hangings and various objects from around the world. On top of a hill with lovely views. There is a large number of rooms but there's also lots of space and Madame's joie-de-vivre ensures that the touch remains personal.

Rooms: 10 double rooms and 2 suites, all with bathrooms.

Price: 230-320 Frs for two, including breakfast.

Meals: Dinner 90 Frs.

Open: All year.

At the end of the world, an old restored farmhouse with lots of beams, white walls and a big fireplace, standing 1000 feet up on 45 hectares of woodland looking out over the valley. Walk or ride straight out into the Pyrenean foothills. The highly entertaining Dutch owners raise horses (which you can ride) and Newfoundland dogs (which you can't). They will regale you, in several languages, with stories of sailing the Atlantic or the Carribean; don't miss dining with them. Superb value; book early.

Rooms: 2 double and 2 twin rooms, all with bathrooms.

Price: 200 Frs for two, including breakfast (320 Frs for two, half-board, if staying for 5 nights).

Meals: Dinner 70 Frs.

Open: All year.

To get there: *From Pamiers, D11 towards Belpech. There, right to La Bastide de Lordat; follow signs to St Felix de Tournegat; signposted 'Montagnac'.*

Map Ref No: 16

To get there: *From Foix, D17 towards Col de Marrous. After 8km, in La Mouline: signposted.*

Map Ref No: 15

Josépha & J-Pierre BERTOLINO
Domaine de Montagnac
09500 St Félix-de-Tournegat
Ariège
Tel: 61 68 72 75
Fax: 61 67 44 84

Bob et Jenny BROGNEAUX
Le Poulsieu
Serres-sur-Arget
09000 Foix
Ariège
Tel: 61 02 77 72

This big old house is relaxed and informal. There are views to the Pyrenees, and a stream running through the garden. Church bells can be heard from the large rooms (good beds and well-stocked bookshelves). The welcome is warm and friendly. Françoise uses organic produce from her sister's farm (vegetarian dishes upon request). Best between May and October.

Rooms: 1 double room and 1 twin room, both with bathrooms. Extra bed available.

Price: 180 Frs for two, including breakfast.

Meals: Dinner 65 Frs, including wine.

Open: Open all year. Best May-Oct.

This old farmhouse set amid cornfields and forest is home to a family and their large dogs. The atmosphere is homely and inviting, with centrally-heated bedrooms with stone walls and a dining-room with huge open fire. There's milk and fruit from the farm; menus are flexible and the family may join guests for dinner. There's riding and a lake nearby.

Rooms: 1 double room and 2 twin rooms, each with own bathroom.

Price: 250 Frs for two, including breakfast.

Meals: Dinner 90 Frs, including wine.

Open: All year.

To get there: *From Pamiers, D119 towards Mirepoix. At "les Issards", D12 to Dun. Right after Post Office, cross bridge, turn left – second house on left.*

Map Ref No: 16

Mme Françoise COPIN
Cambel
09600 Dun
Ariège
Tel: 61 68 69 31

To get there: *From Mirepoix, D6 towards Lavelanet. At Aigues-Vives, left onto D28. Go through Léran and follow signs to B&B on right.*

Map Ref No: 16

Anne-Marie de BRUYNE
Bon Repos
09600 Léran
Ariège
Tel: 61 01 27 83

A former 19th-century farming school; the director's bust presides over the gardens. Still a farm, it's now an informal family home. Guests stay in a separate wing. The light rooms have comfortable beds, pretty rugs on the floors and some period furnishings. Bernadette is young, quietly friendly and helpful. Breakfast, with good home-made cakes, in the guests' living-room. There is a kitchen for guests and a shady garden where you can picnic and idle the day away.

Rooms: 4 double rooms, all with bathrooms.

Price: 230-250 Frs for two, including breakfast.

Meals: Not available.

Open: All year.

Courses in ceramics, painting and weaving are the centre of interest here. The couple also keep a flock of sheep. Their isolated, beautifully renovated old farmhouse looks towards the Pyrenees. The large guestroom is in a separate building with living-room and kitchen facilities. In keeping with your hosts' activities, dinners served 'en famille' may feature home-grown fruit and lamb.

Rooms: 1 double room with bathroom.

Price: 200 Frs for two, including breakfast.

Meals: Dinner 70 Frs, including wine.

Open: All year.

To get there: *From Toulouse, N20 towards Foix. 55km on, at Vernet, D624 left towards Mazères; house is 1km along on right.*

Map Ref No: 15

To get there: *From Pamiers, D11 towards Belpech. After 9km, right towards Pinet and Gaudies, then follow signposts.*

Map Ref No: 16

Bernadette & Casimir GIANESINI
Ferme de Royat
09700 Montaut
Ariège
Tel: 61 68 32 09

Jeanne & Guy GOSSELIN
Certe
09700 Gaudies
Ariège
Tel: 61 67 01 56

An ancient house, gentrified in the 19th century, with breathtaking views of the Pyrenees and the Ariège massif. Manzac d'En Bas has masses of original beams and a huge open fireplace and the English owners bake bread in the old bread oven – as well as producing their own honey. Breakfast in the kitchen is a real celebration. Then sally forth to walk, climb or ride, up hills, down caves, into castles – the area is an inexhaustible treasure-house.

Rooms: 1 double room with bathroom, 2 twin rooms sharing a bathroom.

Price: 180-200 Frs for two, including breakfast.

Meals: Dinner 70 Frs, including wine (advance booking).

Open: All year.

To get there: *From Toulouse, N117 towards Tarbes. Left onto D627, through Daumazan then left onto D19 towards Castex. Right after 2km then left after 600m; house is 200m on left.*

Map Ref No: 15

David & Venetia HOPKINS
Manzac d'En Bas
09350 Castex
Ariège
Tel: 61 69 85 25
Fax: 61 69 85 25

Cantegril is a hamlet-and-riding-stables set in 45 hectares. Its perch 1750 feet above sea level gives spectacular panoramic views of the Pyrenees, with good hiking and fishing. Guestrooms, in an independent building with a living-room, are clean and simple, with stone walls, pine beds and electric heaters. Bathroom facilities vary. Homely regional cooking upon request.

Rooms: 2 double rooms and 2 twin rooms, all with own bathrooms.

Price: 170-180 Frs for two, including breakfast.

Meals: Dinner 60 Frs, including wine (book ahead).

Open: All year.

To get there: *From Foix, D617 towards St Martin-de-Caralp. Turn left onto D145 and left again onto D11. Cantegril is on the left.*

Map Ref No: 15

Mlle Elisabeth PAGES
Ecole d'Equitation de Cantegril
09000 St-Martin-de-Caralp
Ariège
Tel: 61 02 92 73

This is an enchanting family home in an isolated setting, with rides in a horse-drawn cart or fishing and paddling in the mountain stream that gushes past the house. The Piednoëls, smiling and hospitable, genuinely like children. The decor is simple and traditional, the bedding comfortable, the bathrooms new. Straightforward dinners, eaten 'en famille', include cakes and home-grown veg.

Rooms: 1 twin room with own bathroom. Extra bed available.

Price: 190 Frs for two, including breakfast.

Meals: Dinner 65 Frs.

Open: All year.

This elderly couple gives a friendly reception in their bungalow home. The most memorable feature is the riot of flowers all around the south-facing terrace. The guestroom has an immaculate new bed, a mass of books and central heating. The Orient Express loo on the landing will appeal to train buffs. There's plenty of wine with the homely dinners (sometimes 'en famille').

Rooms: 1 double room with own bathroom.

Price: 180 Frs for two, including breakfast.

Meals: Dinner 70 Frs, including wine.

Open: From 15 April to 15 October.

To get there: *From Foix, D21 to Ganac. After 5km take route to Micou "les Carcis". Right just after small bridge.*

Map Ref No: 15

Sylviane PIEDNOEL
Les Carcis
09000 Ganac
Ariège
Tel: 61 02 96 54

To get there: *From Tarascon, D618 towards Massat. 3km after Saurat turn right. Chambres d'Hôtes signposted.*

Map Ref No: 15

Roger & Monique ROBERT
Layroze
09400 Saurat
Ariège
Tel: 61 05 73 24

Set in a mountain valley, this sociable couple's home is reminiscent of a Swiss chalet. He is Dutch, she Norman; both enjoy good conversation. The guestrooms (one with a small sitting area) are traditional in style, with modern bathrooms. In winter, the huge breakfasts set you up for skiing. In summer you can barbecue in the flower garden.

Rooms: 1 double room and 1 twin room, each with own bathroom.

Price: 200 Frs for two, including breakfast.

Meals: Not available.

Open: All year.

To get there: *From Tarascon-sur-Ariège take D8. Follow signpost to Capoulet Junac and B&B on left.*

Map Ref No: 15

M & Mme VAN HOORN
Capoulet Junac
09400 Tarascon
Ariège
Tel: 61 05 89 88

In an area where there is very little accommodation this auberge offers simple, rustic, comfortable rooms with lovely views. Set on the outskirts of a pretty hamlet, the old house is built almost entirely of wood. A typical meal is of vegetable soup, homemade paté, large omelettes and wine for next to nothing! Vegetarians catered for too. Annie and her family are helpful, if a little reserved.

Rooms: 2 double rooms with bathrooms (extra beds available).

Price: 200 Frs for two, including breakfast.

Meals: Dinner from 60 Frs, including wine.

Open: All year.

To get there: *From Toulouse, D632 towards Tarbes. After 75km, right on D90 to Péguilhan; auberge is on left before village.*

Map Ref No: 15

Annie & Jean-François CASTEX
Auberge du Paysan
31350 Péguilhan
Haute-Garonne
Tel: 61 88 75 78

The 18th-century château is surrounded by flat farmlands. Make sure you are expected – there's a locked gate. The comfortable pairs of adjoining bedrooms with period furnishings are ideal for families. The atmosphere is informal, with children's games and a garden. The Baroness is elderly, disarmingly straightforward and unpretentious; she serves dinner herself, and enjoys talking to her guests. Pool 6km.

Rooms: 4 double rooms, all with private bathrooms – 2 extra beds available.

Price: 350 Frs for two, including breakfast.

Meals: 95 Frs for two, including wine.

Open: From Easter to 1 November.

A cereal farm with a handsome 'maison de maître' where you share the lives of your hosts. It has been in their family since 1789 when it was given as a wedding present. This fascinating area is little known to tourists, yet within reach are the Pyrenees, with some of the most spectacular walking in Europe, and Toulouse, an exciting and beautiful city. Nearby, an artificial lake offers all sorts of water sports. Or families can play and swim in the grounds of Mailhol.

Rooms: 1 double room and 1 twin room, with bathrooms.

Price: 325 Frs for two, including breakfast.

Meals: None

Open: All year.

To get there: *From Toulouse, D1 towards Aeroport Cornebarrieu; stay on D1 until St Paul then D87 right to Larra.*

Map Ref No: 15

To get there: *From Toulouse, N20 towards Pamiers. After Les Baccarets, D25 right towards Gaillac-Toulza. House is 2km along this road.*

Map Ref No: 15

Baronne Brigitte de CARRIERE
Château de Larra
31330 Grenade-sur-Garonne
Haute-Garonne
Tel: 61 82 62 51

Marie DUMESNIL
Mailhol
31550 Gaillac-Toulza
Haute-Garonne
Tel: 61 08 90 53

This 1700's abbey hospital, a listed monument, is being slowly restored. The austere guestrooms create a wonderful sense of volume with soaring ceilings and very low beds. One contains the old pharmacist's cupboards. Simple bathrooms. Dinner is served in the kitchen, across the cloister garden, with produce from the small organic farm – Christophe is a man of conviction! Marie-Christine teaches at primary school.

This 17th-century manor-house enjoys sweeping views across a valley to fields and gentle hills. The elegant interior combines antiques, country furnishings and family possessions, with a comfortable lived-in feel. The immaculate bedrooms are charmingly decorated. Madame is usually a conscientious and well-organised hostess. In summer, she serves traditional meals on the terrace overlooking the large garden. Tennis.

Rooms: 2 double rooms with shared bathroom.

Price: 200 Frs for two.

Meals: Dinner 65 Frs, including wine.

Open: All year.

Rooms: 2 double and 2 twin rooms, all with bathrooms.

Price: 320 Frs for two, including breakfast.

Meals: Dinner 120 Frs.

Open: All year.

To get there: *From Toulouse, N117 to Boussens. There, D365 towards Aurignac. In Le Frechet, follow signpost "N.D. de Lorette".*

Map Ref No: 15

To get there: *From Toulouse (23km) along N88 towards Albi. At Montastruc-la-Conseillère, D30 towards Lavour. 4.5km before Montpitol turn right; signposted.*

Map Ref No: 15

M Christophe FERRY
Lorette
31420 Alan
Haute-Garonne
Tel: 61 98 98 84

Claudette FIEUX
Stoupignan
31380 Montpitol
Haute-Garonne
Tel: 61 84 22 02

Josette, a former teacher, and her much-travelled companion, raise sheep and provide warm hospitality. Light, uncluttered bedrooms have sea-green and blue woodwork and ethnic touches – maybe a brass tray or a carved table. The bathrooms are simple but really pretty. Meals cooked with home produce are served in the cosy dining-room. Sitting-room with piano. Enclosed garden.

Rooms: 2 twin rooms with washbasins sharing a bathroom. 2 double rooms with own separate bathrooms. Extra beds available.

Price: 230 Frs for two, including breakfast. Half-board 350 Frs for two.

Meals: Dinner 75 Frs, including wine.

Open: All year.

To get there: *From Toulouse, N117 towards St Gaudens. At Carbonne, D627 to Montesquieu and D628 to Daumazan-sur-Arize; D19 to Montbrun-Brocage. Farm on right 5km after village.*

Map Ref No: 15

Josette PARINAUD-TOMMASI
Hameau de Pave
31310 Montbrun-Bocage
Haute-Garonne
Tel: 61 98 11 25

384

An old manor tucked away in the woods beside a stream at the foot of the Pyrenees – you are forced back into the arms of Mother Nature, to shed your stress and think only of walking, riding, skiing, fishing or painting. Ingeborg is a painter herself, in love with her house, her woods, her adopted country. She'll give you a substantial breakfast, help you plan your day or take you riding. "An extraordinary and beautiful house", said New Yorkers Mr & Mrs Snodgrass (sic).

Rooms: 4 double rooms, 3 with own bathrooms.

Price: 180-260 Frs for two, including breakfast.

Meals: Dinner 70-80 Frs.

Open: All year.

To get there: *From Boulogne-sur-Gesse, D635 towards St Gaudens & Ciaudoux. After about 7km, fork left towards Ciadoux; after a few metres, left down small private road; house on right.*

Map Ref No: 15

Ingeborg ROEHRIG
Ciadoux
31350 Boulogne-sur-Gesse
Haute-Garonne
Tel: 61 88 10 88

385

THE MIDI – PYRÉNÉES

Light floods into the attractive living-room of this converted wine 'chai'. A wooden staircase and gallery lead to the smart bedrooms upstairs. These combine good, old furniture and pretty fabrics with boldly-coloured bathrooms. Roger made the unusual bedside lamps from old pickling bottles. Monique plays the piano and cooks exotic or traditional dishes with equal flair. Smiling, hospitable people.

Rooms: 4 double rooms, all with bathrooms.

Price: 300-350 Frs for two, including breakfast.

Meals: Dinner 200 Frs, including wine.

Open: All year, except January.

This renovated 1840's house, with its pigeon tower, belonged to Madame's grandfather; she, now a retired primary school teacher, was born here. She and her husband are relaxed, cultured hosts who receive their guests as friends. Their local knowledge will be appreciated by the curious. The bedroom, all pink and white, is quiet and welcoming. Breakfast in the living-room or on the terrace, looking onto the neat walled garden.

Rooms: 1 twin room with own bathroom.

Price: 230 Frs for two, including breakfast.

Meals: None.

Open: All year

To get there: *From Toulouse, N124 to Auch. There, D930 towards Condom; after 18km, D103 right towards Fleurance. House is 3.5km after Lavardens.*

Map Ref No: 15

To get there: *From Montauban, D928 towards Auch. After Gimat, right onto D18 and D7 for 4km, then left: house is in hamlet, round to left (signposted).*

Map Ref No: 15

Monique & Roger HUGON
Mascara
32360 Lavardens
Gers
Tel: 62 64 52 17

Mme Solange JEANGRAND
Le Pigeonnier
32380 Pessoulens
Gers
Tel: 62 66 49 25

Friendly, generous hosts and a secluded spot amidst grain fields and pastures. The guestrooms open onto a wooden balcony overlooking the courtyard. Decor is simple: old furniture, white walls with pictures, wooden floors with rugs. Breakfast on rush-seated chairs in the family kitchen with its old cupboards and checked curtains. Guests' living-room with corner kitchen. Garden.

Rooms: 1 double room, 1 triple room and 1 suite ideal for families; each with own bathroom.

Price: 180-220 Frs for two, including breakfast.

Meals: Not available. Self-catering facilities.

Open: All year.

The Vignaux buy farm-reared poultry to make into foie gras and confits, so family and guests share good-value regional cooking. Language barriers are overcome – perhaps with the aid of some local Armagnac! The ivy-covered farmhouse looks out over gentle valleys to the fortified hill-top village beyond. There are flowers everywhere, the rooms are simple and the hosts are friendly. There is a small campsite behind the house but the table d'hôte is reserved for B&B guests.

Rooms: 3 double rooms with own bathrooms; 2 doubles with own showers & shared wc; 1 studio with bathroom & kitchen.

Price: 175 Frs for two, including breakfast.

Meals: Dinner 80 Frs, including wine.

Open: All year, except 1-20 November.

To get there: *From Auch, N21 towards Tarbes. 6km after Mirande, house signposted on left.*

Map Ref No: 15

To get there: *From Condom, D7 towards Lectoure. After Caussens, right onto D204; signposted for 2km.*

Map Ref No: 15

Louis & Marthe SABATHIER
Noailles
32300 St Maur
Gers
Tel: 62 67 57 98

Robert VIGNAUX
Bordeneuve
32100 Béraut
Gers
Tel: 62 28 08 41

Built when Napoleon was waging war across Europe, Madame's exquisite long low house and idyllic gardens are an oasis of calm where peace reigns and you may make a lifelong friend. A coolly elegant entrance hall sets the tone. In the guestrooms, fine furniture, real linen sheets and superb bathrooms speak her pride in her ancestral home. A delicious beautifully-presented breakfast is further enhanced by civilised conversation. Come to unwind – and you may never want to leave.

Rooms: 2 doubles, 1 twin and 1 triple, all with bathrooms.

Price: 240 Frs for two, including breakfast.

Meals: Not available (restaurant 2km).

Open: All year.

A change from many of our 'smarter' places and hardly a conventional B&B, but an admirable cooperative effort to run a family farm and a rambling hostelry offering basic but excellent-value rooms. Views of the rushing Gave de Pau and mountain backdrop are of heartbreaking splendour. 11 clean, freshly-decorated rooms with simple furnishings and cooking facilities in the converted stable (bring your own pots and cutlery!)

Rooms: 4 double, 5 triple, 2 family rooms, most with own shower, sharing wc.

Price: 173 Frs for two, including breakfast.

Meals: None (next door).

Open: All year.

To get there: *From Tarbes, N117 towards Toulouse. At Lannemezan take road to Pinas. Left at church, house on right after 1km.*

Map Ref No: 15

To get there: *From Lourdes, D937 towards Pau. In Peyrouse, house is on left of main road, opposite Mairie.*

Map Ref No: 15

Mme Marie-Sabine COLOMBIER
Domaine de Jean-Pierre
Route de Villeneuve
65300 Pinas
Hautes-Pyrénées
Tel: 62 98 15 08

Josette LADAGNOUS
Le Bourg
65270 Peyrouse
Hautes-Pyrénées
Tel: 62 41 82 66

Close to the Gorges de l'Aveyron, positioned among quiet fields of maize, this 19th-century farmhouse has been carefully restored. The rooms, simply furnished and attractive, are set around a large pool where Véronique and Johnny, a dynamic, well-travelled, generous couple, will happily organise a barbecue for their guests. They enjoy children and the area holds many delights to explore.

Rooms: 1 double & 3 twin rooms, with bathrooms.

Price: 240-280 Frs for two, including breakfast.

Meals: Dinner 90 Frs, including wine (book ahead).

Open: All year.

To get there: *From Cahors, N20 to Caussade then D964 towards Gaillac. At Montricoux, D115 towards Nègrepelisse; after 500m, signposted.*

Map Ref No: 15

Johnny & Véronique ANTONY
Les Brunis
82800 Nègrepelisse
Tarn-et-Garonne
Tel: 63 67 24 08

Michèle is a smiling, big-hearted woman whose whole attitude says 'bienvenue'. Comfortable rooms, though very low beams, but eating is definitely the priority here. Your hostess wins prizes – in Tarn-et-Garonne! – for her recipes, invents sauces, makes her own aperitif. Altogether an exceptional place. Fishing rods are on loan to use in the pond. Footpaths lead out from the gate. The Romanesque treasures of Moissac, lovely villages, caves, are all within easy reach.

Rooms: 1 double and 1 twin, each with own bathroom. Extra beds available.

Price: 220 Frs for two, including breakfast.

Meals: Dinner 80 Frs, including wine & coffee.

Open: All year.

To get there: *From Moissac, D7 towards Bourg-de-Visa about 14km. Before Brassac and just before a bridge, right towards Fauroux. Farm 2km along; signposted.*

Map Ref No: 15

Gilbert & Michèle DIO
La Marquise
Brassac
82190 Bourg-de-Visa
Tarn-et-Garonne
Tel: 63 94 25 16

The English hosts promise a warm welcome to visitors to their 200-year-old 'Quercynois' farmhouse. Set in tranquil wooded grounds, with sweeping views over farmland and hills, it is a peaceful and comfortable base for exploring the surrounding countryside on foot or bicycle. Watersports are also close at hand; take a picnic lunch to the artifical lake and beach, just 5 minutes away by car.

Rooms: 2 double rooms and 1 family room for four, both with bathrooms.

Price: 220-240 Frs for two, including breakfast.

Meals: Dinner 55 Frs, including wine.

Open: From 1 March to 31 October.

Georges was an agronomist in Africa. He and Danielle have sympathetically restored the 1870's hunting lodge with a very personal touch. The huge guestrooms have excellent wide beds and luxury details, including fresh fruit and 'toiletries'. After a swim in the pool, enjoy an elegant dinner with wines from a fine cellar (and a log fire in cold weather). Your hosts like you to stay some time and share their deep knowledge of the region. Excellent value.

Rooms: 1 double, 1 twin & 1 suite for 4, each with own bathroom.

Price: 230-330 Frs for two, including breakfast.

Meals: Dinner 100 Frs, including wine & coffee.

Open: All year.

To get there: *On "Bis" route half way between Périgueux and Toulouse. Sign "Chambres d'Hôtes" on D2, 5km south of Montaigu-de-Quercy.*

Map Ref No: 15

To get there: *From A62, Valence d'Agen exit onto D953 towards Cahors. After Lalande, left on D46. House is after main square in Castelsagrat.*

Map Ref No: 15

Arthur & Deborah HUNT
Les Chênes de Sainte Croix
82150 Montaigu-de-Quercy
Tarn-et-Garonne
Tel: 63 95 30 78

Georges & Danielle JONQUA-CLEMENT
Le Castel
82400 Castelsagrat
Tarn-et-Garonne
Tel: 63 94 20 55

On the pilgrim path to Compostela, the Orsoni estate throbs with animal life (they breed horses) and country delights. Walkers, riders and children love it. A homemade aperitif on the terrace facing the ever-changing Quercy panorama will lighten the soul of any civilised traveller. The welcome is warm, the rooms large, the bathrooms modern and the food fabulous – Edmond comes from Lyon (an excellent gastronomic reference) and cooks with style.

Rooms: 3 double & 1 twin room, all with own bathrooms.

Price: 250-330 Frs for two, including breakfast.

Meals: Dinner 110 Frs, including wine.

Open: All year.

To get there: *From Moissac, D927 + D957 towards Cahors for 6km; fork right on D16 towards Dufort-Lacapelette; left at fork towards St Martin. La Baysse on left before St Martin.*

Map Ref No: 15

Maria & Edmond ORSONI
La Baysse
82200 Montesquieu
Tarn-et-Garonne
Tel: 63 04 54 00

The Franco-Dutch family who spend long summer holidays here have lovingly restored their old stone farmhouse and thoroughly enjoy sharing it and all its leafy, pastoral textures with other families. The local château was once a commandery for the Templars, then for the Order of Malta. It is an area steeped in European history...though somewhat less war-soaked now. Lachapelle offers walks, games and a pool for a really restful holiday.

Rooms: 1 double room (for 2-4) & 1 single room with own bathrooms.

Price: 250 Frs for two, including breakfast.

Meals: Dinner 80 Frs, including wine.

Open: July & August.

To get there: *From Agen, A62 east, exit 8 towards Gramont. After Mansonville, follow signs to Lachapelle; house on right on entering village.*

Map Ref No: 15

M & Mme VAN DEN BRINK
Au Village
82120 Lachapelle
Tarn-et-Garonne
Tel: 63 94 14 10
or (1) 39 49 07 37 (Paris)

Languedoc – Roussillon – Cévennes

An Edwardian folly! And in the humble Aude vineyards, not on the Riviera. Sheer delight, with billiards, ping-pong and pool – many of the elements of the sybaritic lifestyle. But do also visit the reminders of the purer life of those faithful Cathar spirits whose strongholds are here, ruined when their occupants were persecuted for "heresy". The guestrooms are good, spotless (perhaps almost sterile), meals made with home-grown produce and the estate wine very drinkable.

Rooms: 3 double rooms with bathrooms; 1 twin & 1 double sharing a bathroom.

Price: 260 Frs for two, including breakfast.

Meals: Dinner 90 Frs, excluding wine.

Open: 1 April – 30 October.

To get there: *From Carcassonne, N113 to Trèbes then D610 towards Béziers. On entering Puichéric, left towards Rieux and follow signs.*

Map Ref No: 16

Jean et Simone BERGE
Château de Saint-Aunay
11700 Puichéric
Aude
Tel: 68 43 72 20

This is a beautiful, converted farmhouse with its huge beams and fireplace intact. There are five pretty rooms to choose from (one accessible by wheelchair), utter quiet to relax into and wonderful walks. Your hosts will happily share their love of the area, its birdlife, wild flowers, history and wine and a delicious dinner made with local produce and served in the enormous dining-room (or outside in summer).

Rooms: 3 double rooms, 1 twin room, 1 triple room, all with own bathrooms.

Price: 295-315 Frs for two, including breakfast.

Meals: 105-160 Frs, including wine and aperitif (vegetarian dishes available).

Open: All year.

To get there: *From Carcassonne, D142 to Cazilhac. Left in front of Mairie on D56 towards Villefloure (bear left at cemetery). La Sauzette signposted to left after 2km.*

Map Ref No: 16

Christopher & Diana GIBSON
Ferme de la Sauzette
Route de Villefloure, Cazilhac
11570 Palaja, Aude
Tel: 68 79 81 32
Fax: 68 79 65 99

399

Here you are truly miles from anywhere and much closer to yourself. A 14th-century religious retreat (and vineyard) built for the Bishops of Alet, the estate now produces essential oils and offers aromatherapy treatment. An atmosphere of peace and purity pervades. Yann exercises his immense culinary skills on local organic produce; his wife and five daughters have the same radiant presence. A beautiful building and wonderful people in a lovely area.

Rooms: 1 double room and 3 twin rooms, all with own shower room, one with own wc.

Price: 200-250 Frs for two, including breakfast.

Meals: Dinner 80 Frs, including wine and coffee. Picnic lunches available. All organic veg and fruit.

Open: All year except 2 weeks in November.

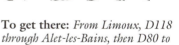

To get there: *From Limoux, D118 through Alet-les-Bains, then D80 to Luc-sur-Aude. Left at cemetery and follow chemin de Castillou; 3.5km of track to house.,*

Map Ref No: 16

Yann & Caroline ROLLAND
Domaine de Castillou
11190 Luc-sur-Aude
Aude
Tel: 68 74 05 31
Fax: 68 74 30 04

400

A fairy-tale 12th-century castle with moats, towers and a monumental courtyart where concerts are given in summer. They even have a resident ghost, la Dame à la Rose! Exceptional bedrooms, some with round tower bathrooms. Madame finds time for her guests despite running a cultural centre in her home. You can expect a warm welcome for adults and children alike and a copious breakfast (as did Mary Stuart (sic) when she came here).

Rooms: 3 double rooms, 2 triple rooms and 1 twin, all with bathrooms.

Price: 400 Frs for two, including breakfast.

Meals: None.

Open: All year.

To get there: *From Avignon, N580 towards Bagnols-sur-Cèze. At junction in L'Ardoise, left along D9 towards Laudun; signposted.*

Map Ref No: 17

Gisèle & Jean-Louis BASTOUIL
Château de Lascours
30290 Laudun
Gard
Tel: 66 50 39 61
Fax: 66 50 30 08

401

This manor-house dates back to the 14th century. The columns of the balcony above the interior courtyard are thought to be Roman! Breakfast is served in a vaulted room. The bedrooms and bathrooms need renovation but this matters little in such a seductive house. Monsieur is an interesting young host; his parents were in the diplomatic service and the house is filled with reminders of their travels. Worth the experience.

Rooms: 3 double rooms, all with bathrooms.

Price: 275 Frs for two, including breakfast.

Meals: Not available.

Open: All year.

To get there: *From Avignon, N580 towards Bagnols-sur-Cèze. At Orange/St-Laurent-des-Arbres roundabout, straight ahead for 200m; left opposite converted chapel; lane on right leads to Beaupré.*

Map Ref No: 17

M Jacques BERARD
Ferme Beaupré
30126 St Laurent-des-Arbres
Gard
Tel: 66 50 01 01

402

An atmosphere of lived-in formality pervades the stately salons with their ancestral portraits and antiques. Immaculately maintained guestrooms include an 18th-century room with marble bathroom. The Count is pleasantly dignified; the Countess is a practical and conscientious hostess. Her 5-course dinners are elegant, convivial occasions. There are invariably 10 people at the table set with silver and crystal.

Rooms: 2 double, 2 twin rooms & 1 suite, all with bathrooms.

Price: 350-600 Frs for two; breakfast not included (40 Frs per pers).

Meals: Dinner 180-200 Frs, including wine.

Open: All year.

An old stone-pillared gate leads to a large, shady courtyard with a small farmhouse facing the substantial 19th-century 'bastide'. The two large rooms ("B&B in the Albert Hall"), with parquet floors and family portraits, are reached by an enormous stone staircase. The Ardèche runs at the bottom of the garden, so enjoy the private "beach" (lucky ones will see otter). There is also a camping-site whose occupants tend to invade the pool.

Rooms: 1 double room and 1 twin, each with own bathroom, sharing wc.

Price: 230 Frs for two, including breakfast.

Meals: None.

Open: All year.

To get there: *From Alès, N110 to Les Tavernes. There, take D106 to Ribaute-les-Tavernes; signposted in the village.*

Map Ref No: 17

To get there: *From A7, Bollène exit onto D994 to Pont-St-Esprit. N86 towards Bourg St-Andéol; signposted before bridge across Ardèche river.*

Map Ref No: 17

Comte & Comtesse CHAMSKI-MANDAJORS
Château de Ribaute
30720 Ribaute-les-Tavernes, Gard
Tel: 66 83 01 66
Fax: 66 83 86 93

403

Mme de LAVAISSIERE
de VERDUZAN
Pont d'Ardèche
30130 Pont St Esprit
Gard
Tel: 66 39 29 80

404

A fine old Provençal mas that has seen better days, it still has some nice heirlooms and the two guestrooms are genuine family rooms with great French charm. Unfortunately they give onto the main road and only have single glazing. The Hansons, a well-organised Anglo-French couple, also run a campsite over the road (B&B guests may use the pool). A useful address for a stopover. Make sure you ask for a room in the main house only.

Rooms: 2 double rooms sharing a bathroom.

Price: 200-350 Frs for two, including breakfast.

Meals: None (in village).

Open: All year.

Roses and lavender framing a kitchen window and a basket of crusty fresh bread set the tone of this house in the middle of the 'garrigue'. Rooms vary in size and style; each features lovely local tiles in the shower and pretty fabrics. The emphasis here is on informality, reflected in the lived-in feel, the hosts' relaxed attitude and the rough paths which scramble up through olive trees to the pool with its stunning views.

Rooms: 3 double rooms and 1 twin room all with own bathrooms.

Price: 350-400 Frs for two, including breakfast.

Meals: None (self-catering possible).

Open: All year.

To get there: *From Vauvert, N572 towards Arles for 5km. House is right on crossroads with D779 to Gallician.*

Map Ref No: 17

To get there: *From Avignon, D2 towards Aramon along Rhône. After 10km, D126 right towards Saze. After 2km, left down track – second house on right with red shutters.*

Map Ref No: 17

Christine HANSON
Mas des Mourgues
Gallician
30600 Vauvert
Gard
Tel: 66 73 30 88

405

Annie & André MALEK
Le Rocher Pointu
Plan de Dève
30390 Aramon, Gard
Tel: 66 57 41 87
Fax: 66 57 01 77

406

A very pretty 18th-century village house with a gorgeous flower-filled garden that makes a delightful contrast with the typical southern village. The Cévennes countryside, of course, is beautiful. St Hippolyte was famous as a silk-making centre and has a silk museum. Rooms are comfortably furnished, large and full of light. There is a magnificent central staircase with an iron balustrade. Madame is well-travelled and sociable.

Rooms: 4 double rooms, all with bathrooms.

Price: 300 Frs for two, including breakfast.

Meals: Not available.

Open: Easter-15 October & 20 December-1 January.

To get there: *From Nîmes, D999 towards Ganges, 50km to St Hippolyte-du-Fort. House in village centre.*

Map Ref No: 17

Mme NAINTRE COLLIN
14 rue Blanqueri
30170 St Hippolyte-du-Fort
Gard
Tel: 66 77 94 10

A flower-filled garden, a house full of books (Madame used to be a librairian) and two superbly appointed rooms (with excellent bathrooms). In the warmer months, after a dip in the pool, breakfast beneath the mulberry tree. In the heart of the Cévennes silk industry, this former silk nursery has fine views of the hills. With advice from your friendly and knowledgeable hostess it is a good base from which to explore the history-laden countryside. Horse-riding can be arranged. Not suitable for children under 7 or dogs.

Rooms: 1 double room and 1 twin room each with own bathroom.

Price: 400 Frs for two including breakfast.

Meals: Dinner 120 Frs, including wine (on reservation only).

Open: All year.

To get there: *From Alès, N110 south, right on D910 towards Anduze; after 500m, left on D24 to Canaules. There, right on D149 to St Nazaire-des-Gardies, right at railway bridge, up hill to Mairie, left to La Fauguière. House at bottom of hill on left.*

Map Ref No: 17

Edna PRICE
Mas de la Fauguière
30610 St Nazaire-des-Gardies
Gard
Tel: 66 77 38 67
Fax: 66 77 11 64

This lovingly renovated old farmhouse stands at the foot of an unspoilt village, visible from pool and guestrooms. The very comfortable rooms are traditional in style (two done in chintz), and named after flowers. Flowers abound; Monsieur is green-fingered, while Madame turns her hand to old porcelain. Guests may use a summer kitchen. Attractive river and waterfall nearby.

Rooms: 3 double rooms, 1 twin room and 2 triple rooms, all with bathrooms.

Price: 250-290 Frs for two, including breakfast.

Meals: None (self-catering).

Open: From Easter to 31 October.

As well as chambres d'hôtes the Simonots run a pottery atelier and the atmosphere is busy and creative. The guestrooms are separate from the main house; bedrooms are simply furnished and there is a sitting-room with fireplace. Breakfast (and dinner on request) is served on the terrace or in the dining-room. Lovely landscape, rolling hills and woods; ideal for hikers as well as potters.

Rooms: 1 twin, 1 double room, each with bathroom.

Price: 230-260 Frs for two, including breakfast.

Meals: Dinner 70 Frs, including wine (book ahead).

Open: All year.

    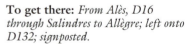

To get there: *From Pont Saint Esprit, N86 towards Bagnols-sur-Cèze. Just before Bagnols right on D980 towards Barjac. After 11km, left on D166 for La Roque-sur-Cèze. House is on left in village, opposite telephone kiosk.*

Map Ref No: 17

To get there: *From Alès, D16 through Salindres to Allègre; left onto D132; signposted.*

Map Ref No: 17

M Pierre RIGAUD
La Tonnelle
30200 La Roque-sur-Cèze
Gard
Tel: 66 82 79 37

Michel & Françoise SIMONOT
Mas Cassac
Allègre
30500 St Ambroix
Gard
Tel: 66 24 85 65

This mediaeval Templar headquarters rises impressively from a frame of well-tended lawns. Monsieur, a stone-mason, has restored the building himself. After bringing up four children, Madame attended agricultural college and now raises sheep and poultry. The very comfortable rooms have big cupboards, fine beds and big bathrooms. There's also a small sitting-room and kitchen, a pool with sweeping views and a warm welcome.

Rooms: 2 double rooms, 1 twin room and 1 suite for two to four people, all with bathrooms.

Price: 260 Frs for two, including breakfast.

Meals: Not available.

Open: All year.

If you love horse-riding and that special arid southern landscape stay here and spend the days exploring the area far from the madding motor on one of M Bonnet's horses. Then plunge into the warm lake before dinner. He also has an agreement with the boating people for canoe rentals. The family are open, welcoming and fun and their table d'hôte has a long-standing reputation for good food and 'ambiance sympathique'. Riding for the experienced only.

Rooms: 3 double, 3 twin rooms, all with own shower & wc.

Price: 220 Frs for two, including breakfast.

Meals: Dinner 90 Frs, including aperitif, wine & coffee.

Open: All year.

To get there: *From Alès, D16 through Salindres, then very soon right on D147 through Cauvas. The mas is out of the village on the left.*

Map Ref No: 17

To get there: *From Clermont l'Hérault, D156 towards Lac du Salagou for 2km; signposted.*

Map Ref No: 16

Mme SORDI
Mas des Commandeurs
30340 Servas
Gard
Tel: 66 85 67 90

411

Christophe BONNET
L'Etrier du Lac
Route du Salagou
34800 Clermont-l'Hérault, Hérault
Tel: 67 96 37 10
Fax: 67 96 38 64

412

Ask for a room at the front to enjoy dramatic views of wine-red hills with the turquoise of the nearby Lac du Salagou beyond. This is a quiet, isolated house with tiny, private terraces outside the bedrooms; these are functional and modern with French rustic decorative overtones. Simple, traditional meals are served al fresco under a pergola with climbing vines.

Rooms: 6 double rooms, all with bathrooms. (Extra beds available.)

Price: 220 Frs for two, including breakfast.

Meals: Dinner 85 Frs, including wine.

Open: All year.

To get there: *From Clermont l'Hérault, D908 towards Bédarieux. After 4.5km. right (D8E) towards Mourèze and Salasc. 1.5km after Salasc, turn left; signposted.*

Map Ref No: 16

Jocelyne & Lionel DELAGE
Ferme-Auberge
Route de Mas Canet
34800 Salasc
Hérault
Tel: 67 96 15 62

413

They have created a garden in the wilderness; they have planted every tree and flowering bush on the rough hillside, and built a house for themselves. A hard-working couple who are justifiably proud of their achievements, they grow vegetables and keep chickens and rabbits, so dinner is a feast of home-grown produce, served on the terrace of a balmy southern evening. Wonderful walks all round.

Rooms: 1 double, 1 twin room sharing wc, 1 suite with own bathroom.

Price: 225-270 Frs for two, including breakfast.

Meals: Dinner 75 Frs, excluding wine.

Open: All year.

To get there: *From Montpellier, N109 towards Millau. After 10km, right onto D111 to Montarnaud. There, right towards Argelliers and Vailhauques. Just before village, turn left up drive: well signposted.*

Map Ref No: 16

Mme FAIDHERBE BOTTINELLI
Mas de la Coste
114 chemin de la Fontaine
34570 Vailhauques
Hérault
Tel: 67 84 41 26

414

An Englishman, a New Zealander ... a French name! They love France, wine, food (Sarah ran a cookery school once), their fine house and this dazzling piece of country. You can walk, ride, climb rocks, swim or canoe in the Orb River, follow your hosts' wine trail, visit the municipal succulent garden – and return drunk with exertion and beauty for a superb meal on the terrace. A delicately-decorated, cool and spacious house, with excellent guestrooms and delightful hosts.

Rooms: 2 double, 1 twin room, 1 suite, all with own bathrooms.

Price: 245-285 Frs for two, including breakfast.

Meals: Lunch or dinner 95-125 Frs, including wine.

Open: All year.

To get there: *From Béziers, take D14 to Roquebrun. House well signposted in village.*

Map Ref No: 16

Denis & Sarah LA TOUCHE
Les Mimosas
Avenue des Orangers
34460 Roquebrun, Hérault
Tel: 67 89 61 36
Fax: 67 89 61 36

415

If it were less off the beaten track this carefully restored farm outbuilding in its beautiful setting, carpeted with wild flowers, would be inundated. The exterior is unimpressive but inside, the blue shutters, pots of geraniums and exposed beams are just what one longs to see in a farmhouse. Eliane offers her guests eggs, chestnuts and fruit from the farm and, exceptionally, a simple meal.

Rooms: 1 double room and 1 twin room, each with bathroom.

Price: 240 frs for two, including breakfast.

Meals: None (self-catering).

Open: From 1 April to 30 September.

To get there: *From Mazamet, N112 towards St Pons-de-Thomières. At Courniou, LEFT to Prouilhe; farm on left.*

Map Ref No: 16

Eliane & Jean-Louis LUNES
La Métairie Basse
Hameau de Prouilhe
34220 Courniou
Hérault
Tel: 67 97 21 59

416

Madame is an artist and sculptor – some of her works are on show here. Her modern house is most agreeably decorated but the surroundings are really what make the place. You are up on the hillside, gently protected by Mediterranean pines, just near the magnificent Lac du Salagou where riding, biking, sailing, swimming are all to be found for the long hot summer days. Madame is charming and only lets both rooms to people travelling together.

Rooms: 2 double rooms with own wc, sharing a bathroom.

Price: 220 Frs for two, including breakfast.

Meals: None (Ferme-auberge 1km).

Open: All Year.

To get there: *From Clermont l'Hérault, D156 towards Lac du Salagou/Liausson; fork left towards Liausson: last house on right before woods.*

Map Ref No: 16

M & Mme NEVEU
Route de Liausson
34800 Clermont l'Hérault
Hérault
Tel: 67 96 30 97 (h)
or 67 96 18 46 (w)

417

Ideal for families, this is a simple, modern house set amongst vineyards and hillsides. It has a pool and a terrace for long hot evenings and the rooms are clean and perfectly adequate. The hosts are simple, farming folk with a friendly and hospitable attitude. Endless supplies of fresh fish can be got from their family who fish in Sète and the fruit, vegetables and salad ingredients come straight from the garden.

Rooms: 3 double rooms, all with own bathrooms.

Price: 200 Frs for two, including breakfast.

Meals: Dinner 80 Frs, including wine.

Open: All year.

To get there: *From Clermont l'Hérault, D908 towards Bédarieux. After 4km, left onto D15 to Cabrières. House is in village opposite Cave Coopérative.*

Map Ref No: 16

Mme ONORATO
Lou Cigalou
Route de Péret
34800 Cabrières
Hérault
Tel: 67 96 36 67

418

M Vaillé produces (highly drinkable) local wines. His is a big village house with lovely old tiled floors. It is simple and his welcome is friendly. Salelles, quiet despite being just off the main road, is an unusual village built in the red stone of the surrounding hills. There are stunning walks to be taken, the 'Causses' are not far away and nearby Lodève has a fine mediaeval cathedral and a lively market on Saturdays.

Rooms: 3 double, 1 twin room, all with own shower & wc.

Price: 200 Frs for two, including breakfast.

Meals: None (self-catering; good choice within 10km).

Open: April to Christmas.

A tall, somewhat forbidding 18th-century Languedocian 'bastide' (stronghouse) approached along a drive lined with plane trees; nothing could be more typical of southern France. There is a lovely pool and an old tennis court; meals are served with fine linen and silver. A sense of enduring old-fashioned lifestyle here (the bathroom facilities are in keeping!). But such atmosphere...plus the delights of Lake Salagou so close at hand.

Rooms: 3 double & 1 triple room, sharing bathroom.

Price: 250 Frs for two, including breakfast.

Meals: Dinner 100-130 Frs, excluding wine.

Open: All year.

  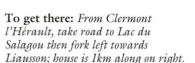

To get there: *From Clermont l'Hérault, N9 towards Lodève. After 8km, right on D140 towards Usclas du Bosc. In Salelles, house opposite church.*

Map Ref No: 16

To get there: *From Clermont l'Hérault, take road to Lac du Salagou then fork left towards Liausson; house is 1km along on right.*

Map Ref No: 16

Bernard VAILLE
1 rue de la Marguerite
Salelles du Bosc
34700 Lodève, Hérault
Tel: 67 44 70 60
Fax: 67 44 73 11

419

Mme VEZIAN
Domaine de Fontenay
Route du Salagou
34800 Clermont l'Hérault
Hérault
Tel: 67 96 19 33

420

A 'terraced château' – yes indeed! – in a quiet street of this charming old village with the Canal de Sète running through it; this is real Languedoc. The Viners are Anglo-Australian and have lovingly restored their 15c-18c house with fine painted ceilings (scènes du Languedoc), large, comfortable rooms and much attention to authentic detail. You are only 5km from the sea.

Rooms: 2 double, 2 twin rooms, 2 sharing & 2 with own bathrooms.

Price: 150-230 Frs for two, including breakfast.

Meals: Dinner 75 Frs, including wine.

Open: All year.

Very convenient for a stopover on your way along the south coast and for Montpellier airport, the Domaine is, unfortunately, just off the motorway so there is inevitably some road noise. A fine old 19th-century wine-grower's house with the remains of a 12th-century chapel. A quiet breakfast can be had in the courtyard in summer or before the kitchen fireplace in winter. Good, clean rooms and a charming hostess who really knows about running chambres d'hôtes.

Rooms: 2 double, 2 twin rooms, all with own bathrooms.

Price: 185 Frs for two, including breakfast.

Meals: None (wide choice nearby).

Open: All year.

To get there: *From Béziers, N112 towards Agde. Pass under motorway then right on D37 into Villeneuve; house in centre opposite Mairie.*

Map Ref No: 16

To get there: *From Montpellier, N113 towards Lunel. House signposted in Baillargues.*

Map Ref No: 17

Andrew & Jennifer-Jane VINER
7 rue de la Fontaine
34420 Villeneuve-lès-Béziers
Hérault
Tel: 67 39 87 15
Fax: 67 39 87 15

421

Mme Michèle VITOU
Domaine de St Antoine
34670 Baillargues
Hérault
Tel: 67 70 15 58

422

Alexis and Françoise are dairy farmers 1275 metres up in a stunning spot on one of the national Grande Randonnée paths, ideal for walking, skiing or pony-trekking. Passionate about their organic produce, they also make cheese and are almost entirely self-sufficient (dinner for 24 guests in two sittings catered for!). The rooms may be small and cluttered, the shared facilities basic, but the people are open and unpretentious in the spirit of the Accueil Paysan association. Much used by hikers.

Rooms: 2 double rooms with hand-basins; shared bathroom.

Price: 280 Frs for two, half-board only.

Meals: Dinner (with wine) included in price.

Open: All year.

Near the Spanish border, this fine old Catalan "mas" nestles amongst cypresses and vineyards – a retreat from the harsh southern sun. Annie and Paul Favier greet their guests with a spontaneous southern warmth. There are four big, stone-walled rooms upstairs with views over the farm plus two others in "la petite maison". Excellent regional food served in the huge dining-room; altogether a perfect base for Pyrenean explorers.

Rooms: 4 double rooms (+single bed in each) & 1 suite, all with bathrooms.

Price: 250 Frs for two, including breakfast.

Meals: Dinner 95 Frs, including aperitif, wine & coffee.

Open: All year.

To get there: *From Mende, N88 to Châteauneuf-de-Randon. There, D985 and D3 to Arzenc-de-Randon. House is on D3, 4km after village.*

Map Ref No: 16

To get there: *From Perpignan, N114 towards Elne. Left onto D62 to Saleilles; through village then D22 towards Alenya; signposted to left between the two villages.*

Map Ref No: 16

Alexis & Françoise AMARGER
Le Giraldes
48170 Arzenc-de-Randon
Lozère
Tel: 66 47 92 70

423

Annie & Paul FAVIER
Domaine du Mas Bazan
66200 Alenya
Pyrénées-Orientales
Tel: 68 22 98 26
Fax: 68 22 97 37

424

This is Catalunya! In a quiet valley of the Pyrenean foothills, dominated by the great Canigou, the traditional 'mas' (old stone farmhouse) overlooks the Mediterranean and the Roussillon vineyards. Hot sunny days – visit Matisse's beloved Collioure – leading to long evenings over local seafood, sheep's cheese and olives. Inside, the owners have kept the warm Catalan stone, the rough beams and the wooden floors of the old house. They are pleased and proud to welcome you here.

Rooms: 1 double & 1 twin with own bathrooms; 2 double & 2 twins sharing 2 bathrooms.

Price: 300-350 Frs for two, including breakfast.

Meals: Half-board arrangement with nearby Mas Cammas: add c.120 Frs.

Open: All year.

To get there: *From Perpignan, N9 towards Spain. After 13km, right onto D2 through Villemolaque & Fourques to Caixas. In Caixas, house is next to church.*

Map Ref No: 16

Jane & Ian MAYLES
Mas Saint Jacques
66300 Caixas
Pyrénées-Orientales
Tel: 68 38 87 83

Louis and Chantal are young farmers – they grow organic kiwis! – who have gradually converted this old farmhouse to provide six large functional guestrooms. Floors are tiled throughout for cool; furnishings are simple and practical, showers small and modern. Dine on Chantal's excellent Catalan cuisine beneath the kiwi trees, share a joke with your good-natured host, enjoy his spontaneous approach to running his B&B ... and see the Pyrenees.

Rooms: 5 double rooms & 1 suite, all with bathrooms.

Price: 185 Frs for two, including breakfast.

Meals: Dinner 75 Frs, including aperitif & wine.

Open: All year.

To get there: *From Perpignan, N114 to Elne. In village take D612 to Bages; signs after 500-600m.*

Map Ref No: 16

Louis & Chantal TUBERT
Mas de la Couloumine
Route de Bages
66200 Elne
Pyrénées-Orientales
Tel: 68 22 36 07

Dark-red old wine casks, polished tables, candles and crystal decanters provide the setting for Monsieur's excellent cooking, served on fine china. A former producer, he and his artist wife have restored this old 'mas' set in 90 hectares of remote hills. Bedrooms are deliberately simple with white walls, terracotta tiled floors and modest furnishings. Madame organises painting courses in winter.

Rooms: 5 double rooms, each with own bathroom.

Price: 400 Frs for two, including breakfast. Half-board – 600 Frs.

Meals: Dinner 110-150 Frs.

Open: From 1 April to 30 September.

This is a converted school-house; Jacques attended school here and his family has lived in the village for generations. Although the interior of the house is modern, family traditions persist, such as the hand-picking of the grapes to make the household wine. The food is good, solid fare, best enjoyed on the terrace outside rather than in the dining-room.

Rooms: 1 double room and one twin room, each with own bathroom.

Price: 210 Frs for two, including breakfast.

Meals: Dinner 73 Francs, including wine.

Open: All year.

To get there: *From A9, exit Perpignan-Sud: left to Thuir. Left before Thuir's first Total garage. After second Total garage, right on D615 towards Fourques, then onto D2. Large casks at entrance, 4km after "les Hostalets".*

Map Ref No: 16

To get there: *From Gaillac, D964 towards Castelnau-de-Montmirail. There, turn off for Les Barrières and follow sign for "Chambres d'Hotes". House next to the country church.*

Map Ref No: 16

M Jacques VISSENAEKEN-VAES
Mas Cammas
66300 Caixas
Pyrénées-Orientales
Tel: 68 38 82 27

Jacques & Huguette CAMALET
Saint-Jérôme
81140 Castelnau-de-Montmirail
Tarn
Tel: 63 33 10 09

A dream for horse-riders and lovers of the Midi. Marc and Claudine have restored a fine 17th-century manor, built a covered riding school and now breed horses and ponies, organising long or short country rides and walks. They also provide huge, soberly-decorated rooms with old beams, long views across the hills, excellent dinners in the large dining-room or on the terrace in summer. They are quiet and attentive hosts who really enjoy horses and guests in equal measure.

Rooms: 2 suites and 3 double rooms, all with own bathrooms.

Price: 310-380 Frs for two, including breakfast.

Meals: Dinner 103 Frs (67 Frs for children); wine 10 Frs.

Open: April to October.

Light streams onto polished antiques in this elegantly restored farmhouse. There's a cosy rich-red sitting-room; restful, comfortable bedrooms. The Crétés have spent much of their lives in Madagascar; Bernadatte likes to cook exotic meals as well as typical regional dishes. They enjoy a comfortable country existence and there's a happy, hospitable family atmosphere. Large informal garden.

Rooms: 1 double room and 1 twin room, both with bathrooms.

Price: 230 Frs for two, including breakfast.

Meals: Dinner 85 Frs.

Open: All year.

To get there: *From Albi, D999 towards Millau. Just before Alban, right on D86 towards Réalmont then 2nd left and follow signposts (not into Paulinet).*

Map Ref No: 16

To get there: *From Rabastens, D12 towards Giroussens. Before bridge over motorway, left on C15 towards Loupiac. After 3km, just after 'Stop' sign, C9 towards Loupiac. Left after 200m – La Bonde is 450m on left.*

Map Ref No: 16

Marc & Claudine CHOUCAVY
Domaine des Juliannes
Paulinet
81250 Alban
Tarn
Tel: 63 55 94 38

Maurice & Bernadette CRETE
La Bonde
Loupiac
81800 Rabastens, Tarn
Tel: 63 33 82 83
Fax: 63 57 46 54

This 1903 Italianate villa still has much of its original Empire furniture. An unusual lounge with galleried staircase and large portraits on warm yellow walls leads to the straw-yellow and grey dining-room. Breakfast in the apricot-coloured heavy pine kitchen. The luminous bedrooms have lots of character. Madame, informal and enthusiastic, welcomes guests with fruit juice and cakes.

Rooms: 2 twin rooms, each with own bathroom.

Price: 250-300 Frs for two, including breakfast.

Meals: Dinner 100 Frs.

Open: From 1 April to 31 October.

To get there: *From Revel, D622 towards Castres. After 9km, D12 to Lempaut. There, left on D46 towards Blan; house is on second turning on left.*

Map Ref No: 16

Mme DELBREIL
Villa des Pins
81700 Lempaut
Tarn
Tel: 63 75 51 01

Before you are the glorious green hills of the Quercy region, at your back the recent additions to this typical 1800s pantiled pale stone house, now restored to its former elegance, including a very fine wooden front door. A relaxed family atmosphere, though the owner lives in an adjoining flat and you make your own breakfast. Perfect for exploring the towns and countryside of this richly historical area. Don't miss the centre of Montauban – deceptively unappealing from the outside.

Rooms: 2 double rooms & 1 suite, all with bathrooms.

Price: 200 Frs for two, including breakfast.

Meals: None (self-catering; in Gaillac 7km).

Open: Mid-September – mid-June.

To get there: *From Gaillac centre, towards Montauban. After level crossing, right onto D32 towards Barat. 5km after crossing D18, lake on left with drive beyond signposted Le Noyer Blanc; up hill, house on right.*

Map Ref No: 16

Mme Frankie McMAHON
Le Noyer Blanc
81310 Lisle-sur-Tarn
Tarn
Tel: 63 57 26 32
Fax: 63 41 05 70

35 hectares stocked with cows and poultry where guests can discover the joys of country living: children come for camp and love it! The guestrooms, all alike in a purpose-converted barn, lack charm but the place has a kind of magic – a big rambling chaotic farm run by kind unprententious people who serve homemade bread. It is off the beaten track and utterly genuine.

Rooms: 3 double and 2 twin rooms, all with own shower & wc.

Price: 190 Frs for two, including breakfast.

Meals: Dinner 50-70 Frs, including wine (book ahead).

Open: All year.

A perfect example of an aristocratic 17th-century townhouse, the Pinons' home will give you a taste of life in a small southern French town: large, cool rooms in grand Napoleon III style, an airy terrace for breakfast overlooking the square and a certain formality behind shutters closed against the heat. After a day exploring the wine cellars and other local delights, come back to rest, change for dinner with the family and relish the utter Frenchness.

Rooms: 5 double rooms, 1 twin room, all with own bath or shower room.

Price: 220 Frs for two, including breakfast.

Meals: Dinner 90 Frs, including wine (book ahead).

Open: All year.

To get there: *From Mazamet, D118 towards Carcassonne. Right on D53 to Aiguefonde; signposted.*

Map Ref No: 16

To get there: *In centre of Gaillac, directly opposite abbey church as you come in across bridge from A68 Toulouse-Albi road.*

Map Ref No: 16

Véronique PECH
Le Fourchat
Aiguefonde
81200 Mazamet
Tarn
Tel: 63 98 12 62

Lucile PINON
8 place Saint-Michel
81600 Gaillac
Tarn
Tel: 63 57 61 48

This authentic mediaeval château is quite an experience! It is in an advanced state of decay but as you go up the ancient, crumbling staircase to the bedrooms, two with their Renaissance coffered wood ceilings, you feel the frisson of 'the real thing' The beds are made with old French linen and breakfast is served by the very elderly and friendly Madame Rahoux in a kitchen dominated by a huge fireplace.

Rooms: 2 double rooms, shared bathroom.

Price: 200 Frs for two, including breakfast.

Meals: Not available.

Open: From May to November.

A square, solid, friendly old "maison de maître" set in rolling fields of sunflowers and vines, the Mas de Sudre is the new home of an English couple who love this area and produce real French food (including hot chocolate in bowls for breakfast). If you feel totally at home in their free and easy atmosphere, they will be happy. If you stay long enough to learn to appreciate their bit of France in depth, they will be pleased as Punch.

Rooms: 2 double & 2 twin rooms, all with own shower & wc.

Price: 250 Frs for two, including breakfast.

Meals: Dinner 70 Frs, including wine.

Open: All year.

To get there: *In Noailles, coming from Cordes, turn left. The Château is on your right, beside the river.*

Map Ref No: 16

To get there: *From Gaillac centre, D4 across railway. Across junction with D18. After 1.5km, left at "Mas de Sudre" sign.*

Map Ref No: 16

Gabriel & Félicie RAHOUX
Le Château
81170 Noailles
Tarn
Tel: 63 56 81 26

435

Pippa RICHMOND-BROWN
Mas de Sudre
81600 Gaillac
Tarn
Tel: 63 41 01 32

This neat, pleasant old house has a slightly formal interior but there are touches of artistic fantasy, from the stained-glass window to the stencilled trellises of flowers on the furniture. Your elderly hosts offer unobtrusive hospitality and breakfast in the old-fashioned blue and white kitchen is a delight.

Rooms: 3 twin rooms with own bathrooms; 2 twin rooms with shared bathroom.

Price: 300 Frs for two, including breakfast.

Meals: Dinner 100 Frs, including wine.

Open: From 1 April to 1 November.

Utterly charming, Monique Sallier takes charge of things in this family-style château, serving breakfast in her farmhouse kitchen so that she can chat more easily to her guests while she prepares the evening meals. The bedrooms have a comfortable, lived-in feel and have kept their original 19th-century charm. Altogether a very welcoming country house comfortably worn around the edges, with pool and tennis court.

Rooms: 1 twin room and 1 suite, each with private bathroom.

Price: 350-400 Frs for two, including breakfast.

Meals: Dinner 90-140 Frs, including wine.

Open: All year.

To get there: *From Revel, D622 towards Castres. After 9km, D12 towards Lempaut and left on D46 towards Blan. 1km along, left by cemetery; second house on right.*

Map Ref No: 16

M et Mme Adolphe SALLIER
Monpeyroux
81700 Lempaut
Tarn
Tel: 63 75 51 17

To get there: *From Revel, D622 towards Castres. 9km along, left on D12 to Lempaut. At Lempaut, right on D46. La Bousqueterie is on your left.*

Map Ref No: 16

Monique & Charles SALLIER
La Bousqueterie
81700 Lempaut
Tarn
Tel: 63 75 51 09

Four of the beamed, double-glazed guestrooms look out onto the square of this picturesque mediaeval village (the others overlook a courtyard). Decor varies, from exposed stone walls and parquet floors to pink-and-green wallpaper and carpeting. Breakfast in a room opening onto the arcade. The friendly hosts divide their time between farming, guests, post office work and new projects.

Rooms: 5 double rooms, 2 suites and 1 single room, each with own bathroom.

Price: 190-210 Frs for two, including breakfast.

Meals: None (restaurants in village).

Open: 1 April to 1 November.

This beautiful ivy-clad château stands proudly above the surrounding farmland. Both rooms, with excellent bathrooms and views over the park, are grand but tiled floors and rugs make them warm and homely. Great fun in colder weather when you dine in the kitchen then go into the sitting-room with a log fire. Nice in summer too, when breakfast and dinner are served on the terrace beneath a pine tree. A great base for visiting Toulouse ... and delightful hosts.

Rooms: 2 double rooms with own bathrooms.

Price: 300 Frs for two, including breakfast.

Meals: Dinner 80 Frs, including wine.

Open: All year.

To get there: *From Gaillac, D922 north then D964 towards Caussade. Castelnau is 10km from Gaillac; Place des Arcades is in village centre.*

Map Ref No: 16

To get there: From Lautrec take the road for Roquecourbe. The château is signposted 4km along on the left.

Map Ref No: 16

Mme Christine SALVADOR
Place des Arcades
81140 Castelnau-de-Montmirail
Tarn
Tel: 63 33 17 44

Laurent et Françoise VENE
Château de Montcuquet
81440 Lautrec
Tarn
Tel: 63 75 90 07

You will be serenaded by birds, bees and sheep in this lovely and largely undiscovered part of France. Your Anglo-French hosts have converted their 200-year-old farmhouse into a deliciously secluded place to stay and walk or bike out into the country. They grow their own vegetables and in summer they serve meals on the terrace overlooking the Tarn valley. Local sheep farmers (who supply Roquefort with milk) will happily show you their milking sheds.

Rooms: 1 twin and 1 triple room with own bathrooms, 1 twin sharing a bathroom.

Price: 200 Frs for two, including breakfast.

Meals: Dinner 90 Frs, including wine.

Open: All year.

To get there: *From Albi, D999 towards Millau. At La Croix Blanche (25km), left down to Caubon du Temple and up to La Barthe on D163. Turn right; house is first on left.*

Map Ref No: 16

Michèle & Michael WISE
La Barthe
81430 Villefranche d'Albigeois
Tarn
Tel: 63 55 96 21
Fax: 63 55 96 21

In several acres of wooded parkland, the 18th-century Château du Plaix has been home to the de Montaignac family for more than 300 years. Splendid rooms with period furnishings, fine food, and the setting to enjoy it. Nearby is the thermal spa town of Néris-les-Bains with an interesting Romanesque church. Fishing, tennis and swimming close by. Children over seven welcome.

Rooms: 1 suite for 2-4 people and 1 twin room, both with bathrooms.

Price: 450 Frs for two, including breakfast.

Meals: Not available.

Open: All year (reservation only between October and May).

The Auvergne

To get there: *From Montluçon, N145 towards Chamblet; signposted on the right.*

Map Ref No: 11

Yves & Jacqueline de
MONTAIGNAC
Château du Plaix
03170 Chamblet
Allier
Tel: 70 07 80 56

442

A perfect place to unwind in the calm green Aveyron where there is so much space. Your comfortable room has a private terrace looking out over a typical old château sold to your hosts for a 'franc symbolique' on condition they maintain it. They are eager to make your stay memorable, to help and provide for all your needs. Our inspectors said that the food was 'outstanding and imaginative' – Peter and Monique used to run a restaurant.

Rooms: 1 double room with own bathroom.

Price: 200 Frs for two, including breakfast.

Meals: Dinner 80 Frs, including wine & coffee.

Open: All year.

A pony often browses in the orchard opposite the modernised farmhouse. The rooms offer clean, basic accommodation and firm mattresses. Madame is robust and cheerful; Monsieur, quietly smiling, helps their son on the dairy farm. Home-smoked hams, fresh eggs and homemade paté go into good farm dinners eaten with the hosts on their plant-filled veranda.

Rooms: 3 double rooms with shower-rooms; 1 double room with shared bathroom.

Price: 150 Frs for two, including breakfast.

Meals: Dinner 60 Frs, including wine.

Open: 15 February to 15 November.

To get there: *From Villefranche, D922 towards Albi through Sanvensa. 600m after village, right towards Monteillet, through hamlet then Chambres d'Hôtes signposted.*

Map Ref No: 16

Monique & Peter BATESON
Monteillet-Sanvensa
12200 Villefranche-de-Rouergue
Aveyron
Tel: 65 29 81 01

To get there: *From Albi, D999 towards Millau. At St Sernin, on square opposite Hotel Inter, take road signposted "P" and Monteils; left in church square and follow signs.*

Map Ref No: 16

Monique & Marcel CAMBON
Monteils de la Serre
12380 St Sernin-sur-Rance
Aveyron
Tel: 65 99 62 73

High on a plateau of sheep-grazed heath, this restored 15th-century château with terraced gardens dominates the village. There are fine views from the well-kept guestrooms adorned with watercolours by Madame, an artist. Monsieur loves to cook, using organic fruit and vegetables in dishes such as Lamb with Pears, served in a room with a large fireplace. His English is superb. He is an engaging and cultivated man whose delight in people and his countryside is as genuine as it is rare.

Rooms: 1 double and 2 triple rooms, all with bathrooms. (Extra bed available.)

Price: 400 Frs for two, including breakfast.

Meals: Dinner 130 Frs, including wine.

Open: All year.

To get there: *From Millau, D911 towards Pont-de-Salars. After 13km, left onto D529 to St Léons. Château visible as you enter village (or signposted if you enter from west).*

Map Ref No: 16

Marc & Odile CHODKIEWICZ
Château de Saint Léons
12780 Saint Léons
Aveyron
Tel: 65 61 84 85
Fax: 65 61 82 30

445

The Monts du Cantal slope down to this tiny hamlet. The 5 Laurens children and their large placid dog greet guests. The main house, converted workers' cottages attached to the local château (where Monsieur's parents live), has a characteristic steep shingle roof. Here are 3 light, fresh-looking rooms. The newer studio rooms, one fully equipped for disabled guests, are in an annexe. The hosts keep dairy cows; Madame is charming and serves delicious, varied breakfasts.

Rooms: 2 double rooms, 1 twin room, 2 studio rooms, all with bathrooms.

Price: 250-350 Frs for two, including breakfast.

Meals: None (restaurants nearby).

Open: All year.

To get there: *From Entraygues, D904 towards Mur-de-Barrez. 4.5km after Lacroix-Barrez, right to Vilherols; signposted.*

Map Ref No: 11

Catherine LAURENS
Vilherols
12600 Lacroix-Barrez
Aveyron
Tel: 65 66 08 24
Fax: 65 66 19 98

446

In an unspoilt village in the lush rolling country of the upper Lot valley, this is a luxurious and handsome 'château privé'. Renovated in 1993 it has large, beautifully-decorated rooms with modern en-suite bathrooms. Victoria cooks superb French dinners, Cliff organizes tours by bike, by car or on foot to local sites. Or relax completely in the two sitting-rooms, the library, the pool, the landscaped gardens. American comforts, French style and a warm welcome.

Rooms: 8 double and 2 twin, all with own bathroom. Apartment for 4 with wheelchair access.

Price: 520-800 Frs for two, including breakfast.

Meals: Dinner 165 Frs, excluding wine (excellent cellar).

Open: All year, except February & March.

To get there: *From Séverac-le-Château, N9 north; D2 to St Saturnin-de-Lenne (12km); right into village, left after church. Château 100 yards on left.*

Map Ref No: 16

Cliff & Victoria LENTON
Château St Saturnin
12560 St Saturnin-de-Lenne
Aveyron
Tel: 65 70 36 00
Fax: 65 70 36 19

Véronique was a vet until she decided to make this house into her dream home. Jean is a cabinet-maker; he made all the pine furniture in the bedrooms. Refined, traditional dishes such as Tarte aux Asperges and Dinde Farci are served by Jean who also loves to talk to guests about the area. Stunning views over the southern Aveyron. Superb walking close by.

Rooms: 5 double rooms and 1 room for four, all with bathrooms.

Price: 250 Frs for two, including breakfast.

Meals: Dinner 80 Frs, excluding wine.

Open: April to November.

To get there: *From Millau, N9 towards Clermont-Ferrand. At Aguessac, D907 to Compeyre; signposted as you enter village.*

Map Ref No: 16

Jean & Véronique LOMBARD-PRATMARTY
Ferme Auberge de Quiers
12520 Compeyre
Aveyron
Tel: 65 59 85 10

The 'mas' basks in a secluded spot surrounded by hills and fields. An adjacent, recently-converted barn provides comfortable guestrooms with large luxurious bathrooms. From the balcony there are views over the lovely garden and beyond. Guests have use of a sitting-room and kitchen. In the morning there's a franglais breakfast with eggs and bacon! Children's games. Busy hosts – best to telephone at mealtimes.

Rooms: 2 twins, 3 doubles, 1 triple, all with bathrooms. Extra beds available.

Price: 320 Frs for two, including breakfast.

Meals: None (self-catering; restaurant 2km).

Open: 1 May – 31 October.

The Viguiers have lived in Ols for centuries and their farm is a centre of activity in this small hamlet. A traditional farmhouse in the remote, rather wild Aveyron area, its style is simple and your hosts' kind reception is genuine. Sit outside in their pleasant garden chairs and admire the ever-changing view. There are delightful footpaths to explore from the house or you can hire a horse or a bike locally.

Rooms: 2 twin rooms, 2 double rooms, one with an extra single bed; shared bathroom.

Price: 240 Frs for two, including breakfast.

Meals: Dinner 70 Frs, including wine.

Open: All year.

To get there: *From Figeac, N122 towards Villefranche-de-Rouergue. In Villeneuve d'Aveyron, D48 towards Cajarc and Ols. In Ols, right following signpost for "Chambres d'Hôtes".*

Map Ref No: 16

To get there: *From Villefranche-de-Rouergue, D922 towards Figeac. Right 800m after St Rémy.*

Map Ref No: 16

Isabelle & Pierre SALVAGE
Mas de Jouas
Villefranche
12200 St Rémy, Aveyron
Tel: 65 81 64 72
Fax: 65 81 50 70

449

Marie-José & Gaston VIGUIER
Ols
12260 Villeneuve
Aveyron
Tel: 65 81 61 47

450

THE AUVERGNE

The 17th-century house is set on a hillside among lush fields grazed by cows. A flower garden tumbles down the hill in front of the house and a peacock struts exotically. The interior oozes character, with centrally-heated, comfortable rooms. Make sure you are expected; the hosts, who raise cattle, are a mite vague! Farm dinners eaten 'en famille'. Half-board only.

Rooms: 5 double rooms, all with bathrooms.

Price: 360 Frs for two, half-board only.

Meals: Dinner included in price.

Open: All year.

This friendly old couple provide genuine, simple hospitality in their modernised farmhouse on a working dairy farm. A solid 1930s walnut bed, with immaculate white crocheted cover and huge pillow, dominates the small guestroom overlooking meadows. The shared bathroom is very basic. The small twin room is ideal for children. Breakfast with farm milk in the formal, rustic dining-room.

Rooms: 1 double room and 1 twin room with shared bathroom.

Price: 190 Frs for two, including breakfast.

Meals: Not available.

Open: All year.

To get there: *From Aurillac, N122 towards Massiac for 8kms. At Giou de Mamou, follow signposts.*

Map Ref No: 11

To get there: *From St Flour, N9 towards Montpellier. At Bellevue-Bellegarde, right on D250 towards St-Georges Bourg. House is on right.*

Map Ref No: 11

Pierre & Isabelle BRETON
Barathe
15130 Giou de Mamou
Cantal
Tel: 71 64 61 72

Henri & Odette PORTEFAIX
La Valette
15100 St Georges
Cantal
Tel: 71 60 01 44

Like the rest of the attractive old village, this house, dated 1777, is built from volcanic stone. Monsieur's shop down below sells "objets" in the same stuff. Superb views of the (extinct) volcano from the rear of the house; try to get one of these rooms. They are all identical, quite small but functional. Your hosts are young and welcoming and breakfast on the terrace is a treat with fresh bread and piping hot coffee (not as easy to get as you might expect in France).

Rooms: 6 double rooms, all with shower-rooms (extra beds for children available).

Price: 210 Frs for two, including breakfast.

Meals: None.

Open: All year.

To get there: *From Aurillac, D922 towards Mauriac. After 35km, right on D680 to Salers. From Place Tyssandier d'Escour, take first left; signposted 'Chambres d'Hôtes'.*

Map Ref No: 11

M Philippe PRUDENT
Rue des Nobles
15410 Salers
Cantal
Tel: 71 40 75 36

Rosa and André raise sheep, working from their 19th-century farmhouse near the village centre, and are the best type of hosts, unpretentious like their house. Their quiet cheerful manner makes you glad you ventured into this untouched part of France. Don't miss dinner before the huge open hearth: simple cooking with many home-produced ingredients (cheese and yoghurt, organic veg, Madame's foie gras). A good base for summer walking and winter cross-country skiing.

Rooms: 1 double, 1 twin & 1 triple room, all with own shower & wc.

Price: 160 Frs for two, including breakfast.

Meals: Dinner 60 Frs, including wine.

Open: 15 January – 15 December.

To get there: *From Le Puy-en-Velay, D589 to Saugues then D585 towards Langeac, turning left onto D32 to Venteuges.*

Map Ref No: 11

Rosa & André DUMAS
Le Bourg
43170 Venteuges
Haute-Loire
Tel: 71 77 80 66

THE AUVERGNE

A new house across from the modern farmhouse provides simple, quiet rooms with tiled floors, hand-made pine furniture and firm mattresses. Dinner 'en famille' with almost everything home-produced, from the milk and sausages to the blue cheese! Young hosts; Jacky, an electrician turned dairy farmer, is quite shy, while Brigitte is more talkative.

Rooms: 6 twin rooms, all with own bathrooms.

Price: 180 Frs for two, including breakfast.

Meals: Dinner 60 Frs, including wine.

Open: All year.

Elisabeth's lovely 18th-century family home is in a tiny hamlet set beneath the first range of Auvergne volcanoes. A fine, solid house with well-preserved outbuildings of great character, it is absolutely right in its environment. The interior is uncluttered, sober and furnished with antiques and soft textiles. There is a gentle garden where you may enjoy country breads and homemade jams for breakfast in the morning sunshine.

Rooms: 3 double rooms, all with bathrooms.

Price: 290 Frs for two, including breakfast.

Meals: Dinner 100 Frs (book ahead).

Open: All year (1 Nov-31 March advance booking only).

To get there: *From Puy-en-Velay, D589 towards Saugues. Just before Saugues, left on D32 towards St Préjet-d'Allier. After 200m right; third house on the right.*

Map Ref No: 11

Jacky & Brigitte MARTINS-ITIER
Rue des Roches
43170 Saugues
Haute-Loire
Tel: 71 77 83 45

455

To get there: *From A71, Riom exit, N144 towards Combronde and Montluçon. After 10km, right onto D122 to Chaptes.*

Map Ref No: 11

Elisabeth BEAUJEARD
Chaptes
Beauregard-Vendon
63460 Combronde
Puy-de-Dôme
Tel: 73 63 35 62

A fine 17th and 19th-century building (and a 12th-century vaulted chapel) in acres of parkland with a walled garden and quite magnificent rooms: vast salon and dining-room with period furniture, beautiful bedrooms with views over Puy-de-Dôme and Mont Dore, canopied beds and excellent bathrooms. Perfect hosts, Monsieur and Madame make you feel immediately at ease and offer the best of help planning your day, all over a most delicious breakfast. A delightful place.

Rooms: 2 double, 1 twin, 1 single room & 1 suite, all with bathrooms.

Price: 365 Frs for two, including breakfast.

Meals: Dinner 120 Frs, including wine (book well ahead).

Open: April – mid-November.

To get there: *From Clermont-Ferrand, A75, Issoire exit then D996 to Parentignat. There D999 towards St Germain-l'Hermite; signposted on right.*

Map Ref No: 11

Henriette MARCHAND
Château de Pasredon
63500 St Rémy-de-Chargnat
Puy-de-Dôme
Tel: 73 71 00 67

457

As the name suggests, this farmhouse on the outskirts of a pretty village is near a small waterfall. All the guestrooms are on the ground floor with views over the garden and hills behind. Madame enjoys weaving, pottery and cooking, using poultry from the farm and organic produce from her garden. Dinner is eaten 'en famille'. Trails for walkers pass near the house.

Provence – The Mediterranean

Rooms: 2 doubles, 1 twin & 3 rooms for 4, all with bathrooms.

Price: 260-290 Frs for two, including breakfast.

Meals: Dinner from 75 Frs, excluding wine.

Open: All year except November and 1 week in February.

To get there: *From Grasse, D2085 to Châteauneuf and D3 to Bramafan. There, right to Courmes. Follow signs from village centre for 0.6km.*

Map Ref No: 18

Patrice BARACCO & Isabelle DUPIN
La Cascade
06620 Courmes
Alpes-Maritimes
Tel: 93 09 65 85

Set in 5 hectares of old parkland, far from traffic and tourists, with a fountain and an old wood oven, this manor house has been sensitively · restored using appropriate materials and techniques. The guestrooms, with original frescoes, have views over the park and an old monastery. The atmosphere is of elegance, warmth and character, reflecting the artistic leanings of the hosts. They speak excellent English.

Rooms: 2 double & 2 twin rooms, all with bathrooms.

Price: 280-400 Frs for two, including breakfast (2 nights minimum).

Meals: Dinner 90-120 Frs, excluding wine.

Open: All year.

This late 19th-century Italianate townhouse is only 5 minutes drive from the centre of Nice but insulated from the noise and bustle of the city. Madame's attention to detail is professional, as might be expected from an ex-hotelier. Guestrooms, irreproachable and supplied with 'toiletries', have views over a terraced flower garden and hills. The huge breakfast buffet includes homemade cakes and compôtes.

Rooms: 3 double rooms with bathrooms.

Price: 430 Frs for two, including breakfast.

Meals: None (vast choice in town).

Open: All year.

To get there: *From Menton, D2566 to Sospel; at 'Mairie', left towards Col de Turini for 1.9km then left towards "Camping". Domaine is 1.3km along on right.*

Map Ref No: 18

Mme Marie MAYER
Domaine de Paraïs
Chemin du Paradis
La Vasta
06380 Sospel, Alpes-Maritimes
Tel: 93 04 15 78

459

To get there: *In Nice, from Place St Philippe, take Ave Estienne d'Orves. Over level crossing. After sharp bend, turn into small private road left of the hill; second house.*

Map Ref No: 18

Mme Jacqueline OLIVIER
Le Castel Enchanté
61 route de St Pierre-de-Féric
06000 Nice, Alpes-Maritimes
Tel: 93 97 02 08
Fax: 92 15 07 87

460

This modern house with its terraced garden carved into the steep hillside is a far cry from the seething tourism on the coast. The guestroom, with its tiled floor, country furniture, and white walls hung with woven rugs, is a delight. Extra touches, such as the books, old boat-ladder-cum-towel-rack and hand-pressed flowers, are original. The table d'hôte, prepared on demand, is very good value.

Rooms: 1 room for up to four people; private bathroom.

Price: 190 Frs for two, including breakfast.

Meals: Dinner 65 Frs, including wine (book ahead).

Open: All year.

A comfortable 1930's family house on the outskirts of the village, with gorgeous views down to the Cap d'Antibes. In keeping with the traditions of the area the host is a sculptor and his wife manages an art gallery. Rooms are large and well-furnished. Breakfast is served on the terrace. There is a swimming pool and an attractive garden.

Rooms: 1 double with own bathroom; 2 doubles and 1 single with shared bathroom.

Price: 300 Frs for two, including breakfast (minimum 2 nights stay).

Meals: Not available.

Open: All year.

To get there: *From Nice, D19 towards Levens. 2km before Levens, after Restaurant "La Chaumière", right onto Chemin de l'Ordalena; house is No 367.*

Map Ref No: 18

To get there: *From A8, St Laurent du Var exit onto D118 then D18 to St Jeannet, crossing D2210 at le Peyron; in the village.*

Map Ref No: 18

Mme Yves PLAT
Chemin de l'Ordalena 367
06670 Levens
Alpes-Maritimes
Tel: 93 79 77 84

Benoît SERE
136 rue St Claude
06640 St Jeannet
Alpes-Maritimes
Tel: 93 24 78 91

This modern, Provençal-style house sits high above the surrounding vineyards and orchards as if in a Cézanne painting; the view of the Montagne Sainte Victoire is quite breathtaking. A fabulous base for a family holiday: a large guestroom with mezzanine and kitchenette, a very fine pool, the sea 45 minutes away and the lovely town of Aix within easy reach. The Babeys have four sons, are relaxed and easy and provide table tennis and boules for all.

Rooms: 1 double room with mezzanine, bathroom and kitchenette

Price: 260 Frs for two, including breakfast.

Meals: None (self-catering).

Open: All year.

To get there: *From Aix, N7 towards Nice for 20km. Left after La Bégude; Chemin des Prés is on right. House at end .*

Map Ref No: 17

Jean-Pierre & Sophie BABEY
Les Bréguières
Chemin des Prés
13790 Rousset
Bouches-du-Rhône
Tel: 42 29 01 16

463

The early 19th-century townhouse is five minutes' walk from the centre of Aix-en-Provence. The guestroom is clean and comfortable, decorated in traditional Provençal style; an extra bed is available and is free to under-15's. Breakfast is on the terrace, or in the family dining-room; there is room service. Madame is most kind and enjoys children (she has four of her own).

Rooms: 1 twin room with own bathroom. (Extra bed available.)

Price: 300 Frs for two, including breakfast.

Meals: Not available.

Open: September – July (closed August).

To get there: *In Aix, from 'Place de la Rotonde' take Blvd de la République; Ave de Lattre de Tassigny; right at 4th traffic light; 50m after Pharmacie is a red-brick building – Bastide Brunet is behind this.*

Map Ref No: 17

Mme GREYFIE de BELLECOMBE
Bastide Brunet, Verte Colline
13090 Aix-en-Provence
Bouches-du Rhône
Tel: 42 96 42 83

464

Ten minutes walk from the centre of Aix, this relatively modern house, in a residential area next to an old castle, was designed by Monsieur himself. Rooms are large and decorated with taste. There is a swimming pool in the garden and olive trees from which the hosts, a lively and sympathetic couple, make their own oil. Children are welcomed.

Rooms: 2 double rooms and 1 twin, all with bathrooms.

Price: 250-400 Frs for two, including breakfast (2 nights minimum stay).

Meals: Not available.

Open: All year.

A 20th-century house with all the appearance of an old Provençal mas. It has patina, old furniture and lovely pottery. Even the stables where Monsieur keeps his horses have the same charm. The atmosphere is refined yet informal and the gardens are cool and well-tended. A symphony in local colour, perfectly orchestrated by Hélène who is a decorator. Bruno is an open, friendly host and Mollégès is typically Provençal, so what matter the slightly small rooms?

Rooms: 2 double & 3 twin rooms, each with own bathrooms.

Price: 450 Frs for two, including breakfast.

Meals: None (wide choice in St Rémy – 9km).

Open: All year.

To get there: *In Aix, from Place de la Rotonde, past Tourist Information, turn into Blvd V. Hugo. At 9th traffic light, turn into Rte du Tholonet; l'Enclos is at second roundabout – white gate on right.*

Map Ref No: 17

To get there: *From Mollégès, D31 towards St Rémy. After 2km, left at sign to Mas de l'Ange.*

Map Ref No: 17

Mauricette IUNG
L'Enclos, route du Tholonet
2 av du Général Préaud
13100 Aix-en-Provence
Bouches-du-Rhône
Tel: 42 96 40 52

465

Bruno & Hélène LAFFORGUE
Mas de l'Ange, Petite route de St Rémy
13940 Mollégès,
Bouches-du-Rhône
Tel: 90 95 08 33
Fax: 90 95 68 49

466

At the heart of the pretty village of Peynier, this 18th-century bastide, which used to belong to the painter Vincent Roux, has been beautifully restored in appropriate Provençal style. The one guestroom has antique furniture and a lovely, traditionally-tiled bathroom; there are views of Cézanne's Montagne-Ste-Victoire. Guests tend to return year after year. Older children welcome.

Rooms: 1 double room with own bathroom; extra bed available.

Price: 300 Frs for two, including breakfast.

Meals: Not available.

Open: All year, except first three weeks of August.

This Arabian horse stud-farm faces the Alpilles. The house itself is built of old materials. Guestrooms (some in a separate building) are very comfortable and centrally-heated. There is a pool and a living room with a piano. The Petits, politely friendly, dine with their guests. All the vegetables and wine in the generous 5-course dinners are organic; vegetarian meals upon request.

Rooms: 6 twin rooms (2 on ground floor), all with bathrooms.

Price: 500-700 Frs for two – half-board only.

Meals: Included in price above.

Open: All year.

To get there: *From Aix-en-Provence, A8 towards Nice. Canet exit on D6 towards Trets. 4km before Trets, right on D57 to Peynier.*

Map Ref No: 17

To get there: *From St Rémy-de-Provence, D99 towards Cavaillon. After 9km, right on D74a to Eygalières.*

Map Ref No: 17

Mme LAMBERT
Mas Ste Anne
3 rue d'Auriol
13790 Peynier
Bouches-du-Rhône
Tel: 42 53 05 32

467

Nicole & Serge PETIT
Le Haras d'Eygalières
Chemin de Cantos
13810 Eygalières
Bouches-du-Rhône
Tel: 90 90 60 12

468

A long avenue of plane trees leads to the house and 18th-century stone farm buildings. Monsieur Pinet, a former antiques dealer, has done the house up with great care and taste, filling it with fine old furniture and paintings. Breakfast is a delight, especially when served on the old threshing floor – now a terrace. Cool, shaded garden.

Rooms: 3 double rooms and 1 triple, all with bathrooms.

Price: 350 Frs for two, including breakfast.

Meals: Not available.

Open: All year.

Cats occupy all the cosiest corners of this restored 'mas', which has lots of interesting bits and pieces, such as an old water pump and some carved stones. The amiable owners have amassed a collection of books about the region. 'Objets' and pretty fabrics complement antiques in the simple rooms (unheated). Copious breakfasts are served under plane trees or in the dining-room in an old barn.

Rooms: 2 double rooms and 1 twin room, all with own bathrooms but 2 sharing a wc.

Price: 250 Frs for two including breakfast.

Meals: None (restaurant in village.)

Open: 1 April to 10 September.

To get there: *From Avignon, D571 towards Châteaurenard, then D34 towards St Rémy-de-Provence. At Eyragues, D29 to Verquières (you will cross D30).*

Map Ref No: 17

To get there: *From Avignon, D571 to Châteaurenard and D571 towards Eyragues. After 3.5km take a small road left; signposted.*

Map Ref No: 17

M René PINET
Mas de Castellan
13670 Verquières
Bouches-du-Rhône
Tel: 90 95 08 22

Mme POLI
Le Mas des Chats qui Dorment
Chemin des Prés
13630 Eyragues
Bouches-du-Rhône
Tel: 90 94 19 71

Madame has used her expertise (she owns an antique shop) to furnish her 18th-century home with taste and comfort. The spacious guestrooms, overlooking a tiny garden, are most elegant, with thick wool carpets, antiques, fine linens and large bathrooms. Breakfast is served on old silver. The enthusiastic hosts like to share their love of music and Provence. On-street parking.

Rooms: 1 double room and 1 triple room, with bathrooms.

Price: 450 Frs for two, including breakfast.

Meals: Not available.

Open: Easter to 30 October.

Valérie and Rémy have recently taken over the summer family residence and converted it. A 17th-century farmhouse, it is in the most beautiful area, nestling among pine forests beside a lake. They grow vegetables and organic fruit and keep some laying hens. Dried flowers adorn the small but pretty rooms. Horse-lovers will enjoy the stables here.

Rooms: 4 double rooms, all with bathrooms.

Price: 450 Frs for two, including breakfast.

Meals: Not available.

Open: All year.

To get there: *From Arles, D17 to Fontvieille; in the town.*

Map Ref No: 17

To get there: *From A7, Cavaillon exit, on D99 to St Rémy. There, D5 towards Maussane; left towards 'Le Lac de St Rémy'; pass the lake – it is the last house.*

Map Ref No: 17

M et Mme RICARD DAMINOT
Le Mas Ricard
107 avenue Frédéric Mistral
13990 Fontvieille, Bouches-du-Rhône
Tel: 90 54 72 67
Fax: 90 54 64 43

471

V.SCHNEIDER & R.REBOUL
Mas de Gros, Route du Lac
13210 St-Rémy
Bouches-du-Rhône
Tel: 90 92 46 85
Fax: 90 92 47 78

472

This beautifully restored 18th-century farmhouse has superb views of the neighbouring 12th-century château, the vineyards, river and hills beyond and actually produces its own wine. The large, Provençal-style bedrooms and guests' sitting-room are in a separate wing. Breakfast is served on the terrace or in the dining-room. Monsieur, an historian, is happy to share his encyclopaedic knowledge of the monuments and sights of the area.

Rooms: 2 twin rooms & 1 suite for 4, all with bathrooms.

Price: 280-300 Frs for two, including breakfast.

Meals: Dinner 90 Frs, including wine.

Open: All year.

To get there: *From A8, St Maximin/La Ste Baume exit onto D560 through Barjols. There, continue D560 towards Draguignan; entrance opposite D60 turning for Pontèves.*

Map Ref No: 18

Guillaume & Armelle de JERPHANION
Domaine de Saint Ferréol
83670 Pontèves, Var
Tel: 94 77 10 42
Fax: 94 77 19 04

473

Well-integrated into its tranquil site, surrounded by pine forest, a modern house with very pretty gardens and a shaded terrace. Rooms, with views of a wooded valley, are decorated around the theme of plants (lavender, pine, etc.). The dining area is sunlit and looks out onto the magnificent new pool, stone-built with a waterfall and lovely shrubs.

Rooms: 2 double, 2 twin and 1 suite for 3-4 people; all with bathrooms.

Price: 290 Frs for two, including breakfast.

Meals: Dinner 95 Frs, including wine.

Open: All year.

To get there: *From Vidauban, D48 towards Lorgues. House is 5km along on the right; signposted.*

Map Ref No: 18

Dino & Teresa DISCACCIATI
La Matabone
Route de Vidauban
83510 Lorgues
Var
Tel: 94 67 62 06

474

A converted 19th-century farmhouse set among vineyards and orchards in a delectable corner of Provence. Superb for a dream family holiday, with farmyard animals, outdoor games, harvesting to be done, delicious home-produced food to be enjoyed and a delightful, energetic hostess who manages to look after her guests while preparing her next market delivery.

Rooms: 2 suites for 4, 1 double room, all with own bathroom.

Price: 280 Frs for two, including breakfast.

Meals: Dinner 90 Frs, including wine; vegetarian dishes available.

Open: All year.

To get there: *From Salernes centre go 200m towards Entrecasteaux, turn right over bridge then left; right at fork. House is 2.5km further on down a track.*

Map Ref No: 18

Karel & Caroline HENNY
La Bastide Rose
Quartier Haut-Gaudran
83690 Salernes, Var
Tel: 94 70 63 30
Fax: 94 70 77 34

475

Beautiful views of the Alps across vineyards and hills, and a warm welcome, await you at this 19th-century farmhouse. The bedrooms feature typical Provençal fabrics and antiques, and the bathrooms are new. Breakfast and dinner are served on the private terrace or in the dining-room. Monsieur farms his land and loves to talk about his 'métier' and village. Madame is a kindly hostess and an excellent cook.

Rooms: 1 double and 1 twin, with private bathrooms.

Price: 260 Frs for two, including breakfast.

Meals: Dinner 90 Frs, including wine.

Open: All year.

To get there: *From Aups, D9 and D30 to Montmeyan. There, D13 towards Quinson. House is on left of road, 1km along; signposted.*

Map Ref No: 18

M & Mme Vincent GONFOND
Route de Quinson
83670 Montmeyan
Var
Tel: 94 80 78 03

476

A 17th-century farmhouse, surrounded by arable fields, that has guestrooms in a new wing with its own entrance and a small terrace with wicker furniture. The place is a working cereal farm and has an organic vegetable garden. Rooms are modest but comfortable in a simple, country style. Madame Grech is extremely helpful and welcoming, glad to share her knowledge of the area. She also serves a wholesome family supper.

Rooms: 3 double rooms and 1 twin, all with bathrooms.

Price: 280 Frs for two, including breakfast.

Meals: Dinner 100 Frs, including wine.

Open: All year.

To get there: *From Rians, D23 towards Ginasservis; right on D30 towards La Verdière. After 3km, you will see grain silos; house is 300m along.*

Map Ref No: 18

An 18th-century farmhouse, in a beautiful hillside position with olive groves and orchards, that produces chutneys and jams (50 types!), almonds and olive oil for sale. The guestroom is comfortable and independent, with old furniture, and opens onto a garden with a summer kitchen. There is a shaded terrace and a living-area too, with stunning views over a spring-fed fountain to Montagne Ste. Victoire.

Rooms: 1 double room with own bathroom.

Price: 350-400 Frs for two, including breakfast.

Meals: Not available.

Open: All year.

To get there: *From Draguignan, D557 through Villecroze, to Aups. From Aups, D77 towards Tourtour; signs after 4km.*

Map Ref No: 18

Mme Paule GRECH
Domaine Espagne
83560 Ginasservis
Var
Tel: 94 80 11 03

477

Micheline MAILAENDER
La Tuillière
Route de Tourtour
83630 Aups
Var
Tel: 94 70 00 59

478

This 18th-century farmhouse, built on the site of a Roman 'villa', has four big, airy, uncluttered guestrooms and is run by an Anglo-French couple who know and love their region. Take Michel's accompanied walk out of the farm and you will learn about the local flora and fauna by looking, smelling, touching. The reading room, a few beautiful and unusual objects and a happy, united family add to the aura of peace in stunning natural surroundings.

Rooms: 2 suites (for 3 & 4), 2 twin rooms, all with own bathrooms.

Price: 390 Frs for two, including breakfast.

Meals: Dinner 100 Frs, including aperitif, wine & coffee (½ price for under tens); vegetarians catered for.

Open: All year.

To get there: *From St Maximin, D560 towards Barjols; 6.1km after leaving Brue Auriac (which is also 1.7km from Barjols), left and follow signs to St Jaume for 500m and enter by red gate.*

Map Ref No: 18

A gorgeous 'domaine viticole', a late-18th-century manor, still under restoration, that produces organically-cultivated wines, with a cellar and tasting. The house overlooks vine-covered hillsides, within easy reach of several charming Var villages. Rooms are decorated and furnished in a traditional Provençal style and have independent kitchen facilities. The menu features vegetables, fruit and wine from the estate.

Rooms: 3 double rooms and 1 twin, all with bathrooms.

Price: 280-300 Frs for two, including breakfast. (Minimum stay 3 nights in July and August.)

Meals: Dinner 90 Frs, including wine.

Open: 1 March – 30 November.

To get there: *From A8, Brignoles exit north onto D554 through Le Val; then D22 through Montfort-sur-Argens, towards Cotignac. 5km along, turn left; signposted.*

Map Ref No: 18

Michel & Stephanie PASSEBOIS
Séjours Découverte et Nature
Saint Jaume
83670 Barjols
Var
Tel: 94 77 18 01

479

M & Mme ROUBAUD
Domaine de Nestuby
83570 Contignac
Var
Tel: 94 04 60 02
Fax: 94 04 79 22

480

Close to the mediaeval village of Castellet and the beaches of Bandol, a pleasing, modern house, designed by its architect-owner and thoughtfully integrated into its surroundings. There is a large, shaded and beautifully-kept terraced garden, with a swimming pool. Rooms are decorated in Provençal style and are very comfortable; one has its own garden with table and chairs. The hosts are cultured and welcoming.

Rooms: 1 double room, 1 twin and 1 suite for four people, all with own bathrooms.

Price: 350-400 Frs for two, including breakfast.

Meals: Dinner 90 Frs, including wine.

Open: All year.

A place full of history: this big, attractive, Italian-style house stands on a site once occupied by Cistercian monks and then by the Templars, today a haven of peace. There is even a private chapel. Madame is charming and has three superb guestrooms, carefully furnished with a mix of old and new, though TV in each room might encroach on the "haven" feel. The views are worthy of the area, the bathrooms marble and breakfast is a banquet.

Rooms: 1 double and 2 triple rooms, with bathrooms.

Price: 440-550 Frs for two, including breakfast.

Meals: Not available.

Open: All year (November-Easter by reservation only).

To get there: *From Toulon, N8 to Le Beausset. At roundabout, D26 to Le Castellet. After 300m (supermarket), right up hill for 1.5km. 100m after a right bend, left up track; signposted.*

Map Ref No: 18

To get there: *From Orange, D950 then D977 towards Vaison-la-Romaine and D88 towards Séguret; left along 'Montvert-L'Esclade' road; signposted.*

Map Ref No: 17

Charlotte & Marceau ZERBIB
Les Cancades
Chemin de la Fontaine
83330 Le Beausset, Var
Tel: 94 98 76 93
Fax: 94 90 24 63

481

Gisèle AUGIER
St-Jean
84110 Séguret
Vaucluse
Tel: 90 46 91 76

482

Lavender fields surround this 17th-century farmhouse and sweep up to great cliffs. This is wild and inspiring countryside. Monsieur, formerly a theoretical physicist, looks after the lavender fields and listens to jazz. Madame restores paintings and picture frames. Together they are gradually renovating this Italianate house. Accommodation is rustic and spacious with new bathrooms. The village is a 500m walk and there is climbing and riding nearby.

Rooms: 3 double rooms, each with own bathroom.

Price: 200-300 Frs for two, including breakfast.

Meals: Not available.

Open: All year.

To get there: *From Avignon. N100 to Apt. There, D113 to Buoux; house surrounded by meadows and lavender fields.*

Map Ref No: 17

M Jean-Alain CAYLA
La Grande Bastide
84480 Buoux
Vaucluse
Tel: 90 74 29 10

The recently-restored farmhouse and courtyard of this vegetable-producing farm are on a quiet road. The guestrooms overlook the fields and are simply furnished, with good beds and Provençal covers. According to one of our readers: "Madame is a star with a lovely sense of humour"; she likes cooking simple Provençal food and she and her family create a very special atmosphere round the table.

Rooms: 3 double rooms, all with own bathrooms.

Price: 280 Frs for two, including breakfast. (400 Frs for two, half-board.)

Meals: Dinner 70 Frs.

Open: All year.

To get there: *From Apt, N100 towards Avignon. At Lumières, D106 towards Lacoste, then D218 to Ménerbes; second farm on the left.*

Map Ref No: 17

Maryline & Claude CHABAUD
Mas Marican
84220 Goult
Vaucluse
Tel: 90 72 28 09

Beautiful countryside, a working vineyard, a large, bright house with Provençal tiles, a pool to swim in as you step into the garden ("you feel you're swimming in a vineyard"), and real Provençal cooking in the evening – all this at a reasonable price? Yes; it's a lovely place and very 'typique'. Perhaps a trifle hotel-like, but there are compensations galore, including an exceptionally friendly family and an equally easy-going old dog!.

An 18th-century 'mas de vigneron' (the vats are still intact) that has been well renovated by the current owners, a Swiss couple formerly in the book trade. The rooms are immaculate, each named after a Provençal author and stocked with their books! The hosts' attention to detail is superb: desks with headed paper, lavender bouquets, childrens' toys and, downstairs, a summer kitchen, table-tennis and a drinks fridge.

Rooms: 4 double rooms and 1 twin, all with bathrooms.

Rooms: 3 double rooms, 1 triple and 1 for four people; all with bathrooms.

Price: 240 Frs for two, including breakfast.

Price: 240-330 Frs for two, including breakfast.

Meals: Dinner 120 Frs, including wine.

Meals: None (BBQ facilities during summer).

Open: 1st March – 31st October.

Open: 1 April – 31 October.

To get there: *From Carpentras, D7 through Aubignan to Vacqueyras. In Vacqueyras, find Bar aux Dentelles; turn left and follow signs.*

Map Ref No: 17

To get there: *From A7, Bollène exit onto D994 and D8 towards Carpentras. At La Begude, D977 to Violès; signposted in the village.*

Map Ref No: 17

Mme Jeanine CHABRAN
Domaine l'Ousteau des Lecques
84190 Vacqueyras
Vaucluse
Tel: 90 65 84 51
Fax: 90 65 81 19

485

Augustine & Jean-Claude CORNAZ
La Farigoule
Le Plan de Dieu
84150 Violès
Vaucluse
Tel: 90 70 91 78

486

A recently-renovated 18th-century 'mas' with 2 hectares of organic cherry and plum orchards; there's locally-produced fruit juice at breakfast. Copious, delicious dinners, after which the widely-travelled Grecks join guests to chat. They have exposed the old stone walls on the ground floor and the ceilings are pure Provençal. Each bedroom is different, modern, with attractive fabrics and good bedding.

Rooms: 6 twin rooms, all with bathrooms.

Price: 450-480 Frs for two, including breakfast.

Meals: Dinner 130 Frs, excluding wine.

Open: All year.

This new house is built around a patio and terraced gardens against the hillside. Madame Guillaumé teaches relaxation therapies and a spring next to the house is symbolic of her concern that a stay here should be a "ressourcement" (a moment of renewal). There are quiet corners and music. Each of the spruce, modern rooms (one in a tiny old pavilion next to the pool) has a little breakfast terrace.

Rooms: 3 double rooms and 1 suite, each with own bathroom.

Price: 380 Frs for two, including breakfast.

Meals: Not available.

Open: All year.

To get there: *From A7, Avignon-Sud exit, D22 towards Apt; house is 2km after the signpost 'Petit Palais', near junction with N100.*

Map Ref No: 17

To get there: *From Cavaillon, D2 and N100 towards Apt. 3km after Apt, D174 right to Saignon. At bottom of village, right then left after 100m; signposted.*

Map Ref No: 17

Monique & François GRECK
Le Mas du Grand Jonquier
84800 Lagnes
Vaucluse
Tel: 90 20 90 13
Fax: 90 20 91 18

487

Hélène GUILLAUME
La Pyramide
Quartier du Jas
84400 Saignon, Vaucluse
Tel: 90 74 46 86
Fax: 90 74 28 03

488

This finely-decorated modern house (hand-painted doors throughout), in traditional Provençal layout, is more luxurious and expensive than most B&Bs. But its position just 15 minutes walk from Ménerbes, an engaging little hill-top village, is seductive, the view stunning and the garden a delight. Your charming hostess speaks 6 languages and simply loves entertaining; expect impromptu suppers or musical evenings bathed in the wonderful air of the Lubéron.

Rooms: 1 double suite with own bathroom, 1 independent studio, 2 double rooms sharing a bathroom.

Price: 400-600 Frs for two, including breakfast (minimum stay 3 days).

Meals: Dinner (served in pool house) 100-120 Frs, including wine (book ahead).

Open: All year.

To get there: *From Avignon, N100 towards Sisteron and Apt. After about 20km, just before Les Beaumettes, right towards Ménerbes. The Mas is 2km from the turning, on left.*

Map Ref No: 17

Mme Monika HAUSCHILD
Mas du Magnolia
Quartier le Fort
84560 Ménerbes, Vaucluse
Tel: 90 72 48 00
Fax: 90 72 48 00

489

This 16th-century manor-house is a sheer delight. Modern comforts blend unobtrusively with books, deep armchairs and old Provençal furniture. Rooms are comfortable, the vast garden wonderful for children. "Country guest house" is the right name for this estate with self-catering apartments as well as B&B. The swimming pool and tennis court are unexpected luxuries. Monsieur, a keen mountain cyclist, is happy to suggest itineraries.

Rooms: 4 double rooms, all with own bathrooms.

Price: 320-360 Frs for two, breakfast 35 Frs extra per person.

Meals: None

Open: 1 March to 1 November.

To get there: *From Avignon towards Villeneuve-lès-Avignon, crossing Daladier Bridge. Right on D228 following sign for Ferme Jamet. After 2km, at roundabout, follow orange signpost.*

Map Ref No: 17

Martine & Etienne JAMET
Ferme Jamet
Ile de Barthelasse
84000 Avignon, Vaucluse
Tel: 90 86 16 74
Fax: 90 86 17 72

490

Monsieur, an architect and Madame, an English art historian, have lovingly restored this 18th-century stone farmhouse set among vineyards near Bonnieux. Guests are offered the warmest of welcomes, peace, quiet and all mod cons. Rooms, delightfully furnished with country antiques, are in a converted "bergerie" that opens directly onto the garden with fine trees around pool and summer kitchen. Spectacular views over olives, lavender and vines to Mont Ventoux.

Rooms: 1 double and 3 twin rooms, all with bathrooms.

Price: 400-450 Frs for two, including breakfast.

Meals: Not available.

Open: 1 March – 31 October.

To get there: *From Avignon, N100 towards Apt. 10km after Lumières, right towards Bonnieux, Pont Julien. Cross Roman bridge and take D149 towards Bonnieux for 2km; signposted on right.*

Map Ref No: 17

Shirley & Ian KOZLOWSKI
Jas des Eydins
Route du Pont Julien
84480 Bonnieux, Vaucluse
Tel: 90 75 84 99
Fax: 90 75 96 71

491

The interior of this former 17th-century 'relais de poste' has been decorated with great refinement and filled with antiques and lovely fabrics. Monsieur is an interior decorator and his shop is on the ground floor. There are mountain bikes for guests' use – Madame is a keen cyclist, ready to advise on routes. For the less athletic there's a cool, shaded garden.

Rooms: 2 double and 3 twin rooms, all with bathrooms.

Price: 300-400 Frs for two, including breakfast.

Meals: Not available.

Open: All year.

To get there: *From Aix-en-Provence, N96 and D556 to Pertuis. There, D973 to Cadenet and then D943 towards Bonnieux until you reach Lourmarin.*

Map Ref No: 17

M & Mme LASSALLETTE
Villa St Louis
35 rue Henri de Savornin
84160 Lourmarin, Vaucluse
Tel: 90 68 39 18
Fax: 90 68 10 07

492

Built of old stone in traditional style, this house has fine views over the valley towards Bonnieux and the Lubéron. The Lawrences worked abroad for 40 years, he in public works, she in the diplomatic service. Their home is witness to their travels and they speak several languages. Guests are pampered and comfortable; there is a dressing-room and the bedroom is air-conditioned.

Rooms: 1 triple room with bathroom.

Price: 250 Frs for two, including breakfast.

Meals: Not available.

Open: All year.

To get there: *From Avignon, N100 towards Apt. At Coustellet, D2 for Gordes. After Les Imberts right on D207 and D148 to St Pantaléon. Pass church, stay on D104 for 50m, left onto small uphill road; 1st drive on the right.*

Map Ref No: 17

Pierrette & Charles LAWRENCE
Villa La Lebre
St Pantaléon
84220 Gordes
Vaucluse
Tel: 90 72 20 74

This typical Lubéron stone farmhouse, with vineyards and cherry orchards, within walking distance of the picturesque village of Lacoste, has clean, homely rooms and lovely views across the Mont Ventoux. Madame serves Provençal food with their own vegetables and local wine. The number of rooms and the little reception desk verge on the institutional but, apart from Olivier's baseball cap and the ubiquitous photo's of off-road vehicles, the house is thoroughly French. Children over six welcome.

Rooms: 2 double rooms, 2 twin, 1 triple room and 1 room for four, all with bathrooms.

Price: 500 Frs for two, including breakfast.

Meals: Dinner 100 Frs, excluding wine.

Open: All year.

To get there: *From Avignon, N100 towards Apt. At Lumières, D106 towards Lacoste; left onto D108; house is on left.*

Map Ref No: 17

Lydia & Olivier MAZEL
Layaude-Basse
84710 Lacoste
Vaucluse
Tel: 90 75 90 06
Fax: 90 75 99 03

Madame is warm and delightfully enthusiastic about her fine old farmhouse; it has a huge stone fireplace and immaculate light-filled rooms decorated with the help of a designer friend in feminine but unfussy style. Monsieur is a creative cook, bringing the fresh produce and aromatic herbs of Provence to your table. Add the incomparable light, the spreading lime tree on the terrace with views over lavender fields and so many places to visit – you'll want to stay a month.

Rooms: 2 suites and 3 double rooms, all with own bathrooms.

Price: 250-400 Frs for two, including breakfast.

Meals: Dinner 120 Frs, including wine.

Open: All year.

To get there: *From Carpentras, D941/D1 to Sault (41km) then D942 towards Aurel. Just before Aurel, left at signpost.*

Map Ref No: 17

Christian & Visnja MICHELLE
Richarnau
84390 Aurel
Vaucluse
Tel: 90 64 03 62

495

Just outside the pretty village of Le Thor, this house is set in an oasis of cool, green gardens. The hosts go out of their way to make guests feel good; there is a separate kitchen in the guests' wing (where Madame prepares breakfast), and rooms are quiet and comfortable, with lots of books and paintings. The Mourges' sometimes take their guests on walks or visits.

Rooms: 3 double rooms, all with bathrooms.

Price: 360 Frs for two, including breakfast.

Meals: Dinner 90 Frs, including wine (book ahead).

Open: All year (book in advance in winter).

To get there: *From A7 exit Avignon-Sud, towards Cavaillon for 1km then left to Caumont. After village, D1 to Le Thor and once there, telephone.*

Map Ref No: 17

André MOURGES
La Palasse
Route de St Saturnin D98
84250 Le Thor, Vaucluse
Tel: 90 33 92 38
Fax: 90 33 76 05

496

The Ricquarts lived in Morocco and Egypt before retiring in 1972 to this old mill on the Mède river. They spent 15 years restoring the house, which they have filled with souvenirs of their travels. The stone walls keep the house cool and there is a pool in the large landscaped park surrounding it, though the busy road tends to make its presence felt. The shaded terrace provides a perfect setting to begin the day over breakfast.

Rooms: 2 double rooms and 1 twin room, all with own bathrooms.

Price: 280-320 Frs for two, including breakfast.

Meals: Not available.

Open: All year.

To get there: *From Carpentras, D974 towards Bédoin and Mont Ventoux. 1km after Crillon-le-Brave turn-off, left to house; signposted.*

Map Ref No: 17

Bernard & Marie-Luce RICQUART
Moulin d'Antelon
84410 Crillon-le-Brave
Vaucluse
Tel: 90 62 44 89
Fax: 90 62 44 90

The narrow, cobbled streets of the mediaeval quarter lead to this house – formerly part of the 17th-century Bishop's palace. The Verdiers' love of antiques is reflected in their impeccably-furnished home. Guestrooms are comfortably rustic in style and there are wonderful views from the breakfast terrace. The friendly, welcoming hosts are keen walkers and wine buffs. Guest salon with fireplace. Parking on street near house.

Rooms: 2 double rooms and 2 twin rooms, each with own bathroom.

Price: 360-400 Frs for two, including breakfast.

Meals: Not available.

Open: All year, except 2 weeks in November.

To get there: *From Orange, D975 to Vaison. In town, follow "ville médiévale" signs.*

Map Ref No: 17

Aude & Jean-Loup VERDIER
L'Evêché, Rue de l'Evêché
84110 Vaison-la-Romaine
Vaucluse
Tel: 90 36 13 46
Fax: 90 36 32 43

Raymond and Elise will greet you warmly and share their passion for the soul and story of this ancient mediaeval fortress with its later, Renaissance, 'conversion'. Each high moment in the history of France has left its mark here and the tradition of hospitality and celebrations (concerts, shows, exhibitions) is still followed today. The oldest (12th century) wing has been converted into superb guestrooms. An exceptional place to stay.

Rooms: 5 suites, each with antechamber and bathroom.

Price: 400 Frs for two, including breakfast.

Meals: None.

Open: All year.

The Alps – Jura

To get there: *From Gap, D994 towards Veynes. 4km before Veynes, take D320 towards Dévoluy; Montmaur is 2km on, visible from the road. Drive along château wall then towards church.*

Map Ref No: 18

Raymond & Elise LAURENS
Château de Montmaur
05400 Veynes
Hautes-Alpes
Tel: 92 58 11 42

Unbridled luxury and comfort are the order here and your fun-loving hosts are concerned that you should want for nothing (they bring their standards from their previous home on the Riviera). And want you do not, unless it is the homely feel. It is slightly hotelly, with carefully coordinated satins and super-mod bathrooms. But dinner is excellent, breakfast is a banquet (10 homemade jams, brioche, cake, and more and more), the half-acre garden most restful and Madame charming.

Rooms: 3 double, 1 twin, 2 suites, all with own bath and wc.

Price: 350-450 Frs for two, including breakfast.

Meals: Dinner 150 Frs, including (abundant) wine.

Open: All year.

To get there: *From Lyon, A43 Chimilin/Les Abrets exit towards Les Abrets and follow signs.*

Map Ref No: 12

Christian & Claude CHAVALLE REVENU
La Bruyère
38490 Les Abrets, Isère
Tel: 76 32 01 66
Fax: 76 32 06 66

500

Nicole and Jean-Pierre run an auberge as well as their B&Bs; a little business-like but their hospitality is absolutely genuine. Good food (vegetarians catered for), dinner being rounded off with Nicole's own delicious "alcool de fruits". Jean-Pierre shares his love of the area and offers to take you to see it on horse-back...or on a bike, or you can walk straight out into the countryside. The old farmhouse is traditionally decorated and the rooms well-equipped.

Rooms: 4 double, 1 twin room, all with own bath or shower & wc.

Price: 250 Frs for two, including breakfast.

Meals: Dinner 90 Frs, including wine and aperitif.

Open: All year.

To get there: *From A48, exit 3 (Bourgoin-Jallien) then N85 towards Grenoble. After 4.5km, left onto D520 to Biol then left to Torchefelon; signposted.*

Map Ref No: 12

Jean-Pierre & Nicole PIGNOLY
"Le Colombier"
La Taillat
38690 Torchefelon, Isère
Tel: 74 92 29 28
Fax: 74 92 27 33

501

The Oppelts and their fabulously renovated neo-classical house can be unhesitatingly recommended for an authentic taste of château living. The rooms have fine period furniture, are decorated with engravings and family portraits and look out over the park. Madame, as elegant as her house, provides for all without being invasive and Monsieur is pleased to be told that 8 years of painstaking work have all been worthwhile.

Rooms: 3 double rooms & 1 suite, all with bathrooms.

Price: 450 Frs for two, including breakfast.

Meals: None.

Open: All year.

To get there: *From Besançon, N73 to St Vit. Then left through town and right onto D203 to Salans; château in village.*

Map Ref No: 12

Mme Béatrice OPPELT
Château de Salans
39700 Salans
Jura
Tel: 84 71 16 55

Here you sleep on superb mattresses in large rooms in a converted stable block. Decorated with subtlety (dried flowers and books) they have good bathrooms and are excellent value. A quiet village house, despite the nearby airport, with a large garden, gregarious host and good food (Madame's dinner always includes regional specialities using home-grown produce). Visit the pretty town of Dôle for interesting urban architecture or the River Loue for swimming.

Rooms: 3 double & 2 twin rooms, all with bathrooms.

Price: 200 Frs for two, including breakfast.

Meals: Dinner 100 Frs, including wine.

Open: All year.

To get there: *From A39, exit Dôle-Sud, then follow signs to Genève. 1st village on right, 2nd house on left after church.*

Map Ref No: 12

Danielle & Roland PICARD
3 rue du Puits
39100 Gevry
Jura
Tel: 84 71 05 93
Fax: 84 71 08 08

Steeped in history, this ferme-auberge dates from the 1100s. Most of the existing building is 16th century; the ground floor is completely vaulted. But the 1st-floor guestrooms, though up a steep staircase, are thoroughly modern. The flower-decked façade overlooks enchanting countryside near arcaded Lons-le-Saunier, birthplace of the composer of the Marseilleise. Madame serves superb meals in a happy atmosphere; home-produced fromage blanc is a must.

Rooms: 3 double rooms, 1 twin room, each with own shower & wc.

Price: 220 Frs for two, including breakfast.

Meals: Dinner 70 Frs, excluding wine (book ahead).

Open: All year.

To get there: *From Lons-le-Saunier, D117 through Macornay to Géruge; 1st left at entrance to village; La Grange Rouge at end of winding road.*

Map Ref No: 12

Henri & Anne-Marie VERJUS
La Grange Rouge
39570 Géruge
Jura
Tel: 84 47 00 44

What excellent value! A typical Savoy chalet-cum-farm, whence fresh milk and cheese for breakfast. Leave the front door on your cross-country skis or take a nearby lift. Madame is down-to-earth, loves children and her house. She runs a real chambre d'hôte: you feel you are her personal guest in one of the simply-furnished homely rooms or taking breakfast in the small kitchen. No wonder the first visitors stayed a week.

Rooms: 1 double, 1 triple and 1 family room for 4-5 people; all with own bathrooms.

Price: 170 Frs for two, including breakfast.

Meals: None.

Open: All year.

To get there: *From Albertville, N212 towards Megève. 1.5km after Flumet, at Notre Dame de Bellecombe junction, go towards "Téléski Les Seigneurs"; house is 300m along, after "Fromagerie"; signposted.*

Map Ref No: 13

Béatrice BURNET-MERLIN
La Cour
Les Seigneurs
73590 Flumet
Savoie
Tel: 79 31 72 15

A farm, but with a difference – it has been in the family for 5 generations and produces organic fertilizers! Madame's unaffected warmth melts any shyness you may feel. She once ran an art gallery; her love of art is reflected in the decoration and all the "objets". She will sometimes play the piano, Monsieur might play the accordeon, there is classical music almost all the time (meals may be less important?). Horses for experienced riders, very comfortable rooms and good "presence".

Rooms: 2 double, 2 twin, 1 triple room, all with own shower & wc.

Price: 280 Frs for two, including breakfast.

Meals: Dinner 75 Frs, including wine.

Open: All year.

Another Savoyard farm, another stupendous set of views across the surrounding massif. Masses of home-grown vegetables and meat from the farm. Dinner around a huge dining table, en famille, with regional specialities centre stage. These are down-to-earth working people who know that, while sleeping quarters can be on the small side, proper food is essential for those planning to explore their area, be it on skis or on foot. Half board only.

Rooms: 2 double/quadruple (bunk beds) rooms, each with own shower & wc.

Price: 400 Frs for two, including breakfast and dinner.

Meals: Included in half-board arrangement.

Open: All year.

To get there: *From Aix-les-Bains, D913 to Trévignan ("direction Le Revard") then follow signs.*

Map Ref No: 13

To get there: *From Albertville, N212 towards Megève. After 22km, left to St Nicolas-la-Chapelle; follow signs.*

Map Ref No: 13

Mme Daniel CHAPPAZ
La Jument Verte
Place de l'Eglise
73100 Trévignin
Savoie
Tel: 79 61 47 52

506

André & Michelle JOLY
Le Passieux
Ferme du Mont Charvin
73590 St Nicolas-la-Chapelle,
Savoie
Tel: 79 31 62 89 or 79 31 69 37

507

They are off-beat, amusing and very good hosts! Top-class bedrooms and bathrooms in a Hitchcock-like house with grounds (monkey-puzzle trees), views (Alps with snow) and fabulous meals by Philippe. He left acting for cooking but will entertain you with after-dinner sketches once you have been filled with good wine, music and the gentle vapours of fresh flowers. Anne-Charlotte enjoys the comedy of life: her family used to own the fine château you can see opposite.

Rooms: 1 twin room, 2 double rooms, 1 suite and 1 flat for 2-4; all with bathrooms.

Price: 390 Frs for two, breakfast 65 Frs extra per person.

Meals: Dinner 150-250 Frs, excluding wine.

Open: All year except 2-15 January.

To get there: *From A41, Pontcharra exit; D925 towards Albertville. At La Rochette go to Hôtel de Ville and take road for Arvillard. The Châtaigniers is 200m along on the left.*

Map Ref No: 13

Philippe & Anne-Charlotte REY
Les Châtaigniers
Rue Maurice Franck
73110 La Rochette, Savoie
Tel: 79 25 50 21
Fax: 79 25 79 97

508

The heart fills upon arrival at this house on the edge of the Vanoise national park, up 1350 metres near the Italian border. Bernard is a qualified summer and winter guide for walkers and the Trigons do know about walking; delicious packed lunches are easily made and dinner in the stone-vaulted dining-room is a convivial feast. Rooms are large, sober, just right. Authenticity abounds: hamlet, house, hills and mountains, food, activities and atmosphere. You will want to stay on...and on.

Rooms: 3 twin rooms, 1 triple room, all with own bathrooms.

Price: 360-370 Frs for two, including breakfast & dinner.

Meals: Dinner included in half-board arrangement.

Open: All year.

To get there: *From Chambéry, N6 towards Turin. 4km before Modane, left to St André/L'Orgère. Through village then signs on left to Le Villard.*

Map Ref No: 13

Bernard & Michèle TRIGON
Le Villard
73500 Saint-André
Savoie
Tel: 79 05 27 17

509

Hospitality is a family tradition; Anne-Marie also keeps horses and organizes rides up to the Alpine pastures above the valley. You should see chamois and marmots if you go far enough. The chalet houses a 'museum' depicting life on an Alpine farm in the old days. Best of all is dinner at the long wooden table with grandmama's recipes cooked on a wood-fired stove: "simple ingredients well prepared and delicious cheeses". You may be greeted by a Union Jack....

Rooms: 1 triple room with bathroom, 5 doubles sharing 3 showers & 3 wcs.

Price: 320 Frs for two: half-board only.

Meals: Dinner included in price.

Open: All year.

To get there: *From Thonon-les-Bains, D26 towards Bellevaux; house is 2km before Bellevaux on the left – signposted.*

Map Ref No: 13

Anne-Marie FELISAZ-DENIS
Le Chalet
La Cressonnière
74470 Bellevaux
Haute-Savoie
Tel: 50 73 70 13

510

Honey from the hive, cheese from the udder (well, almost), eggs of the minute and bits of the 15th century in the building. Do you need more? A magnificent lake 10km away, fine ski slopes on the doorstep, a refreshingly authentic feel here, amongst real farming folk. Dinners consist of home-produced-practically-everything. For the adults, there are beams and books galore in the guestroom and stunning country outside; for the young, plenty of farmyard animals to talk to.

Rooms: 1 triple room with own shower & wc.

Price: 195 Frs for two, including breakfast.

Meals: Dinner 70 Frs, including wine (book ahead).

Open: All year.

To get there: *From Annecy, N201 for Aix-les-Bains. At Chaux Balmont, right onto D38 to Chapeiry. House is first farm on right in village.*

Map Ref No: 13

Michel & Cécile FILLIARD
Chef-Lieu
74540 Chapeiry
Haute-Savoie
Tel: 50 68 28 28

511

A 200-year old Savoyard farmhouse that still houses a farming family and has three attractive guestrooms with wood, stone and white paint in harmony and lovely shower rooms. There is a sitting-room for guests with an unusual half-moon window at floor level, the result of a clever conversion. Madame will do anything to help, dines with her guests and still finds time to work on the farm, whence fresh vegetables for dinner.

Rooms: 1 double room, 2 twin rooms, each with own shower & wc.

Price: 246 Frs for two, including breakfast.

Meals: Dinner 80 Frs, including wine.

Open: All year.

To get there: *From Annecy, N201 towards Geneva. 1km after Cruseilles, D27 left to Copponex. Through village, left at cemetery; signs to Chambres d'Hôtes Châtillon. House on right.*

Map Ref No: 13

Suzanne & André GAL Châtillon
74350 Copponex
Haute-Savoie
Tel: 50 44 08 94

Halfway between Annecy and Geneva, France and Switzerland, in green hilly country, another Savoyard chalet, this one built by the owner himself. You will warm to his rough, jovial manner and appreciate Madame's enthusiastic welcome. The guestrooms are functional. Dinner dishes are Savoyard with ingredients from the large kitchen garden and poultry farm (now run by younger members of the family).

Rooms: 1 double room, 1 double/suite, both with bathrooms.

Price: 190 Frs for two, including breakfast.

Meals: Dinner 80 Frs, including wine.

Open: All year except November & January.

To get there: *From Annecy, N201 towards Geneva. Soon after Cruseilles, left onto D27 to Copponex. Through village then left at cemetery; sign for Chambres d'Hôtes Châtillon – 1.5km.*

Map Ref No: 13

Maryse & Aimé GAL Châtillon
74350 Copponex
Haute-Savoie
Tel: 50 44 22 70

"With a view like this one needs nothing else." At breakfast, in front of the picture window, you look straight across to Mont Blanc and the Glacier des Bossons. All is rock, snow and sunlight. It will take your breath away. You are in a chalet set quietly above Chamonix proper. Your hosts, educated, sensitive folk who look after you unobtrusively, know and love their mountains. And, moreover, Madame's dinner is of the "cuisine raffinée" kind. An exceptional place; book well ahead!

Rooms: 1 double room, 2 twin rooms, sharing bathroom.

Price: 260 Frs for two, including breakfast.

Meals: Dinner 120 Frs, including wine.

Open: All year.

In mind-boggling Alpine beauty, this 19th-century chalet embodies the very best in the tradition of French B&B. From the moment you arrive you are one of the family, welcome to join in Madame's activity – for active she will be! Dinners are solid Savoyard affairs where you may sit with guests staying a week or two. Footpaths lead up the valley to a small lake, and up, and up, and up ... for the more adventurous.

Rooms: 4 double & 1 twin room, all with bathrooms.

Price: 220 Frs for two, including breakfast.

Meals: Dinner 65 Frs, including wine.

Open: All year.

To get there: *From Geneva, A40, Chamonix Sud exit; turn left, cross 2 small roundabouts. At traffic lights, straight on: signposted.*

Map Ref No: 13

To get there: *From Thonon-les-Bains, D26 to Bellevaux. There, left to La Clusaz then towards La Chèvrerie; house is along on right.*

Map Ref No: 13

Pierre & Georgette GAZAGNES
46 chemin de la Persévérance
74400 Chamonix Mont Blanc
Haute-Savoie
Tel: 50 53 37 58

Francis & Geneviève PASQUIER
La Clusaz – Vallon
74470 Bellevaux
Haute-Savoie
Tel: 50 73 71 92

This lovely, rather austere old house stands on the slope of an extinct volcano, whence stupendous views. In a recently-converted 'bergerie', the guestrooms have an air of luxury and are decorated with obvious flair. Skilfully-presented meals are made with organic fruit and vegetables from the garden, local meat and cheeses and homemade desserts. Monsieur speaks fluent English and both hosts are kind, cultured and generous.

Rooms: 3 double rooms, 1 twin room, 1 suite, each with own bathroom.

Price: 420 Frs for two, half-board only.

Meals: Dinner with wine included in price.

Open: All year, except for two weeks in June and two weeks in September.

To get there: *From A7, Loriol exit, N104 to Privas, then towards 'les Ollières'. At Petit Tournon, D260 left to Pourchères and follow signposts.*

Map Ref No: 12

The Rhône Valley

Marcelle & Jean-Nicolas GOETZ
07000 Pourchères
Ardèche
Tel: 75 66 81 99

Tucked away in beautiful wooded Ardèche country, Myriam, Claude and their two children surely inhabit a corner of paradise; come commune with Nature. Claude will ride horseback with you, there are magnificent walks, river pools for swimming, a very special meal to come back to with home-produced cheese, honey, fruit, vegetables...and a chance to hear Claude's traveller's tales (the quacamayo came back with him from South America!).

Rooms: 1 double room with bathroom, 2 doubles & 1 twin with shower each but sharing wc.

Price: 220-270 Frs for two, including breakfast.

Meals: Dinner 75 Frs, including wine.

Open: All year.

In spring, blossom and buzzing bees greet you; in summer, the lavender scent wafts over you and cicadas scrape all day. Long views over vineyards and hills, only Nature's noises breaking the peace; you can make your own supper and sit on the guests' terrace all evening. So if Madame is rather shy and the mix-and-not-match decoration is unfortunate, it matters not – the rooms are a good size (though with thin walls), the beds firm and the environment unique.

Rooms: 3 double rooms with own bathrooms.

Price: 170-190 Frs for two, including breakfast.

Meals: None (self-catering in 2 rooms & good choice locally).

Open: All year.

To get there: *From Montélimar, N102 to Aubenas; N104 towards Alès 16km; right onto D5 to Largentière; D24 towards Valgorge 12km then left into Rocles; 300m after church.*

Map Ref No: 17

Myriam & Claude ROUVIERE
La Croze
07110 Rocles
Ardèche
Tel: 75 88 31 43

517

To get there: *From Nyons, D538 towards Valréas. After 7km, continue D538 right to Rousset-les-Vignes. 3km after Rousset, left at sign & follow signs for 800m.*

Map Ref No: 17

Rémy & Marie-Noëlle BARJAVEL
26770 Montbrison-sur-Lez
Drôme
Tel: 75 53 54 04

518

Set in vineyards facing Mont Ventoux, this 400-year-old farmhouse provides honest country hospitality. Small, basic guestrooms, but excellent value and Madame's cooking merits a slot in the local good food guide: good Provençal dishes – soupe au pistou and maybe some local stuffed peaches. The locality is also full of "musts" to explore (Vaison-la-Romaine, Mont Ventoux, hill-top villages, wine cellars...la Provence quoi!).

Rooms: 3 double, 2 twin and 1 family room, all with own shower & wc.

Price: 185 Frs for two, including breakfast.

Meals: Dinner 75 Frs, including wine.

Open: 15 February – 15 November.

A trout river tumbles within earshot. The old stone farmhouse faces the Vercors mountains. The Cabanes, their children, a grandmother and a centenarian relative all live here. Warm and friendly, they are good story-tellers! Guestrooms have polished wooden floors and old "armoires". The house breathes country comfort. At dinner, local wine, garden produce, soups and local dishes; at breakfast, grandmother's jams. The farm produces organic walnuts.

Rooms: 1 double room (with extra bed) and 1 twin room; own bathrooms, shared wc.

Price: 160 Frs B&B for two; 330 Frs half-board for two; 380 Frs full-board for two.

Meals: Lunch and/or dinner available on half-board.

Open: All year.

To get there: *From Vaison-la-Romaine, D938 towards Malaucène; after 2km, left onto D54 to Entrechaux, then D13 and D5 to Mollans-sur-Ouvèze, then D46 towards Faucon for 2km.*

Map Ref No: 17

To get there: *From Valence, D68 to Chabeuil. There, cross river and take D154 towards Combovin for 5km; signposted.*

Map Ref No: 12

René & Rose-Marie BERNARD
Quartier Ayguemarse
26170 Mollans-sur-Ouvèze
Drôme
Tel: 75 28 73 59

Mme Madeleine CABANES
Les Péris
CD 154
26120 Châteaudouble
Drôme
Tel: 75 59 80 51

Exposed stone, beams and terracotta tiles are combined with antiques to create an elegant, restful interior to this farm. Immaculate, heated bedrooms have period furnishings and firm beds with latex mattresses. At dinner, mouthwatering regional dishes! The owners cultivate 28 hectares of AOC vines. Monsieur's joviality complements Madame's professional efficiency. Courtyard garden and peaceful 'garrigue' setting.

Rooms: 4 double rooms and 1 triple room, all with bathrooms.

Price: 310 Frs for two, including breakfast.

Meals: Dinner 130 Frs, including wine (book ahead; except Sundays).

Open: All year.

To get there: *From Montélimar, N7 towards Orange. At Bollène, D994 to Suze-la-Rousse. There, D59 towards St Paul-Trois-Châteaux; right on D117 to La Baume-de-Transit; signposted.*

Map Ref No: 17

Ludovic & Eliane CORNILLON
Domaine de Saint-Luc
26790 La Baume-de-Transit
Drôme
Tel: 75 98 11 51
Fax: 75 98 19 22

521

A perfect place for lovers of art (summer exhibitions and courses), crafts (Madeleine makes china dolls) and ecology (the house is renovated with authentic materials, meals made with organic produce, every care taken with natural resources). The Goldsteins are a sensitive, unconventional 'ex-60s' couple with a rare creative flair married to sound practical skills. An original and desirable place for like-minded souls.

Rooms: 2 double rooms & 1 suite for 4, all with own bathrooms.

Price: 250-380 Frs for two, including breakfast.

Meals: Dinner 85-100 Frs, including wine.

Open: All year.

To get there: *From Chabeuil, D538 towards Crest for 5km (ignore signs for Montvendre). Left at sign 'Les Dourcines'; house 700m on right next to Auberge-Restaurant sign.*

Map Ref No: 12

Bernard & Madeleine GOLDSTEIN
Les Dourcines
26120 Montvendre
Drôme
Tel: 75 59 24 27

522

In a quiet setting at the foot of Mont Vercors your hard-working hosts run a poultry and frog farm...and, needless to say, are launching an ostrich project next year. When work allows they like chatting with guests but rarely have the time. The rooms are well-furnished if smallish and have separate entrances. Dinner was reported by one of our readers as "quite delicious with ample wine" and breakfast "a magnificent spread", both served outside in good weather.

Rooms: 3 double rooms with own bathrooms and 2 double rooms sharing a bathroom. Extra bed available.

Price: 255 Frs for two, including breakfast.

Meals: Dinner 67 Frs, including wine.

Open: All year.

Evelyne is an artist, she loves people, lots of people, and in summer throws her house and garden open to groups doing meditation, music and massage. There are children, animals and lots of activity; more peaceful out of season. Her rooms are large, simply but artistically furnished, her meals based on organic produce. You can walk in the park (4 hectares), swim in the Drôme (100m away) or climb the Vercors hills. Always book ahead for this wild and beautiful country was long ago 'discovered' by the French.

Rooms: 3 double rooms sharing bathroom and wc.

Price: 240 Frs for two, including breakfast.

Meals: Dinner 90-100 Frs, including wine.

Open: All year (advance booking only).

To get there: *From Chabeuil, D119 to St-Didier. Then follow Gîtes de France signs for 3.3km. House down short track on right.*

Map Ref No: 12

To get there: *From Crest, D93 to Mirabelet Blacons. Château on left as you leave village with sign "Galerie Arbre de Vie" on wall.*

Map Ref No:

Christiane & Pierre IMBERT
Le Marais
26300 St Didier-de-Charpey
Drôme
Tel: 75 47 03 50

Evelyne LATUNE
Château de Blacons
26400 Crest
Drôme
Tel: 75 40 01 00

A genuine B&B in the owners' farmhouse where you have the feeling you really are their personal guests. They are a cultivated couple living quietly in a lovely setting. There is a fine piano for those with talent. The rooms are furnished with a mix of old (an antique writing-desk, a fine old clock, one bathroom even has an inherited 19th-century loo!) and new. Mick, your hostess, is organised and welcoming and her excellent dinner may include home-grown truffles.

Rooms: 1 double & 1 triple room sharing a bathroom, 1 suite (5-6 people) with bathroom.

Price: 190-230 Frs for two, including breakfast.

Meals: Dinner 80-100 Frs, including wine.

Open: All year except 15 Dec- 15 Jan.

To get there: *From Montélimar, D540 towards Dieulefit for 7.4km (ignore signs for Montboucher). Left at sign for 300m.*

Map Ref No: 17

François & Mick PROTHON
Le Vermenon
26740 Montboucher-sur-Jabron
Drôme
Tel: 75 46 08 37

525

Surrounded by Beaujolais – go wine-tasting, riding or walking. This is the perfect centre for exploring a gentle, fascinating region. Yet the château itself is rather forlorn. Fine floors, grand rooms, tall windows over the 19th-century park but stonework and staircase worn. The guestrooms, however, are light and airy with sumptuous lacy linen. The public rooms retain their charm and splendour. These echoes of a more gracious past will appeal to many and Monsieur is a most attentive host.

Rooms: 1 suite of 3 double or twin rooms, 1 suite of 2 double or twin rooms, each with own bathrooms.

Price: 400-500 Frs for two, including breakfast.

Meals: Not available.

Open: All year (minimum stay 2 nights in winter).

To get there: In Villefranche head towards Roanne then D31 through Chervinges. 4km after Chervinges, Bois Franc signposted on left.

Map Ref No: 12

Monsieur DOAT
Château de Bois Franc
69640 Jarnioux
Rhône
Tel: 74 68 20 91
Fax: 74 65 10 03

526

THE RHÔNE VALLEY

The goats provide the very special atmosphere of this memorable house. Their gentle mastications lull you to sleep and you awake to a hissing sound; milk in the pail, perhaps. So goat's milk for breakfast is no surprise; try it with coffee... something to ruminate on. Then the cheeses, graded according to strength, mostly at the top end of the muscle-range. As you leave you are helped on your way by these gentle quadrupeds. Book early – your hosts need time to remove the previous occupants from the room.

Rooms: 1 ground-floor area, sharing wc.

Price: Varies according to numbers sharing.

Meals: Available 24 hrs a day; cheese-based.

Open: Breeding season.

To get there: Follow your nose.

Map Ref No:

M & Mme BLITTE
Maison des Cabris
Odeur-sur-Pestilence
12345 Mamelle
Gaule

TIPS FOR TRAVELLERS IN FRANCE

● Buy a phone-card *(télécarte)* on arrival; they are on sale at post offices and tobacconists' *(tabac)*. Keep some small change for non-card phone-boxes; phone-boxes are generously distributed throughout France.

● Be aware of public holidays; most national museums and galleries close on Tuesdays and may also alter opening times on these days:

New Year's Day (1 January)   Bastille Day (14 July)
Easter Sunday and Monday   Assumption of BVM (15 August)
May Day (1 May)   All Saints (1 November)
Liberation 1945 (8 May)   Armistice 1918 (11 November)
Ascension Thursday   Christmas Day
Whit Sunday and Monday

● Beware also of the mass exodus over public holiday weekends, both the first day – outward journey – and the last – return journey.

Medical and emergency procedures.

● If you are an EC citizen, have an *E111 form* with you for filling in after any medical treatment. You will subsequently receive a refund for *part* of your payment, so it is advisable to take out private insurance.

● French emergency services are:
– the public service called *SAMU*
– the private service called *SOS MEDECINS*

Roads and driving.

● Current **speed limits** are: motorways 130 kph (80 mph), "RN" national trunk roads 110 kph (68 mph), other roads 90 kph (56 mph), in towns 50 kph (30 mph). The road police are very active and can demand on-the-spot payment of fines.

● You will get used to driving on the right fairly fast but complacency leads to trouble; take special care coming out of car-parks, private drives, narrow one-lane roads and coming onto roundabouts.

French motorways (autoroutes) are   *Autoroutes à péage*
mostly toll-paying
BLUE signs = motorways   *Autoroutes*
GREEN signs = alternative routes   *Itinéraires bis*
Many roads coming from the right   *Priorité à droite*
have priority; expect it **always!**
"Use engine braking" down steep
hills means ... KEEP IN LOW GEAR
Diesel   *Gasoil – Gazole*
Unleaded   *Sans plomb*

Talking to your hosts and others.

(For those with reasonable French). We all know how the French like a good debate. Here are a few topical and slightly (or very!) controversial subjects which should make for lively conversation. But do remember that we all harbour deep-seated prejudices and that "rivalry" between France and England has been **the** cross-Channel sport for centuries, long before rugby was invented.

Le Tunnel..
.Trains on both sides of the Channel.
English wine (this will get them going).
Vegetarianism (still an occult science to many French people).
Le Franglais, the Minister of Culture Jacques Toubon (known as Jack Allgood by the French chattering classes) and the Académie Française.
Corruption in sport.
Hypermarkets v village shops.
The pub v the café.
The weather (yes, the French talk about it just as much as we do, in the northern half of France at least).
'Tu' and 'Vous'.
And, as ever, the European Union …

If you are worried about getting into controversy … go ahead! Isn't that what adds spice to a conservation? Isn't that what makes an encounter real?

Before arriving (therefore over the telephone).

Do you have a room for tonight?	*Avez-vous une chambre pour ce soir?*
How much does it cost?	*Combien coûte la chambre?*
I/we shall be arriving about 4 p.m.	*J'arriverai/nous arriverons vers seize heures.*
I'm/we're lost	*Je suis/nous sommes perdu(s).*
I am in the phone box at …	*Je suis dans la cabine téléphonique à …*
I am in the Café des Sports at …	*Je suis au Café des Sports à …*
Can you tell the owner how to find your house	*Pouvez-vous expliquer au patron comment trouver votre maison.*
Do you have any animals? I'm allergic to cats	*Avez-vous des animaux? Je suis allergique aux chats.*

On arrival

Hello Mrs/Mr X. I'm Mrs/Mr Y.	*Bonjour Madame/Monsieur X. Je suis Madame/Monsieur Y.*
I found your name in Alastair Sawday's Guide.	*J'ai trouvé votre nom dans le Guide Alastair (sic).*
Can I put this picnic food/these ice blocks in your refrigerator?	*Pourrais-je mettre ces restes de piquenique/ces blocs réfrigérants dans votre frigidaire?*
Could I heat up the baby's feeding bottle?	*Pourrais-je réchauffer ce biberon?*
Can the children sleep in sleeping bags on our floor?	*Est-ce que les enfants peuvent dormir dans leur sac de couchage par terre dans notre chambre?*
How much will you charge for that?	*Ça coûtera combien?*

Things you need/that go wrong.

Can I have pillows instead of the bolster/some more blankets?

Pourrais-je avoir des oreillers à la place du traversin/encore des couvertures?

The mattress is too soft/hard.
Le matelas est trop mou/dur.

Clothes hangers
Cintres

The water is cold/too hot.
L'eau est froide/trop chaude.

Do the chickens usually sleep in this room?
Est-ce que les poules dorment toujours dans cette chambre?

Our tap is dripping.
Notre robinet fuit.

The gas bottle is empty
La bouteille de gaz est vide.

I've forgotten how to light the cooker.
J'ai oublié comment allumer la cuisinière.

Could I have some matches?
Pourrais-je avoir des allumettes?

Where can I hang these wet clothes?
Où pourrais-je mettre ce linge à sécher?

How the house works.

Can we use our room/the sitting room during the day?
Pouvons-nous utiliser notre chambre/le salon dans le journée?

Do you leave any lights on during the night?
Est-ce que vous laissez la lumière allumée la nuit?

Can the children play in the garden/explore the farm?
Est-ce que les enfants peuvent jouer dans le jardin/visiter la ferme?

Is there any danger?
Est-ce que c'est dangereux?

Can we/they help?
Pouvons-nous/peuvent-ils aider?

Can we leave the children this evening?
Pouvons-nous laisser les enfants ce soir?

Can you find us a babysitter?
Pouvez-vous nous trouver une babysitter?

I'm so sorry about the mess in our room.
Excusez le désordre dans notre chambre.

Please let me clear it up.
Laissez-moi ranger.

Feel free to express your anger to the children.
Ne vous gênez pas pour gronder les enfants s'il y a un problème.

Local information.

How far is it to the sea/petrol station/nearest shops?
A combien de kilomètres est la mer/la station d'essence/les magasins les plus proches?

Is there a small restaurant suitable for children near here?
Y a-t-il un petit restaurant où on peut amener les enfants?

What do you suggest we do after dinner this evening?
Que pourrions-nous faire après le dîner ce soir?

On leaving.

What time must we leave?
A quelle heure devons-nous partir?

May I pay my bill?
Je voudrais vous régler, s'il vous plaît.

How much do I owe you?
Combien je vous dois?

We've had a very pleasant stay.
Nous avons passé un très bon moment chez vous.

Thank you so much!
Merci mille fois!

The photo IS supposed to frighten you! It certainly frightened us, because inside the van were Guy Hunter-Watts and Patti Herrera Cornejo ... our inspectors! They escaped unhurt, short on teeth and long on bruises.

Most accidents are, of course, minor ... but they always involve you in frustration, anxiety, expense and wasted holiday time.

So, do read the next page ...

COVER FOR YOUR CAR – THE ETA

The Environmental Transport Association is the 'green' version of the AA and RAC, sparked off by the huge success of similar groups in Switzerland and Germany. It is the only organisation for environmentally-conscious (and perhaps reluctant) motorists who nevertheless still need the best possible cover.

European Cover. There is automatic cover throughout Europe, so you are fully covered when driving in France. So, for as little as £62 you can have ETA membership plus full European cover ... less than you would pay for European cover elsewhere.

How Good Is It? Well, the February 1994 issue of "Car Week" described the ETA as the Best Value for Money; and Which? magazine has rated it highly. Its contracted network of garages has over 4,000 recovery vehicles ... often used, by the way, by the AA and RAC when they cannot cope.

How Does It Work? The ETA car-recovery system is not a collection of rickshaws and horses but is contracted out to an extensive network of the best garages. Recovery is efficient and very fast, second to none. Every rescue-vehicle can also tow you home or on to your destination, so you never have to await a tow-truck if the first man on the scene cannot fix the fault.

How Is It Green? The ETA campaigns for better public transport and a more intelligent overall transport policy. It lobbies Parliament and produces excellent reports. The AA and RAC, on the other hand, have always lobbied for more road-building, whatever the damage to the environment and our health. If you belong to them you are, perhaps unwittingly, supporting the bulldozing of our countryside.

How To Join. Send in the form at the bottom of this page and you will be sent an application form with further details. When you join you will receive a £5 discount off the membership fee as a reader of this Guide. *(Note that the ETA WON'T inundate you with junk mail!)*.

Voilà ... a marvellous way of helping yourself and the environment at the same time. If you have not heard of it before it is because it has only been going a few years in the UK; it now has over 10,000 members and is firmly established.

To: The ETA, The Old Post House, Heath Rd, Weybridge KT13 8RS
Please send me a membership application form.

NAME: _____

ADDRESS: _____

_____

_____

Post Code: _____

☐ *Please tick this box if you do NOT want to receive mailings from other organisations.*

Were these first ferries a Good Thing? (Discuss on the journey down through France).

With the arrival on the scene of the Chunnel the ferry companies of today must feel like the person who said 'Just as you think you have made both ends meet someone moves one end". (A bottle of Burgundy for the first person to tell us who said that.)

But they are fighting back, and if you join Eurodrive you can get some marvellously low fares.

EURODRIVE

The ferry doesn't HAVE to be expensive ...

If, like me, you feel slightly powerless when buying your ferry tickets, confused by price rises and conflicting advice and resenting what appears to be a seller's market ... read on.

What Is Eurodrive? In a nutshell ...... it is a company that offers you big discounts on the price of cross-channel ferry trips.

It is part of the ABTA-bonded travel company, Leisure Directions Ltd, and buys space allocations on the ferries.

How Does It Work? It acts rather like airline 'consolidators', selling the ferry space on to members for discounts of up to 50%. You have probably never heard of it because it rarely advertises in its own name. However, they are the people behind most of the ferry promotions offered by others, such as newspapers.

General Advice on ferry prices is easy to obtain through Eurodrive as they are the specialists, with up-to-date information on all prices and sailings at their fingertips.

Special Offer For Our Readers. Applying for membership with the slip at the bottom of this page will get you free membership (usually £8) ... and some big savings on your ferry trip.

To: Eurodrive Leisure Directions, 3-5 Crouch End Hill, London N8 8DH
Please enrol me as a member of Eurodrive.

NAME: _____

ADDRESS: _____

_____

_____

_____ Post Code: _____

☐ *Please tick this box if you do NOT want to receive mailings from other organisations.*

Alastair Sawday Publishing

These two young monks adorn this page largely because we like the photo!
(Taken by Quentin Craven)

But they can claim a right to be here because they were pouring tea for our 1993 group to Ladakh, the eastern part of what is now Kashmir. Do YOU put such exuberance into pouring tea?

Our JOURNEYS take you to beautiful places all over the world where you invariably have encounters with many people as beguiling and interesting as these boys.

JOURNEYS

If you have enjoyed the new experiences that this Guide has provided then you will probably be fascinated by JOURNEYS. Read on ...

As well as publishing this Guide we also run a small but unusual travel company, which is why we know France and its Chambres d'Hôtes so well. We have now launched a new programme under the name Alastair Sawday's 'JOURNEYS' ... the first of its kind in the UK.

In the next century tourism will be the world's biggest 'industry'. Most tourists travel with little regard for their impact on the places they visit. You doubtless share my sadness at such things as the loss of forests, the construction of huge hotels, and the displacement of people to make way for a new and invasive culture. (You will know what I mean if you have seen a video shop in the Himalayas.)

SO, JOURNEYS almost certainly has something for you:

•• Inexpensive journeys to some of the world's most fascinating places: PERU, ETHIOPIA, KENYA, SOUTH AFRICA, INDIA (Ladakh, Garhwal, Kerala and the south), THAILAND, BELIZE and EUROPE (biking and walking in Andalusia, and biking in the UK).

•• Journeys that have minimal impact on other cultures and environments. You stay in villages, visit development projects, hike in mountains, learn a lot and ... enjoy yourselves hugely.

•• Journeys that benefit the indigenous people. There are, perhaps, two vital elements to this:

1. We plan to use, where possible, local voluntary organisations to 'handle' us (rather than for-profit agencies)
2. We share the net profit from the trips with environmental or development organisations.

FOR EXAMPLE: In Ladakh our 'agent' is the Women's Rural Development Movement; they organise our treks and take us to their homes to stay. We then share the profits with the Ladakh Ecological Development Project, which encourages cultural and economic independence from the invading consumer culture which we all know so well.

I would enjoy saying more, but write or telephone for our brochure:

Alastair Sawday's JOURNEYS: 44 Ambra Vale East, Bristol BS8 4RE. Tel: 0117 9299921

Please send me a Journeys brochure.

I am particularly interested in _____ ;

please send me a detailed itinerary for that country.

NAME: _____

ADDRESS: _____

_____

_____ Post Code: _____

☐ *Please tick this box if you do NOT want to receive mailings from other organisations.*

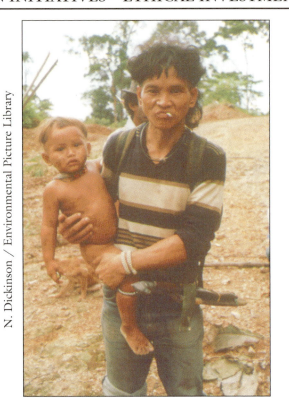

N. Dickinson / Environmental Picture Library

Just having a quiet fag?

Or is this a depressing example of the transfer of one of our bad habits to people who have enough on their plate as it is?

Many of us are passive investors as well as passive smokers. But others, aware of the ethical dilemmas, have found the beginnings of a solution.

GREEN INITIATIVES – ETHICAL INVESTMENT

This page is a sort of commercial plug, but it sits well with the rest of the book, I think. It introduces what for many of you may prove to be a new and interesting set of ideas.

I am counting on your goodwill having survived intact this far. If you have had one or two beautiful experiences in Chambres d'Hôtes you may be willing to trust me and read a little further.

Green Initiatives is a small company I launched to promote green products and services. One of them is Ethical Investment. Read on ...

Why Even Think About It? Many of you reading this Guide are investors of one sort or another. If you have a few hundred, or thousand, pounds stashed away somewhere you are an 'investor', perhaps letting someone else make all the decisions for you.

Do you KNOW what is being done with your money ... whether in a bank, Building Society, pension fund, or shares? Have you asked yourself if the managers of your portfolio (or bank, or pension fund) have ANY priority other than profit? If not, what ... it is fair to ask ... are the consequences?

You may be a perfectly honourable person, doing your best to lead a decent life. Perhaps you are kind to children and dislike smoking ... but is your money helping to sell cigarettes to African children? Perhaps you are as enthusiastic about Chambres d'Hôtes as I am ... but do you have shares in a company which is building those monstrous modern hotels I referred to in the Introduction? Do you know?

What To Do? 5 years ago it was considered foolish to invest 'ethically'. Now it is firmly established as a viable, and often advisable, option for those whose conscience is an irritant. It is entirely feasible to switch from one pension to another, one stock to another, and to gain in the process.

How To Do It? Send in the slip at the bottom of this page and you will be contacted by Holden Meehan, our local ethical investment brokers. We know them and trust them, and they are among the best ... far-sighted leaders in what has been a sceptical market. If you do invest or take out insurance or pension etc through them then Green Initiatives receives a (very) small commission.

A Last Peroration. If you are genuinely concerned about the long-term state of our environment then the ETA (see preceding pages) is an easy and sensible way to have your cake and eat it while driving a car.

The same applies to ethical investment. You can now invest with a good profit AND a clear conscience. (Just in case ... yes, my company HAS taken out ethical pensions!)

To: Green Initiatives, 44 Ambra Vale East, Bristol BS8 4RE

Please send me details of Ethical and/or Green Investment etc.

NAME: _____

ADDRESS: _____

_____

_____

_____

Post Code: _____

Please tick this box if you do NOT want to receive mailings from other organisations.

Alastair Sawday Publishing

FOR FURTHER INFORMATION:

I would like to receive advance notice of new editions and new publications, and even perhaps news of special Chambres d'Hôtes.

To: Alastair Sawday Publishing, 44 Ambra Vale East, Bristol BS8 4RE. Tel: 0117 9299921

NAME: _____

ADDRESS: _____

_____

_____

Post Code: _____

How many times do you travel to France each year? _____

Do you take a car to France?   ☐ YES   ☐ NO

Do you intend to use the Channel tunnel?   ☐ YES   ☐ NO

Which countries in Europe do you most often visit? _____

_____

_____

☐ *Please tick this box if you do NOT want to receive mailings from other organisations.*

Alastair Sawday Publishing

ORDER FORM

Alastair Sawday's Guide to French Bed & Breakfast

Title: Mr/Mrs/Miss/Ms/Other _____

Surname _____ Initials _____

Address _____

_____

_____ Postcode _____

Daytime telephone no. _____

Order date _____ No. of copies ordered _____

Delivery address – if different from address above

Title: Mr/Mrs/Miss/Ms/Other _____

Surname _____ Initials _____

Address _____

_____

_____ Postcode _____

I enclose CHEQUE payable to:
Alastair Sawday Publishing, 44 Ambra Vale East, Bristol BS8 4RE, UK

	for: 1 copy	(£11.95)	_____
	2 copies	(£23.90)	_____
	3 copies	(£35.85)	_____
4 or more copies @ £10 each	(£ .)		_____
	plus: P&P	(£2.00)	

Signed _____ TOTAL _____ DATE _____

REPORT FORM

Comments on existing entries and new discoveries.

If you have any comments on existing entries –
anything from details on prices to the reception you
got, the atmosphere, the hosts, the house –
then please let us have them.

If you have a favourite spot which you are willing to
share with us, so we may feature it in our next edition,
let us know.

Please fill in the following information:

Report on:
Entry no. _____   Date _____

Names of owners _____

Name of house _____

Address _____

_____

_____ Tel. No.: _____

Please tick the appropriate box:

☐   Should continue as a main entry

☐   Should not be continued

☐   Should be considered for inclusion as a main entry

My reasons are _____

_____

_____

_____

(continued)

_____

_____

_____

_____

_____

_____

Any of the following additional information will be appreciated.
(Please tick)

☐ I enclose a photograph of the property
    (We cannot return material sent to us)

☐ I am happy for you to use an edited version of
    my description

☐ I am happy for my name to appear
    in the book

Name _____

Address _____

_____

Tel. No.: (only if you don't mind) _____

I am not connected in any way with the owners of this property

Signed _____

Please send the completed form to:
Alastair Sawday Publishing, 44 Ambra Vale East,
Bristol BS8 4RE, UK.

THANK YOU SO MUCH FOR YOUR HELP!

INDEX of OWNERS

NAME	PLACE	Entry No.
ABIVEN-GUEGUEN	St Martin-des-Champs	120
ACHARD de LELUARDIERE	Caumont l'Eventé	41
AMARGER	Arzenc-de-Randon	423
ANFREY	Conteville	60
ANNERON	Asnières-sur-Vègre	276
ANTONY	Nègrepelisse	392
ARCHER	Mouleydier	332
ARMITAGE	Hautefort	333
ARNAULT	Brissac	249
AUCLERT	Quiberville	106
AUGIER	Séguret	482
AUGUSTIN	Auxi-le-Château	13
AUNAY-STANGUENNEC	Rouen	107
BABEY	Rousset	463
BADIN	Marcigny	188
BAHUAUD	Grez-Neuville	250
BAILLIOU	Montreuil-sur-Loir	251
BARACCO & DUPIN	Courmes	458
BARBARIN	St Savin	303
BARBARIN	Parigny-les-Vaux	177
BARJAVEL	Montbrison-sur-Lez	518
BARTHELEMY	Dieuzé	165
BASTID	Saumur	252
BASTOUIL	Laudun	401
BATAILLE	St Aubin-Lebizay	42
BATESON	Villefranche-de-Rouergue	443
BAXIN de CAIX de REMBURES	St Denis-sur-Loire	237
BEAUJEARD	Combronde	456
BEAUPERE	St Michel-de-Plélan	112
BECQUET-CHATEL	Forest l'Abbaye	26
BEGHINI	Boncourt	61
BELIERES	Loubressac	349
BELL	Rignac	350
BELLEE	La-Haye-du-Puits	73
BENHAMOU	Méobecq	221
BERARD	St Laurent-des-Arbres	402
BERDE	Unac	367
BERGE	Puichéric	398
BERGEROLLE	Le-Puy-Notre-Dame	253
BERNARD	Mollans-sur-Ouvèze	519
BERRIDGE	Brix	74
BERTHOLOM	Ste Sabine	334
BERTIN	Le-Clion-sur-Mer	146
BERTOLINO	St Félix-de-Tournegat	368

INDEX

BESNARD	Houlbec Cocherel	62
BILLAT	Montlieu-la-Garde	290
BINNS	La Guiche	189
BLANCHET	Ste-Mère-l'Eglise	75
BLIAUT	Les Authieux-du-Puits	97
BLITTE	Mamelle	527
BODET	Continvoir	229
BOHIC	Carantec	121
BONNET	Clermont l'Hérault	412
BOUANT	Le-Buisson-de-Cadouin	335
BOULLOT	Caumont l'Eventé	43
BOURGAULT	Le Sap	98
BOURGEOIS	Heudreville-sur-Eure	63
BOURGES	St Cyprien	336
BOURVEAU	Quéméneven	122
BOUSSEMAERE	Echinghen	14
BREMAUD	Mouterre Silly	304
BRETON	Giou-de-Mamou	451
BRETON	Muncq Nieurlet	15
BRIEUX	St Emilion	315
BROGNEAUX	Foix	369
BROSSIER-PUBLIER	Kerdruc-en-Nevez	123
BRUNOT	Mont-St-Sulpice	199
BUGE	St Bonnet-l'Enfantier	323
BUISSON	Villiers Fossard	76
BULTEY	Beuzeville	64
BURGI	St Révérien	178
BURNET-MERLIN	Flumet	505
BUTLER & KIRK	Ticheville	99
CABANES	Châteaudouble	520
CAILLET	Bergerac	337
CALOT	Neuillé	254
CAMALET	Castelnau-de-Montmirail	428
CAMBON	St Senin-sur-Rance	444
CANTEL	Bretteville-sur-Laize	44
CARCAILLET	Le Lion d'Angers	255
CARRUTHERS	Verteillac	338
CASPER	Saint Adjutory	287
CASTEX	Péguilhan	379
CAYLA	Buoux	483
CAZUC	Plouenan	124
CESNE	Carteret-Le Cap	77
CHABAUD	Goult	484
CHABRAN	Vacqueyras	485
CHAINIER	Salles-d'Angles	288
CHAMBRIN	St Germain-des-Bois	208
CHAMSKI-MANDAJORS	Ribaute-les-Tavernes	403
CHANUDET	Laurière	362
CHAPPAZ	Trévignin	506
CHARRIER	Plassay	291
CHARTIER	St Mariens	316
CHAUVEAU	Panzoult	230
CHAVALLE REVENU	Les Abrets	500
CHEILLETZ-MAIGNAN	Locqueltas	149
CHERVAUX	Cruzy-le-Châtel	200

CHEVALLIER	Marcigny	190
CHODKIEWICZ	St Léons	445
CHONE	Venoy	201
CHOQUET	Noyer	238
CHOUCAVY	Alban	429
CHRISTAENS	Clermont-en-Argonne	162
CIROTTE	Sancerre	209
CLAY	St Nicolas de Pierrepont	78
CLAYS et VENON	Troo	239
COLIBET	Charcé	256
COLLET	Pluvigner	150
COLLOT	Maisons-en-Champagne	157
COLOMBIER	Pinas	390
COPIN	Dun	370
CORNAZ	Violès	486
CORNILLON	La-Baume-de-Transit	521
CORPET	Trévières	45
COSTAILLE	Ste Magnance	202
COUILLAUD	St Fort-sur-Giron	292
CREPELLE	Vauchelles-les-Quesnoy	27
CRETE	Rabastens	430
CURFS	Monmort Lucy	158
CUZON du REST	St Philibert	151
DALLE	Saulty	16
DARTOIS	Châtillon-sur-Seine	171
DAUGE	Fontevraud-l'Abbaye	257
de BELLEFON	Lannion	113
de BONFILS	St Florent-le-Vieil	258
de BOSREDON	Issigeac	339
de BRUYNE	Léran	371
de CARRIERE	Grenade-sur-Garonne	380
de CHAMPSAVIN	Aignay-le-Duc	172
de GIAFFERRI	Chauvigny	305
de JERPHANION	Pontèves	473
de KERMEL	Pommerit-Jaudy	114
de la BUSSIERE	Bissy-sous-Uxelles	191
de la MONNERAYE	Herbignac	147
de la RAITRIE	Bouglon	354
de LAMARLIERE	Caours	28
de LATAILLADE	St Lon-les-Mines	320
de MEIXMORON	Bayonville	156
de MONTAIGNAC	Chamblet	442
de MONTIGNY	Belle-et-Houllefort	17
de MORCHOVEN	Plouaret	115
de PREAUMONT	Thiberville	65
de ROCQUIGNY	Foucaucourt	29
de ROQUEFEUIL	Plougrescant	116
de SALCHER EVIDE	Outre-Tombe-en-Mer	314
de SAULIEU	Grande-Rullecourt	18
de VERDUZAN	Pont St Esprit	404
de VILLOUTREYS de BRIGNAC	Lavoux	306
de VITTON	St Sauveur-de-Flée	259
DEFRANCE	Senan	203
DEFRANCE	Riville	108
DELAGE	Salsasc	413

INDEX

DELAROCQUE	Senoville	79
DELBREIL	Lempaut	431
DELCAMBRE	Banteux	6
DELISLE	Hébécrevon	80
DELTOUR	Châtillon-en-Bazois	179
DENECK	Wy-Dit-Joly-Village	40
DEPREAY	Grévilly	192
DESALASE	Desvres	19
DESCHAMPS	Aumagne	293
DESCHAMPS	Royère-de-Vassivière	330
DHUIT	Châtenoy	242
DIO	Bourg-de-Visa	393
DISCACCIATI	Lorgues	474
DOAT	Jarnioux	526
du MANOIR	Buzançais	222
du MONTANT	Eymoutiers	363
DUBOIS	Ladornac	340
DUBOIS	Oizé	277
DUBOST	Yvetot Bocage	81
DUCHET	Saint Loup	180
DUFAYET	Bussy-en-Othe	204
DUFFIE	Missy-sur-Aisne	1
DUFOUR	Thillombois	163
DUGUEPEROUX	Macey-Pontorson	82
DUHAMEL	St Pierre-sur-Dives	46
DUMAS	Venteuges	454
DUMESNIL	Gaillac-Toulza	381
DUPIN	Nontron	341
DURET	Port-de-Lanne	321
DURIEUX	Vendoire	342
DUSAUTOIR	Haut-Locquin	20
DUSSARTRE	Fourmetot	66
EARLS	La Trimouille	307
EDON	Maunit-Chemellier	260
ELMES	St Savinien	294
ENGEL	Villé	168
EVENO-SOURNIA	Volnay	278
FAIDHERBE BOTTINELLI	Vailhauques	414
FALLELOUR	Antezant	295
FAUVEL	Ecrammeville	47
FAVIER	Alenya	424
FAVREAU	Routot	67
FAYOLLE	Prémery	181
FELISAZ-DENIS	Bellevaux	510
FERCHAUD	Marennes	296
FERRY	Alan	382
FIEUX	Montpitol	383
FILLIARD	Chapeiry	511
FORGET	Ecoyeux	297
FOUGERIT	Trizay	298
FOUQUENET	Monts-sur-Guesnes	308
FRANCOIS	Baracé	261
FRANCOIS	Briare	243
FRAPPIER	St Jean-d'Angély	299
FRENKEL	Thevet-St-Julien	223

FROGER	Ste Solange	210
GABROY	Monfarville	83
GAGNARD	Monbazillac	343
GAL	Copponex	512
GAL	Copponex	513
GALLAUD	Marcigny	193
GARNIER	Pontigny	205
GAUDIN	Bouzillé	262
GAUTHIER	Trambly	194
GAVARD	St James	84
GAZAGNES	Chamonix Mont Blanc	514
GEDOUIN	Servon	85
GENCE	St Riquier	30
GIANESINI	Montaut	372
GIBSON	Palaja	399
GINISTY	Vézelay	206
GIORGI	Nuits-St-Georges	173
GITTERMAN	Amblainville	7
GLEMOT	Cherrueix	140
GODFREY	Carrouges	100
GOETZ	Pourchères	516
GOETZ	Marlenheim	169
GOISQUE	Digeon	31
GOLDSTEIN	Montvendre	522
GOMIS	La Couyère	141
GONFOND	Montmeyan	476
GONIDEC	Douarnenez	125
GOSSELIN	Gaudies	373
GOUNAND	Darcey	174
GOURLAOUEN	Nevez	126
GRANDCHAMP	Le Rozel	86
GRECH	Ginasservis	477
GRECK	Lagnes	487
GREENWOOD	Nonards	324
GRESSIN	Montigny	211
GREYFIE de BELLECOMBE	Aix-en-Provence	464
GRIMM	Vosne-Romanée	175
GROS	Boussac	331
GROSSET	St Pierre-de-Plesguen	142
GUENY	Tintury	182
GUEZENEC	Montreuil-Bellay	263
GUILLAUME	Saignon	488
GUILLOU	Querrien	127
HAMEL	Isigny-sur-Mer	48
HAMELIN	Betz	8
HANSON	Vauvert	405
HASQUENOPH	Chauffours	216
HATTE	Isdes	244
HAUSCHILD	Ménerbes	489
HENNY	Salernes	475
HENRIET	Beaulieu-sur-Dordogne	325
HENRIO	Cléguérec	152
HERE	Mareil-sur-Loir	279
HOPKINS	Castex	374
HUEZ	Montreuil-Juigné	264

INDEX

HUGON	Lavardens	386
HUNT	Montaigu-de-Quercy	394
HUTTON & PAGE	Loches	231
IMBERT	St Didier-de-Charpey	523
IUNG	Aix-en-Provence	465
JAMBOU	Meslan	153
JAMES	Fressin Hesdin	21
JAMET	Avignon	490
JAMIN	Les Essards	300
JANDET	Ste Marie	183
JANSEN de VOMECOURT	St Léonard-de-Noblat	364
JAUBERT	Eymoutiers	365
JEANGRAND	Pessoulens	387
JOLY	St Nicolas-la-Chapelle	507
JONQUA-CLEMENT	Castelsagrat	395
JUBARD	Le Blanc	224
KITCHEN	Le Vieil Baugé	265
KOZLOWSKI	Bonnieux	491
KREBS	Beaumont-en-Véron	232
KRUST	Lassy	143
LA TOUCHE	Roquebrun	415
LADAGNOUS	Peyrouse	391
LAFFORGUE	Mollégès	466
LAFOND	Argentat	326
LAIGNEL	Occagnes	101
LAISNE	Granville	87
LAJUS	St Perdon	322
LALLEMAN	Brémoy	49
LALLEMAND-LEGRAS	Bémécourt	68
LAMBERT	Peynier	467
LANGER	St Xandre	301
LANGLAIS	Onzain	240
LANGLAIS	Champfleur	280
LANNEAU	St Vivien-de-Médoc	317
LARDNER	Albussac	327
LARRIBEAU	Cancon	355
LARUE	Genneteil	266
LASSALLETTE	Lourmarin	492
LATUNE	Crest	524
LAUGERETTE	Charolles	195
LAURENS	Lacroix-Barrez	446
LAURENS	Veynes	499
LAWRENCE	Gordes	493
LAWRENCE	Loudun	309
LE BOUTEILLER	Crennes	102
LE GALL	St Yvi	129
LE GOASTER	Paimpol	117
LE GOFF	Château-du-Loir	281
LE LAY	Gien	246
Le MARCHAND de SAINT PRIEST	Le Coudray St Germer	9
LE PLATRE	Richelieu	233
LE ROUZIC	La Trinité-sur-Mer	154
LEBATARD	Pont d'Ouilly	50
LEDE	Plancoët	118
LEE & SIMONDS	Onlay	184

LEEMANN	St Estèphe	318
LEFEBVRE	St Denis-d'Anjou	272
LEFLOCH	Douarnenez	128
LEFRANC	Châtillon-sur-Loire	245
LEGON	Sigogne	289
LEGRAND	Bayeux	51
LEGRAS-WOOD	Montreuil-Poulay	273
LEJAULT	Alluy	185
LEMAITRE	Creuse	32
LENDRUM	Quettehou	88
LENTON	St Saturnin-de-Lenne	447
LEROUX de LENS	Arçay	310
LEROY	Marles-sur-Canche	22
LESAGE	Banville	52
LESENECHAL	Servon	89
LESPAGNOL	Château-Chervix	366
LETANNEUX	Dissay-sous-Courcillon	282
LETHUILLIER	Senneville-sur-Fécamp	109
LETURGIE	Ardres	23
LEVY	Monségur	319
LIBEAUT	St Laurent-Nouan	241
LINOSSIER	Durtal	267
LOLLIER	Spézet	130
LOMBARD-PRATMARTY	Compeyre	448
LONHIENNE	Archigny	311
LORIEUX	Mamers	283
LOTHON	Faverolles	217
LOURADOUR	Plassay	302
LOUREIRO	Bonvillers	10
LUNES	Courniou	416
MAIGNAN	Bubry	155
MAILAENDER	Aups	478
MAILLARD	Abbeville	33
MALEK	Aramon	406
MALLOWS	Argentat	328
MANSSENS	Lignière-en-Berry	212
MARCHAND	St Rémy-de-Chargnat	457
MARECHAL	Boutigny-Prouais	218
MARESCASSIER	Beaumont-du-Périgord	344
MARESCASSIER	Mazeyrolles	345
MARIE	Isigny-sur-Mer	55
MARIE	Bernesq	54
MARIE	Roullours	53
MARLIERE	Amboise	234
MARTIN	Loigny-la-Bataille	219
MARTIN	Braine	2
MARTINS-ITIER	Saugues	455
MARTNER	Vic-sur-Aisne	3
MARZELIERE	Nozay	148
MASSIAS	Clairac	356
MATHIS	Morhange	166
MAURICE	Aubry-en-Exmes	103
MAURICE	Berzy-le-Sec	4
MAYER	Sospel	459
MAYLES	Caixas	425

INDEX

MAZEL	Lacoste	494
McMAHON	Lisle-sur-Tarn	432
MICHEL-QUEBRIAC	St Pierre-de-Plesguen	144
MICHELLE	Aurel	495
MITCHELL	Tendu	225
MONCORGER	Ozolles	196
MOREAU	Roiffé	286
MOREAU	Charenton Laugère	213
MORHAIN	Cuvry	167
MORINIERE	Bouzillé	268
MOURGES	Le Thor	496
MURRELL	Quettreville-sur-Sienne	90
NAINTRE COLLIN	St Hippolyte-du-Fort	407
NAY	Mézangers	274
NEVEU	Clermont l'Hérault	417
NICOURT	Vanne-sur-Cosson	247
NOIROT-NERIN	Asnières	69
NOVAK	Carhaix	131
O'NEILL	Lézigné	269
O'NEILL	Quettreville-sur-Sienne	91
OGOR	Guilers	132
OLIVIER	St Pierre-de-Féric	460
ONDER DER LINDEN	Le Mazis	34
ONORATO	Cabrières	418
OPPELT	Salans	502
ORSONI	Montesquieu	396
PAGES	St Martin-de-Caralp	375
PANNETIER	Devillac	357
PARINAUD-TOMMASI	Montbrun-Bocage	384
PARIS	Tourville-la-Campagne	70
PASQUET	Neuvy-sur-Loire	186
PASQUIER	Lalbenque	351
PASQUIER	Bellevaux	515
PASSEBOIS	Barjols	479
PATIZEL	Les Charmontois	159
PAUWELS	Eperlecques	24
PECH	Mazamet	433
PENN	Scaër	133
PERNET	Bretoncelle	104
PERRIER	Bazoches-de-Morvan	187
PESSEL	Pouligny-St-Martin	226
PETIT	Eygalières	468
PETITON	Livry	56
PEUBRIER	St Chartier	227
PICARD	Pouant	312
PICARD	Gevry	503
PIEDNOEL	Ganac	376
PIGNOLY	Torchefelon	501
PINET	Verquières	469
PINIER	St Mathurin-sur-Loire	270
PINON	Gaillac	434
PINOT	St Mars-sur-Futaie	275
PLASSAIS	Pertheville-Ners	57
PLAT	Levens	461
POLI	Eyragues	470

POPPE-NOTTEBOOM	Villeneuve-sur-Lot	358
PORTEFAIX	St Georges	452
POULAIN de SAINT PERE	Dangu	71
PRICE	St Nazaire-des-Gardies	408
PROFFIT	Rians	214
PROTHON	Montboucher-sur-Jabron	525
PRUDENT	Salers	453
QUEGUINEUR	Lanhouarneau	134
RAFFIN	Coullons	248
RAHOUX	Noailles	435
RAMELOT	Gramat	352
RANDJIA	Frise	35
RANNOU	Plonévez Porzay	135
RENAULDON	Bretteville-sur-Dives	58
REY	La Rochette	508
RICARD DAMINOT	Fontvieille	471
RICHMOND-BROWN	Gaillac	436
RICHOUX	Loeuilly	36
RICOL	Marcigny	197
RICQUART	Crillon-le-Brave	497
RIGAUD	La Roque-sur-Cèze	409
RIJPSTRA	St Gaultier	228
ROBERT	Saurat	377
ROBERT	Vouthon-Bas	164
ROBINSON	Plouer-sur-Rance	119
ROCCA	Monflanquin	359
ROEHRIG	Boulogne-sur-Gesse	385
ROLLAND	Luc-sur-Aude	400
ROUBAUD	Contignac	480
ROUSSEL	Montignac	346
ROUSSELOT	Velles	160
ROUVIERE	Rocles	517
RUBBENS	Villars	347
RUHLMANN	Dambach-la-Ville	170
SABATHIER	St Maur	388
SAGUEZ	Dury	37
SALLET	Uchizy	198
SALLIER	Lempaut	438
SALLIER	Lempaut	437
SALVADOR	Castelnau-de-Montmirail	439
SALVAGE	St Rémy	449
SALVAUDON	Availles-Limousine	313
SANDRIER	Nazelles	235
SCHAEPMAN CRAMER	Duras	360
SCHNEIDER & REBOUL	St Rémy	472
SCOTT	Fargues	353
SENECAL	La-Croix-St-Leufroy	72
SENLIS	Duisans	25
SERE	St Jeannet	462
SIMAND	Nonant	59
SIMONNOT	Chérêt	5
SIMONOT	St Ambroix	410
SIOHAN	Lanhouarneau	136
SOLLIEC	Botmeur	137
SORDI	Servas	411

INDEX

SOUCHON	La Celle Condé	215
STENOU	Dinard	145
SYLVAIN	Gevrey-Chambertin	176
TAILLEUX	Sept-Meules	110
TAQUET	Damazan	361
THAON D'ARNOLDI	Erondelle	38
THIBAULT	La Bruère	284
TIFFAINE	St James	92
TONNELIER	Chênehutte-les-Tuffeaux	271
TOUTOUS-JACQUEMET	Brasparts	138
TRIBOULET	Bargny	11
TRICKETT	Bourdeilles	348
TRIGON	St André	509
TROUT	Cerisy-la-Salle	93
TRUMBLE	Picauville	94
TUBERT	Elne	426
TURGOT	Avranches	95
VAILLE	Salleles-du-Bosc	419
VALENGIN	Villers Bocage	39
VAN DEN BRINK	Lachapelle	397
VAN HOORN	Tarascon	378
VASSELIN	Port-Bail	96
VENE	Lautrec	440
VERDIER	Vaison-la-Romaine	498
VERGNAUD	Sepmes	236
VERHOEVEN	Buicourt	12
VERJUS	Géruge	504
VEZIAN	Clermont l'Hérault	420
VIEILLET	Pontvillain	285
VIEL-CAZAL	Montier-en-Der	161
VIGNAUX	Béraut	389
VIGUIER	Villeneuve	450
VILLAMAUX	Caudebec-en-Caux	111
VINER	Villeneuve-lès-Béziers	421
VINET	Bussières	207
VIOLETTE	Pré-St-Martin	220
VISSENAEKEN-VAES	Caixas	427
VITOU	Baillargues	422
WEBB	Beaulieu-sur-Dordogne	329
WILLIAMS	Moelan-sur-Mer	139
WISE	Villefranche-d'Albigeois	441
WORDSWORTH	Exmes	105
ZERBIB	Le Beausset	481